Esther Regina

Rethinking Theory

Esther Regina

A Bakhtinian Reading

André LaCocque

Northwestern University Press
Evanston, Illinois

Northwestern University Press
www.nupress.northwestern.edu

Printed in the United States of America

10 9 8 7 6 5 4 3 2 1

Library of Congress Cataloging-in-Publication Data

Lacocque, André.
Esther Regina : a Bakhtinian reading / André LaCocque.
p. cm. — (Rethinking theory)
Includes bibliographical references and index.
ISBN-13: 978-0-8101-2458-5 (cloth : alk. paper)
ISBN-10: 0-8101-2458-0 (cloth : alk. paper)
ISBN-13: 978-0-8101-2459-2 (pbk. : alk. paper)
ISBN-10: 0-8101-2459-9 (pbk. : alk. paper)
1. Bible. O.T. Esther—Criticism, interpretation, etc. 2. Bakhtin, M. M. (Mikhail Mikhailovich), 1895–1975. 3. Bible as literature. 4. Carnival in literature. I. Title. II. Series.
BS1375.52.L33 2007
222.9066—dc22

2007035875

♾ The paper used in this publication meets the minimum requirements of the American National Standard for Information Sciences—Permanence of Paper for Printed Library Materials, ANSI Z39.48-1992.

To Claire, my wife, and Elisabeth, my daughter—queens in their own right

"We played the flute and you did not dance . . ."
—Matthew 11:17; Luke 7:32

Only by learning to laugh at the hopelessness around us can we touch the hem of hope [for] laughter is hope's last weapon.
—Harvey Cox, *The Feast of Fools*

Contents

Esther Regina

1

The Literary Genre(s) of the Book of Esther

Bakhtin as Pathfinder

The Russian philosopher and literary critic Mikhail Bakhtin (1895–1975) needs little introduction to the English-speaking public aware of literary criticism. He is by now recognized as "the greatest theoretician of literature in the twentieth century."[1] An English translation of most of his works exists, as does a growing literature about him and his literary production. Appended to this essay is a bibliography of studies both by and about Bakhtin. For now, we need only recall that an important theme in his writing is the carnival and the carnivalesque in literature. In fact, two of his books discuss their role in literature in great detail: *Rabelais and His World*, 1965, and the fourth chapter of the second edition of his *Problems of Dostoevsky's Poetics*, 1972. The carnivalesque in literature, Bakhtin complains, has been largely ignored or disparaged by critics. He cites, for instance, Voltaire, who saw in Rabelais's ribald images just "erudition, dirt, boredom."[2] Bakhtin, on the contrary, considers Rabelais to have been one of the three great authors of the novel, along with Dostoevsky and Goethe.

Some recent critics have attacked Bakhtin's idealization of the carnivalesque in literature; for instance, Michael André Bernstein reacts negatively to the Russian thinker's idealization of the Roman saturnalia,[3] and Gary S. Morson and Caryl Emerson see an unfortunate faux pas in Bakhtin's "carnival phase."[4]

Yet I would argue that if we consider Bakhtin's life story, his emphasis on the carnival in literature can be seen to fit within the overall development of his thought. We might even consider this development as, at least, a personal form of revenge directed against the appallingly gloomy *seriousness* of Stalinism. Bakhtin's praise for the irrational in the marketplace—its hawking, its scatological and insulting cries—makes sense when we remember that he wrote his *Rabelais* in the dire conditions of the Stalinist era in the USSR and in hidden opposition to its dogmatic claim to absolute truth.[5]

I want to show in this essay that the book of Esther presents undeniable signs of the carnival and that the carnivalesque spirit of its author is quite evident.[6] This is not surprising once we remember that one of the carnival's Near Eastern ancestors was the widespread pattern of the New Year festival, especially the Babylonian Akitu, celebrating the return of spring, as we shall see below.[7]

Carnival evokes reveling and laughter. But for the book of Esther, *humor* rather than laughter is the more appropriate term. Bakhtin, in praising laughter, went so far as to affirm that "there is no violence lurking behind laughter. . . . [Laughter] does not create dogmas and cannot become authoritarian."[8] Humor, in contrast, can be light or dark; it is light, for instance, when the whole apparatus of the state is mobilized to ensure that the women of the Persian Empire are kept in check by their husbands. It is dark when Haman erects a ridiculously oversized gallows meant for the torture and death of Mordecai.[9] Thus, if we focus below on Purim's laughter, as I shall do shortly, the weaknesses that critics have denounced in Mikhail Bakhtin's concept of carnival will be seen to be felicitously absent from the story of Esther, although the carnivalesque is very much one of its crucial ingredients. To put it another way, Esther may be read from a carnivalesque point of view given the proviso that we acknowledge that it in no way equates "goodness to brute size and crude vitality," as does Rabelais.[10]

Rabelais, to recall, published in 1532 his famous satiric and farcical chronicle of "Pantagruel, king of the Dipsodes and son of the great Giant Gargantua." Under the guise of drollery, Rabelais alludes to details of contemporary French society and praises humanistic ideals. Great master of the comic in universal literature, he uses a multilayered parodic and outrageous picaresque for the pleasure of the populace as well as of the erudite scholars of his epoch. Bakhtin considered him one of the most important literati of all times. Already Victor Hugo had said of him, "Et son e'clat de rire énorme / Est un des gouffres de l'esprit."[11] Bakhtin was attracted to Rabelais because the French satirist had successfully ripped apart with a vitriolic criticism the remnants of mediaeval obscurantism and the sixteenth-century Catholic establishment (the "Papimanes"). Bakhtin thought of himself as enmeshed in a comparable situation within the repressive Stalinist regime, and, like Rabelais but as a literary critic, he chose to praise the carnivalesque in literature and laughter as a powerful weapon to fend off the Soviet establishment's gloomy mood.

How can we say that Esther and *Pantagruel* belong to the same literary genre? We can do so because the very notion of genre is a loose approximation; genres are dynamic and ever changing, although it is also true that within a given group of texts we may discover a family resemblance that allows each to participate in and contribute to our recognition of the genre in question. The differences among the individual family members may be great, but, as long as the *typical* ingredients are present, or at least recognizable, one may speak of an encompassing genre.[12] In other words, a genre exhibits both typical features (in the case of Esther, the carnivalesque, for example) and atypical traits (say, the setting of Esther in a royal court rather than in the marketplace).

In what follows, I shall hold that Esther's overarching genre—for a genre is seldom if ever "pure"—is the novella. More specifically, it is an example of what has been called the *Diasporanovelle.* As a novella, the biblical book is seen as synchronically presenting characteristics recognizable in many ancient or modern works: for example, a Hellenistic novella of the first century C.E.[13] or, in our time, *The Pearl* by John Steinbeck. There is, of course, no question of mutual influence. On this score, the assignment of Esther to the novella genre is ahistorical or transhistorical. At the same time, from a diachronical point of view, by designating the book as a *Diasporanovelle* we do recognize a historical dimension to the tale's composition. I shall return to this point below.

Carnivalesque novella belongs to a "low genre," that is, it derives from the need of the so-called lower classes to find some way to express their response to the contradictions of social life. In Esther, to be sure, the Jewish heroes are said to belong to the court entourage. Hence while the carnivalesque in Esther is not directly dependent on social class, it does stem from a different although comparable social situation, namely, that of the relationship of a minority population to a hostile majority. In other words, if we look at carnival as presenting a *strategy* for negotiating the interface between official and unofficial, the uniqueness of the book of Esther lies in its use of fiction to place the unofficial *inside* the official: Esther is queen of Persia and Mordecai is a courtier. The book's *chronotope*—a favorite term of Bakhtin's as it combines the specific time and the specific place of an occurrence—is the royal palace in the fifth century B.C.E.[14] What the story will show is the deconstruction of this chronotope.[15]

Thus in this essay, Bakhtin's vision of the carnival(esque) in literature is adopted as a *methodological* tool.[16] His heuristic insights on this topic will be taken as the key to understanding the application of a specific literary genre to a biblical book. The usefulness of this approach has been too often overlooked.

The first thing to be emphasized in our inquiry is the *popular* bent of the story told in the book of Esther. The ostensible setting of the tale in a royal court should not blind us to that fact. On the contrary, we recognize a favorite folkloric trait in that very setting and in the placement of the characters in the upper spheres of the social world. Popular tales and legends are fond of taking kings and princesses, knights and courtiers as their characters. In the literary genres influenced by folklore, this type of chronotope still prevails. The heroes have little if anything to do with daily life, in which in any case they do not participate, and they never require public approval or meet public disapproval. But if the tie with the humdrum of most people's daily lives is tenuous, the royal court setting remains, as Humphreys puts it, "designed to reveal the essence of human life, a setting in which the risks are huge and the prizes larger than life itself."[17]

The folkloric in Esther is not limited to its setting, of course. Numerous other elements of the story point in the same direction. Royal banquets lasting six months or more, only to be succeeded by drinking bouts and orgies;[18] the crucial mention of the immutability of the Persian laws; the lethal danger of appearing before the king without first being summoned; the royal decision to annihilate a whole population within the empire; the mass conversion of Persians: all of these factors are constitutive of the story as folkloric.

Mordecai and Esther belong to a different world from that of the populace, making natural their adoption of the aloofness and detachment from ordinary life typical of the folkloric tale. Esther 4:11–14, for example, shows that Esther was indeed tempted at one point by that solution, hoping to extricate herself from the crisis initiated by the confrontation of Mordecai and Haman. But this is only a passing moment in the story, and it serves the purpose of underscoring the risk inherent in the public and popular commitment of the two Jewish heroes. Even if they do belong to the Persian aristocracy, their dedication to their people turns out to be on a par with that of Moses, who was also raised at a foreign royal court (Exod. 2:10). He and they both sacrifice their privacy and the "diplomatic immunity" guaranteed by their public functions to become the saviors of their people.

We are not given biographies of Esther or Mordecai; they are presented wholly from an external and public point of view, and the narrative concerns itself only with their actions, not their sentiments. This lack of intimacy with the heroes' psyches was already felt in the Greek versions of the book of Esther, the translators of which made a real effort to psychologize the story's characters. Thus in the Greek texts the Jewish heroes pray, they faint, they lament, they apologize (especially Esther, for sharing the bed and table of an uncircumcised man), and so forth.[19] But in so doing, the carnivalesque nature of the story became lost, and the literary genre shifted from satire to moralistic apologue. In chapter 7, I shall develop this point further.

Paradoxically, to find the literary genre that the Hebrew version of the story of Esther parodies in a comic-ironic way we need only turn to the subsequent Greek versions of the tale. The latter blot out the former's laughter as unfit for a "serious" document and reintroduce all the religious paraphernalia that the carnivalesque book of Esther had thrown aside. The nature of the story is thus entirely changed. Rather than being a comedy, Esther 1–8 becomes a tragedy. The numbers in the story are taken literally; the history-like narrative becomes real history; and the Jewish heroes become pious, self-effacing, insignificant epigones. In short, what used to be subversive is now tamed, and the extraordinary returns to the habitual, even to the trivial![20]

This glossing process is frequent in literature, including in the Bible. The same middle-of-the-road outlook was imposed on the Greek versions of other biblical documents, such as Daniel, Ecclesiastes, or the Song of Songs (even the Hebrew text of Song of Songs was attributed to King Solomon).[21] The subversive (including laughter, Bakhtin was right!) has never been accepted as such by denizens of diehard reactionary milieus. Irony is disturbing. It makes one think.[22]

As regards the book of Esther, also allegedly in need of a serious "weeding"—an operation performed by the Greek translator-glossarists—its dubious character was even seen as an obstacle to its incorporation into the biblical literature.

Esther in the Canon of Scriptures

The ironic Hebrew text of Esther (and also of its kin-book, Judith) was not easily received into the canon of Scriptures. It is the only biblical book not found at Qumran among the Dead Sea Scrolls. Qumran knew nothing of a Purim festival. The covenanters were perhaps displeased with the absence of any mention of God or of the Holy Land in the book and displeased too with Esther for failing to respect the dietary laws, and for wavering before coming to the aid of her people (4:10–14).[23] And Qumran was not the only site of doubts about the canonicity of the book of Esther. We know of dissenting opinions, down to the third and fourth centuries C.E., reported in the Talmudic tractates Megillah (7a–b) and Sanhedrin (100 a), although Esther does find a place on the list of twenty-four canonical books given in a Baraita of Baba Bathra 14b–15a (second century C.E.).[24] Among Christians in the eastern churches, too, the book of Esther was often considered noncanonical. The New Testament does not even allude to it. There was no Christian commentary on the book of Esther until the ninth century. Even the general welcome that the book received among the Jews at a certain point in history cannot conceal that for a long time the orthodoxy in Zion resisted both its canonization and the celebration of Purim as a bona fide Jewish festival. The chronological gap between possibly the first pre-Masoretic, Mordecai-centered version of the story in the fifth or fourth century B.C.E.[25] and its later versions during the Hellenistic period in Palestine shows how long it took for the idea of a diasporic contribution to Jewish thought to become worthy of consideration and ultimately acceptable.

We must acknowledge that the book of Esther as a *Diasporanovelle* does introduce novel elements (to be spelled out in chapter 3) in the composition of the Judaism of the time. At least this is true of the Hebrew text before its later transformations in the Greek versions. In those translations, as we shall see in chapter 7, a generalized elision of the book's troublesome features occurred (a few of which are noted above in connection with its absence from Qumran). Such a sanitized reading includes early attempts at smoothing the rough angles of the story by interspersing various additions throughout the text. Those Greek additions, six in number, describe premonitory (prophetic) dreams, the prayers of Mordecai and Esther, declarations by the queen that she loathes the Persian food and bed, and so forth.

What we can say at this point is that the book of Esther did provoke various reactions among its readers, ancient (witness the various textual versions) or modern (beginning in the sixteenth century with the Reformers). Much depends, of course, on *how* the book is read.

Esther's Literary Genre in Focus

It is crucial for its understanding to start with the question of what kind of book the tale of Esther is. The style adopted by a writer results less from aesthetic choice than from the selection of an appropriate vehicle for visualizing reality from a specific point of view (mimesis). The point of view represented in Esther is one that prevailed in the Jewish diaspora of the third to the second century B.C.E., a viewpoint that found the novella a fitting idiom for expressing its vision of reality (see, for example, the Joseph story and the books of Jonah, Ruth, or Judith). "New genres reflect changes in real social life," say Morson and Emerson,[26] and, obviously, the creation starting in the fourth century B.C.E. of a Jewish community living elsewhere than in Israel qualifies as a major social, political, and religious change.[27]

The adoption of the novella as a rhetorical vehicle by the Jewish diaspora of the Second Temple period thus corresponds to the social changes taking place. In what follows I shall summarize the characteristics of the novella as they reflect the inner social transformations of the time. In this respect, an initial reflection on the term *diaspora* is appropriate. The word *diaspora* specifically designates the Jewish dispersion in the ancient world. It originated in the Septuagint version of Deuteronomy 28:25 where the Hebrew word *terror* (*zaʿawah*) was rendered in Greek by *diaspora*. In turn, John 7:35 mentions those (Jews) who are "dispersed among the Greeks." James 1:1 is more striking: "James, slave of God and of the lord Jesus Christ, to the twelve tribes of the diaspora"; an echo of this is found in 1 Peter 1:1: "those who live as strangers in the diaspora." Historically, no national dispersion had the impact that the Jewish one has had in terms of both its significance and its duration.[28] Already in the sixth century B.C.E., through their Babylonian exile, the Jews were among the very first people to acquire a vivid consciousness of the unlimited world. As a defense against being simply absorbed by "the world," their sense of universalism was balanced by one of particularism. Incidentally, the discovery of the world at large explains in part decisive earthly concerns of the book of Esther, in contrast to what could have been deemed religious provincialism.

In this world at large during the centuries preceding the Common Era, the literature of fiction saw the blossoming of the Greek romance,[29] which displays a fondness for the discovery of foreign countries, real or imaginary. Now, fondness is a decidedly inappropriate concept with which to describe the view among the Jewish diaspora, but this new literary production did at least express interest in (and concern with) the outer world and especially with foreign courts (Babylon, Nineveh, Susa, and so on). The problem to be faced was one of partial adaptation to unknown milieus, hence the acquisition of a new *wisdom,* for adaptation was a balancing act aimed at protecting Jewish identity and particularism. Esther's story unwinds in Persia, that is, "east of Eden," in an alien world. Nothing there is according to Jewish rules and habits. One cannot count on the "rule-generating force"[30] as applied in one's customary world. In short, the environment is unpredictable, and the center of unpredictability is, of course, the royal palace.

Corresponding to aspects of the Greek romance—with which it shares at least a distinct element of "novel of ordeal"—the Esther novella presents heroes who are courtiers, that is, protagonists who act as their people's antennas and radars attuned to the court's "frequency." In this kind of literature, clever courtesans are promoted to the highest administrative functions in their adoptive countries (as were Joseph, Aḥikar, and Daniel). Writing about Jewish heroes in the court in Persia also offered the literary advantage of allowing negative judgments on the vanity of some of the people in power, even according to their own standards. Esther and Mordecai could have competed for royal favor or to gather ever greater power for themselves. Instead, they risk their own lives for the sake of their people, as Moses, despite his position in the Egyptian court, did before them.

It remains that "Persia," the palace, and the royal entourage, as chronotopes, are too generic to permit any firm conclusions regarding the story's place of composition. Here, exoticism may be a disguise. As happened during the European Renaissance, with its fascination for the new lands of America and India, so too during the Second Temple period, some seventeen to eighteen hundred years earlier, the Jewish *Diasporanovelle* speaks of foreign countries (from the standpoint of Israel) as strange places where unusual things can happen: for instance, the picture of Egypt according to Genesis 47:13–26. Along that line, according to both Esther and Daniel, "Persia" is controlled by a law that is inalterable to the point of absurdity. In these far-off countries, people in power can afford to hold endless banquets, and the king has innumerable concubines, his due as a half-divine being. To come uninvited into his presence is punishable by death, like the fate of an unsavvy worshiper struck by lightning thrown by an irascible god. Furthermore, at the king's whim entire populations of the "Persian" Empire can be disposed of without further ado and without making the least ripple in the immensity of its 127 provinces.[31]

In any case, the novella's exploitation of the theme of exoticism is an effective means of shaking the established order and the habitual, be it "at home" (by favorable or unfavorable comparison with foreigners' ways of life) or "abroad," within the foreign land itself (as in the case of the tale of Esther). On this point again, there is something that recalls Rabelais or, long before him, Lucian's *A True Story.*

The relative pleasantness of the exotic does not prevent Esther, as a *Diasporanovelle,* from dealing with an existential and baleful situation. The "Jewishness" of the immigrants was endangered. Hence we find here a definite accentuation on *ethnicity*: the Jewish minority as such finds itself in a hostile environment and must be prepared for any eventuality. That is one of the main reasons why the author of the Jewish novella parodies the "Persian" world and treats it with irony.

The issue of adaptation or unadaptability is the more urgent in that the immigrants have a vivid consciousness of their remoteness from Zion and from the cultic presence of God. The more they feel the absence of the Land, of priests, prophets, and kings, as well as of altar and sacrifices, of the sacred festivals' ground, the more they develop an exile mentality. It can be expected, therefore, that their understanding of their relationship with God will undergo a profound revision: since God does not reveal himself directly in a foreign land,[32] he is thought of as indirectly providential. Consequently, the accent is now set on peripeteia, on some felicitous turn of fortune, on serendipity. And, because divine providence is experienced within the course of events, narrative emphasis also shifts from charismatic personalities to plot.

Furthermore, a new interest in "exceptional women" arose, women like Naomi, Ruth, Esther, Judith, Susanna, and even Vashti and Zeresh, along with a recuperation both of the ancient heroines' axiological dimension (Rachel, Lea, and Tamar; compare Ruth 4) and of their sexual one (Tamar, Ruth, Esther, Judith, and Susanna). (We will consider this in chapter 4.)

In short, the Jewish diaspora created a new theology and a new anthropology: not a new God, but a new relationship with God, and not the *homo israelitus*, but the *homo judaeus*. The literary genre of the novella was not "designed from the outset to the purpose [it] currently serve[s], but adapted for that purpose from forms previously serving other purposes."[33]

The Jewish Novella and Irony

The book of Esther belongs in large part to a carnivalesque type of literature, and its rejection by many a non-Jewish reader is often due to a fundamental oversight. Reading Esther as a historical record, one moreover allegedly distorted by ultranationalistic interests, might indeed entitle us to judge it to be repulsive or outrageous.[34] It is true that violence plays an important role in the tale and that it even receives justification and praise at a few points.[35] What is more, on the same line with some (very few) writings of the Hebrew Scriptures, it is devoid of all pious discourse and of any allusion to the Holy Land and its "salvation history." Its concern is exclusively with the Jewish diaspora of the East. It seemed evident to many well-meaning Christian readers that no theological or ethical lesson could be drawn from such a narrative. The Church Fathers ignored it completely. Martin Luther, as is well known, was willing to exclude it from the canon, and he would not recommend Christians read it.[36] Although not himself impervious to violence, Luther, like many reflective "people of faith," was unwilling to contemplate violence in Holy Writ.

When the literary genre of Esther is taken seriously, however—that is, as an offspring of folk culture—the unstable position of the book in the canon of Scriptures is not, in fact, made any more secure. As Bakhtin said about Rabelais, "It is uncanonical by its very nature"[37] (a judgment that Bakhtin extended to all carnivalesque novelistic literature).

Areligiosity, cunningness, and violence in the book of Esther will clearly constitute a challenge to be dealt with in this study. Already at this point we can say, however, that a carnivalesque reading radically transforms our understanding of this biblical book. And, in fact, it is not the first time that such a thesis has been proposed. Kenneth Craig touched on this idea in his provocative book, *Reading Esther: A Case for the Literary Carnivalesque.*[38] But, as Barbara Green complains,

> Having made the formal case for Esther's suitability to be read as a carnival, Craig stops short of doing it. . . . [He] fails to follow up with the implications. The book simply ends with the last point of similarity established.[39]

I mean to take up Green's challenge. Rereading Esther in the light of folkloric literature, it occurred to me that it constitutes an ideal test of Bakhtin's ideas. As we shall see, had Bakhtin paid attention to this story as a model of the carnivalesque, I believe he would have achieved significant nuance in his definition. Furthermore, if the following study has merit, it anticipates the Bakhtinian findings by some eighteen centuries! The Russian philosopher would not be surprised, however. He purposely singled out the late Middle Ages for his examination since he was looking for a liminal manifestation of the grotesque before it was tamed, as he thought, by the Renaissance. In fact, he was perfectly aware that any period would do that preceded the rationalization and officialization that came to prevail after Rabelais, for carnival is as old as human socialization, and as ubiquitous.[40]

This essay is thus not a commentary on Esther,[41] but a way of reading the book following the lead of the Russian critic. Other readings are not only possible, they legitimately occupy the shelves of scholars and laypeople alike. If this work is not a commentary, it may still contribute to the understanding of the biblical book, if only, we may say, as a kind of prolegomena to a commentary.

As already stated, Mikhail Bakhtin's analysis of the carnivalesque in literature will be used here heuristically as a methodological guide, and I shall, as much as possible, let him speak in his own voice—about a biblical book that, to my knowledge, he does not even mention in his written works but which could have served as a model for his inquiry (along with Apuleius, Petronius, Rabelais, Cervantes, and many others).

True, the phenomenon of carnival is never as clearly delineable as Bakhtin would like it to be. There is no way that we might construct a patterned "pure" carnival serving as a blueprint to gauge "deviations" in the concrete manifestations of the grotesque. As a prototype, however, late expressions of carnival in the Middle

Ages are applicable, methodologically, to both earlier and later embodiments; as I have said above, the definition of a literary genre can only be approximated by recognizing typical ingredients that have become prototypes by their presence in model texts, thus overcoming atypical differences. Within this perspective, Bakhtin's concept of carnival is definitely valid.[42]

Carnival, nevertheless, is not the exclusive property of the disenfranchised populace. More accurately, a grotesque manifestation of popular discontent with the (political, moral, or religious) authorities can be and actually is often annexed by the powers that be, where it is turned into orchestrated rituals at the service of the status quo. I am referring to what I shall call in what follows in this essay the parody of parody.[43] If, as a matter of fact, carnival is the display of the grotesque deriding the "establishment," it so happens that officialdom—so harshly denounced by Bakhtin—can also gruesomely imitate carnival. This is how the book of Esther starts and how it continues, with descriptions of "Gargantuesque" banquets organized by the king of Persia, Xerxes I, called here Ahasuerus, or by his wife, Vashti.[44]

But things are not as they first appear. The opening words of the Esther story should alert us to this: they are, "It was in the time of . . . ," a phrase that appears five times in the Bible and always as the prelude to a catastrophe (Genesis 14:1–2; Isaiah 7:1; Jeremiah 1:3; Ruth 1:1). Even the summoning of Queen Vashti, who is supposed to expose herself (naked?) to the reveling crowd, is carnivalesque. But these grotesque manifestations sponsored by people in power are a parody of folk comedy, if only because the royal orgy purports to buttress the establishment not to mock the official order.[45]

One of the most striking ironic contrasts in the story of Esther is precisely the sham idyllic environment depicted in Esther 1. In Xerxes' Persia, all seems to be perfect, and people allegedly spend their time reveling, eating, and drinking.[46] The contrast with the Deuteronomistic narrative is stark and has been perceptively drawn by Robert Alter.[47] In Judges, Samuel, and Kings, things are disorderly, and "the recalcitrant facts of known history have to be encompassed." Esther, on the contrary, is "at the other end of the spectrum, near the pole of design."[48]

The regime's display of generosity is simply deceptive. A monstrous tragedy is being hatched, and thousands of human beings are under threat of annihilation. The establishment's carnival spells out not liberation and peace but slavery and destruction. Only a countercarnival can wipe away the sickening grimace on the face of the brute. Esther is the story of conflicting carnivals. We shall have to turn below to one of the false "clowns" of the Esther story, Haman-the-Wicked: Haman is a clown who—true to form—does not laugh, for, as Bakhtin insists, "laughter could never become an instrument to oppress and blind people. It always remained a free weapon in their hands."[49]

The author of Esther has opted for this parody of parody in order to let the carnival spirit permeate his or her narrative from beginning to end.[50] Even the genocide plotted by Haman is, by virtue of its enormous proportions versus its tiny rationale, an element worthy of Rabelaisian extravagance.[51]

Parody of parody is a constant feature in Esther. In a contrasting parallel to the gathering of the Jewish community to begin a collective fast (4:15–17), Haman assembles his wife and friends (5:10). With Esther, the order of the day is to abstain from food and drink; with Haman, the summons occurs between two banquets; Esther gives advice, Haman asks for advice; in both cases, a woman, Esther or Zeresh, provides the impulse to action, and this is not lacking irony, especially with the events of Esther 1:16–22 in the background ("each man shall be master in his household"). Of course, the greatest contrast is that Esther's purpose is to save her people while Haman's is to destroy them (5:14). In all this—and particularly in Haman's boasting before his wife and friends[52]—it feels as if we are reading a Molière comedy or La Fontaine fable.[53]

At the end of the Esther tale, Mordecai commands a Jewish celebration very much on the model of the royal parody with which the narrative started. The issue is most vexing, as it seems to go in the opposite direction from the subversion of the powers that be. Is it not playing into the hands of the enemy to use their own tools and methods? Is it still carnivalesque when Esther and Mordecai become themselves potentates at the Persian court? Is it still parodic when the Jewish courtiers impose the festival of Purim on their people? The objection is serious but, I believe, indecisive. Right before the eruption of the carnival at Purim, there is, as it were, an implosion of the absolute power—almost an apocalyptic pattern. Esther and Mordecai take total power into their own hands, just as Moses and Aaron became themselves magicians to defeat the Egyptian wonder-makers. Then, Aaron's stick became a serpent that swallowed the Egyptian ophidians (Exod. 7:10–12). In Esther, the serpent of absolute power bites its own tail, for the hellish machine of the "Penitentiary Colony," designed to crush all resistance to absolutism, has turned into a self-destructive mechanism. Consequently, the Jewish subversion not only overcame a crowd of anti-Semites but, more decisively, it overcame the machinery of the state itself. The oppressed have captured their enemy's fortress and turned its power against their tormentors. Therefore, what the Jewish authorities originally and paradoxically ordered becomes something the people choose to celebrate (see 9:23, 27–28).

The story's dénouement is a carnival, but the carnival had started, although in a subdued and subtle way, much earlier, namely, when Mordecai stripped off his sackcloth and put on royal vestments (Esther 6) in anticipation of things to come. When the (former) slave rides a horse and the (former) prince walks on foot beside him, it is truly carnival. For Purim also legalizes license and even drunkenness (at least in the traditional perpetuation of the festival among Jews), as was the king's order in Esther 1.[54] Bakhtin notes the brevity of the explosion of freedom on Mardi Gras, and his remark well suits Purim: it lasts only one day (9:17–19), extended by

Mordecai to a second day (9:22, 27, out of compassion for the people?), in contrast with the royal banquet that had lasted 180 days (1:4).

As I said above regarding officialdom's imitation of carnival, had Bakhtin spoken of this obscene parody of folk culture, he would have avoided the scathing criticism of Mikhail K. Ryklin.[55] But to think that Bakhtin remained blind to a phenomenon he witnessed on a daily basis is unimaginable. In truth, it would have been sheer madness to write about it during the Stalinist era. This brings us to the realization that Bakhtin is not only an innovator and mentor but someone for whom indeed carnival was the last impregnable stronghold of liberty, as it had been for the Jews of the eastern diaspora about to be annihilated in the second century B.C.E. Writing more than fifty years later about the book of Esther is, of course, a vastly different matter from Bakhtin's writing about Rabelais in his Kazakhstan exile. It is easy to be dispassionate and "objective," although I refuse to be simply that "after Auschwitz."[56] We may not forget that "there is always going on within us a process of formulation and interpretation whose subject matter is our own self," as the literary critic Erich Auerbach said.[57] My own commitment does, I hope, honor Bakhtin's principles of "outsideness" and "creative understanding." He says, "It is immensely important for the person who understands to be *located outside* the object of his or her creative understanding—in time, in space, in culture."[58] Such reading goes far beyond simply decoding what Bakhtin calls "sentences"—which he contrasts with the much more meaningful complex he dubs an "utterance." True, the book of Esther's language demands to be decoded, but this leads only to a "passive understanding"; Esther's utterance (or "contextual meaning") demands a "creative understanding" achieved by entering into a dialogue with the text, bringing one's own voice into interplay with Esther's voice.[59] In other words, the sentences alone present only a "mono-horizon," whereas the dialogic utterance encompasses a meeting of two horizons, that of the text and that of the reader. "Language lives only in the dialogic interaction of those who make use of it," says Bakhtin.[60]

Along this line, the time has come to emphasize a particular point, to be expounded more thoroughly later. As is carnival in general, the book of Esther and also Purim, the festival instituted in memory of the events narrated in the book, are far from being carefree or anxiety-free. When carnival occurs, it is generally preceded and accompanied by oppression and an ominous threat of worse times to come. Purim, as we shall see, comes more as a pause, a counterpoint, or even as the brave affirmation of another world in the midst of this baleful one rife with the possibility of continued threats to the people's existence.

In this way the festival comes as a welcome "happy end," but an end only to what has preceded it. As such it has the property of allowing the reader to sigh with relief and to wish that such a victory over this ancient enemy of the community might also be true today and always. It gives rise to hope for the otherworld's final victory over the bloody sufferings of the present world. In fact, the events described in Esther are all to be understood as set within the transhistorical and universal context of the "war of the sons of light against the sons of darkness." This war is perpetual, and the victory over evil is never final (*unfinalizability* is a Bakhtinian concept). That is why Israel's wisdom recommends laughing along with the tears of sorrow and weeping along with the tears of laughter (most of the biblical Psalms of lament include a note of joy, and vice versa). Carnival is no effacement of memory but rather the reenactment of a historically endured death that avoids letting that death have the last word. As Bakhtin insists, death in carnival is pregnant with the renewal of life.

When we talk of laughter in Esther, therefore, it is more the laughter of the author than of the characters that is at issue. There is no laughing among the Jew-haters, obviously because they take themselves so seriously, on the model of their leader, Haman. And to the Jews, Haman's threat against their lives is far from comic. On the other hand, we shall have to assess Mordecai as a deliberate jester.[61] On this score, while quite a distance separates the author and her or his characters, it is no chasm.

The author comes *after* the events she or he narrates and knows they end happily, while the characters are in the midst of the "historical" flow and cannot anticipate its ultimate peripeteia.[62] The author's temporality is different from that of the book's heroes. It is only at the end of the story that the two temporalities merge, when the authorial laughter is shared by all the characters. This is one reason for not severing the end of Esther (chapters 9 and 10) from the whole, as some have done.[63]

Moreover, the presence of the carnivalesque in Esther is not to be attributed exclusively to an individual author. Although the book badly lacks the distinct traditional characteristics generally found in ancient Israelite literature, it definitely is a product of popular Jewish culture.[64] As I have insisted elsewhere, and will repeat here, if Esther is not an *Israelite* book, it is nonetheless a thoroughly *Jewish* book.

Focus on the Novella

Above, I spoke of the carnivalesque in Esther as one crucial ingredient in the story. Another generic marker is its presentation in the form of a novella. As I have argued elsewhere,[65] the novella is a literary genre particularly suited to the circumstances of the diaspora, that is, to the situation of a community living as an ethnic minority in the immense expanse of the Persian Empire. The following summary on the nature of the novella by E. K. Bennett is particularly illuminating as to how this literary form functions and why it is so applicable in this situation.

> The Novelle [= novella] is an epic form and as such deals with events rather than actions; it restricts itself to a single event (or situation or conflict), lay-

> ing the stress primarily upon the event and showing the effect of this event upon a person or group of persons; by its concentration upon a single event it tends to present it as chance (*Zufall*) and it is its function to reveal that what is apparently chance, and may appear as such to the person concerned, is in reality fate. . . . It must present some aspect of life (event, situation, conflict) which arouses interest by its strangeness, remoteness from everyday happenings, but at the same time its action must take place in the world of reality and not that of pure imagination. . . . Characteristic of its construction is a certain turning point, at which the development of the narrative moves unexpectedly in a different direction from that which was anticipated, and arrives at a conclusion which surprises, but at the same time satisfies logically. . . . The effect of the impact of the event upon the person or group of persons is to reveal qualities which were latent and may have been unsuspectedly present in them.[66]

In a word, the only basic rule of the novella is verisimilitude; it is a history-like story, even though at times the extreme limits of plausibility are reached. A prophet is swallowed by a fish and lives in its stomach for three days, for example, or an Israelite slave becomes the vizier of pharaonic Egypt—and an insignificant Jewish girl in the Persian diaspora becomes queen.

Another characteristic of the novella worth noting here is the role of recorded dialogues. Although not so extensive as in the novella of Ruth, the dialogic in Esther is also an important element. It is so because it marks the changes the protagonists undergo. The coy Esther changes course, for example, and declares her intention to act on behalf of her people. King Ahasuerus, in a much more frantic way, changes his mind as regards Haman and orders his demise. In a similar manner, Ahasuerus permits the Jewish community to countermand his first edict. In another *Diasporanovelle,* Joseph evolves from a problem-ridden brat to a wise and balanced adult whose discourse is effective in dealing with the situations that confront him.

A parallel has indeed often been drawn between Esther and the narrative about Joseph. The similarities between the two tales are ideological as well as verbal.[67] It is worth noting a similarity on the religious level as well: the Joseph story involves an eclipse, of sorts, of the divine. André Neher has called attention to the absence of divine discourse in the narration in Genesis 37:1–46:2.[68] He correctly points out that the setting of the Joseph story in Egypt renders the direct involvement of God improper. Theophanic dialogue, when it finally occurs, only does so in the land of Israel. On foreign soil the contact is only indirect, through dreams, for instance, or through serendipitous coincidence.

The author of Esther goes even further and avoids any mention of or even any allusion to God in the Persian setting. In other words, there seems to be a theology for the land of Israel and another (or its absence) for the diaspora; or, more accurately, there is a language for those within Israel and another for those without. This is all the more understandable in that the problems are utterly different, depending on their settings. The point of the book of Esther is Jewish survival under the threat of genocide. The solution it gives to that problem is inspired, not by the possible precedent of the exodus from Egypt under the leadership of Moses, but rather in terms of the remembrance of the safe management of Egyptian affairs by Joseph, who stayed in the foreign land and made both his people and the Egyptians prosperous. Esther too deals with a situation in which the danger of Jewish annihilation issues from the setting itself. The foreigners are dangerously ambivalent; their attitude toward the Jews is ambiguous. They may one day command the massacre of all Jews in the whole empire while the next day elevating one of them to quasi kingship; or they may promise half the empire to another because she is attractive or sexy, finally taking sides with those who were at first selected for annihilation.

All of this uncertainty demanded a reassessment of the community's self-understanding. This aggiornamento found expression in a new literary genre. Genre, of course, is a mode of cognition,[69] and the *Diasporanovelle* is a privileged vehicle for conveying a new Jewish approach to reality developed away from the stereotyped religious categories still prevalent at the time in restored Jerusalem. As we shall see in what follows, this new philosophical reflection marks a *reaccentuation* (also a Bakhtinian concept) on the *people* as fated in a grand historical scheme transcending moment-to-moment occurrences. Such an innovation, simultaneously literary and cognitive, at first competed with the scribalism developed in Jerusalem under Ezra and Nehemiah. Eventually, after the catastrophe of 70 C.E., scribalism blossomed into halakhah (the legal system), while the novelistic moved in the direction of the haggadah (the use of narrative to convey a point). Before their junction under the rabbinic umbrella, though, it is important to recognize how distant the aggadic Esther is from any aspect of the halakhah. Esther does not teach a uniquely right way of behavior but a modus vivendi for Jews living in a foreign land. In other words, Esther is a story meant to buttress hope.[70]

What is remarkable about the advent of the novella in literature is that it turns its back on the epos. Whereas the epos is entirely national and traditional, that is, marked by the legendary, the novella is oriented toward the historical present. In fact, the sociohistorical condition of the Jewish community in diaspora had considerable impact on the shift from epos to novella. The new situation demanded a new form of reflection on the question of survival and, beyond it, on identity. In many respects the Jewish diasporic identity was *novel*. In literature, it demanded a new vehicle. That is why stories such as "Joseph in Egypt," "Jonah in Nineveh," or "Esther in Persia" are so different from the patriarchal or matriarchal sagas or from the story of Moses's leadership in the desert, or again (but less so from a stylistic viewpoint) from David's succession story. The biblical novella is generically a *Diasporanovelle*.

From a compositional point of view it is a much freer genre, liberated from religious, at times sclerotic, conceptions such as those that recount direct and personal divine interventions in human history; divine retributive justice; the people's indelible guilt; or the Zion ideology. No other biblical novella went as far in that direction as did the Hebrew text of Esther.[71]

For, just as the novella sets itself at a distance from the epos or the legend, both turned toward a glorious past, in the novella we find that anything that deflects the focus from contemporary events (or those roughly contemporary with the time of composition) is avoided. Such avoidance is quite evident in two examples drawn from Esther. The first one is the Jews' recourse to fasting when they hear of the murderous plan of Haman. As we shall see, the absence of reference to any religious rationale in Esther 4:16 is striking. There is clearly an intentional disregard for the past moorings of the ritual.

The second example is more complex. In addition to the pre-Exodus time (Joseph and the Hebrew settlement in Egypt) and to Exodus (Moses and Passover), another key textual background of the tale of Esther is the confrontation between Saul and Agag, king of Amalek, in 1 Samuel 15. Mordecai is a descendant of Kish, father of King Saul, and Haman is an "Agagite" (see Esther 2:5 and 3:1). Here, as much as in the first examples given, there is an appeal to the past. But just as Purim stands in competition with Passover in relation to Exodus, so too, in relation to 1 Samuel 15, the reference is to an *ignominious* past occurrence in need of closure, where such "closure" is to be sought precisely in the "present" set of events.[72]

Thus here, the issue of the past is primordial. In the novella about Joseph (Gen. 37–50), for instance, the presence of the past, so to speak, was vouchsafed by the towering figure of the father Jacob. In the story of Jonah, the hero is a prophet of an unconventional type, perhaps, but recognizable as a member of the historic guild. Something more or less of the same nature can be said of the Judean exile Daniel in Daniel 1–6. But Esther is no "dreamer" in the manner of Joseph or Daniel, and Mordecai is no prophet in the manner of Jonah. The Septuagint (LXX) of Esther felt so uncomfortable with this qualitative gap that it prefaced the story by recounting a premonitory dream of Mordecai's, making him thus join ranks with Joseph and Daniel. In the Hebrew text, however, Mordecai is no visionary, just a wise courtier. We cannot even speak of him as endowed with mantic wisdom, yet his is a "Jewish" wisdom, by which we must understand a worldview forged by long historical experience, from which nothing religious or ethical is excluded yet without any need to be made explicit.

In this connection, the "presence of the past" is indeed overwhelming. Esther and Mordecai are not international heroes, and the planned genocide does not threaten a community at random. Although the horror would not be diminished in the latter case, it is important for understanding this book to keep in mind that Haman's conspiracy is anti-Semitic. The book of Esther signals the historical beginning of anti-Semitism (in the third or second century B.C.E.). Its precise starting point can be traced to Haman's flimsy rationale in Esther 3:8: the Jews have different laws—which ones and of what worth is unstated.[73] I shall deal with this issue more extensively in chapter 8 below.

The relation to time is precisely where Esther is to be distinguished from an epic. Epic treats the past as absolute, that is, as remote from the historical present of author and audience, thus creating a fictional world at an unbridgeable distance from the present, a "sublime and distant horizon,"[74] having very little to do with the author's life experience.

The yawning gap between fictional hero and audience in epic is, as it were, compensated for by the striking lack of distance within the hero himself between his identity and his actions. "He has already become everything that he could become, and he could become only that which he has already become."[75] The contrast between the book of Esther and epic is reflected in its different anthropology. The epic hero is "fully finished" and "completed," a "ready made . . . entirely externalized" character, "because his fate has been predetermined."[76] By contrast, Mordecai and Esther are fighting against any notion that the past determines the present and even against the idea of an absolute truth. The "hero" who represents absolute truth and determinism is Haman-the-Wicked. As for Esther and Mordecai, their identity transcends all determinism and is much more unfinished, unfinalizable. The very duality of their names (Esther and Hadassah; Mordecai and Kish) proclaims that much. Their teamwork points in the same direction.

On this score, the relationship of Esther to 1 Samuel 15 is of the utmost importance as regards the conception of time. Clearly, here past time is not self-contained, as it would be in the epos. The past is unfinished, incomplete, in need of further development; what is more, as will be shown later, time is teleological. There is no "absolute past," using Goethe and Schiller's terminology,[77] rather the past is open-ended. It is not segmented, but a continuum, not cyclical, but linear; that is, it possesses a beginning, and it strives toward fulfillment.[78] The claim of the book of Esther is that it establishes a link between the past and the future; the book is open toward the past (of Israel's history) as well as toward the future (the "now and ever more" temporality instituted by Purim). This claim represents a sweeping breakthrough on several levels. I shall mention three of them in what follows.

First, 1 Samuel 15 is part and parcel with what theologians and Biblicists call the *Heilsgeschichte* (history of salvation), that is, the history of Israel as seen by its people as being conducted by the "Lord of history" according to a divine master plan, a history in which the reality of the Land plays a central role. Before the conquest of Canaan (*qibbuš kenaʿan*) and after the deportation from Zion, the Land is the magnet. The book of Esther is revolutionary in that it ignores the Land and claims that the *Heilsgeschichte* finds its accomplishment in the Jewish diaspora![79]

Second, 1 Samuel 15 belongs to Israel's sacred tradition—it will find pride of place in the canonized Scripture (first century C.E.). But the contribution of the book of Esther to Israel's memory affirms the incompleteness of this specific tradition. "Scripture" is instead itself a process toward *entelechia*. There is not only an "infinite reading" of it,[80] but it itself is an infinite *écriture* in the sense that Esther "adds" itself to the corpus of the people's traditions. This is an important point in any discussion of the canon of Scripture.

Third, Esther is one more chapter in the ongoing struggle of the forces of good and justice against the forces of evil and inequity. The serpent's head must be time and again crushed underfoot (even under a wounded heel, see Genesis 3:15). The hydra has many hideous heads. Haman is just one of them. The list of historical monsters also is infinite.

Because of the unfinalizability of events according to the dynamic Jewish understanding of history, any noticeable occurrence (such as the war with Amalek in 1 Samuel 15) becomes *figura*—as Auerbach says—that is, a figure that is "real and historical announcing something also real and historical."[81] The protagonists in 1 Samuel 15 are "re-created," as is their combat, the outcome of which in Esther must be what was prefigured in 1 Samuel, namely, that the head of one will be crushed under the heel of the other.[82]

Is There an Evolution of the Characters in Esther?

Esther's change of mind in Esther 4 is insufficient to allow the classification of the book as a *Bildungsroman* (a novel about character development). As for Mordecai, the idea is even less pertinent. Mordecai remains from start to finish who and what he is, maintaining his identity; he is "Mordecai-the-Jew" and, as such, predictable, almost an archetype. The same may be said of Haman, who is less an individual than a stereotype of his nation, Amalek. Through him, it is the whole of his race that is scorned in Esther 6 and destroyed in Esther 7, but as an individual, he does not evolve in the story.[83]

Still we can see a certain movement of becoming in Esther. From obscure immigrant to pageant queen to queen of Persia—and eventually to savior of her people—the transformation is highly dramatic. While Mordecai is a "static unit" around which the action pivots, Esther is comparatively a "dynamic unit."[84] But the opposition between the two characters, Esther and Mordecai, is a relative one. As I shall emphasize later in this study, the two heroes are in fact the two faces of one reality. Even their different genders contribute to their global completeness. At the end of the story, they are practically indistinguishable.[85]

With them, history shifts course; they are threshold heroes at the hinge point of two eras. That is why Esther and Mordecai strive toward a historical (nonbiographical) future. They wittingly disappear behind their people's becoming.[86] Despite their elevated social position at the royal court, they are the servants of their community.[87] They are more public figures than private individuals, and they serve in different capacities. As we see in chapter 4 of Esther, Mordecai is to Esther what institutionalized Judaism, or rather "Jewishness," represents for all Jews, including the most unconventional ones. Esther, compared to him, is much more unruly, more unpredictable. Mordecai could not be conceived other than as performing "a function of the plot fate assigns to him."[88] Esther, on the contrary, must be molded to fit a role she did not even imagine for herself—but which she eventually plays to perfection. She is endowed with "a happy surplus of [her] own."[89] Her personality is more complex and hence more interesting. There is here more of an inner struggle and more of a personal victory and, therefore, a "surplus of meaning" (Ricoeur).[90]

All the same, one cannot speak of the book of Esther as a psychological drama. The characters are not described as struggling with contradictory sentiments or a diversity of options. Mordecai refuses to bow down before Haman and thus jeopardizes the security of the whole Jewish community, but this does not, it seems, involve for him any pangs of existential doubt. Esther shares the table and the bed of a pagan despot, but she does not appear to be troubled by any inner sense of contradiction. And because the characters do not express their feelings, the authorial role gains in importance. The author is omniscient. He or she knows what his or her heroes say and do even in private. Their reactions to different events are no mystery, and the author is privy to the dialogues between Esther and Mordecai, or between Esther and Ahasuerus, and makes no effort to disguise his or her omniscience behind a fictional eyewitness, a maid for instance, a servant, an intimate trustee[91]—or God himself. The absence of God from the story leaves the helm entirely in the hands of the narrator. Simply, the author *knows*, and the reader is implicitly invited to trust this knowledge, a knowledge confirmed by the reported events. There is no doubt that the king was furious at Vashti's noncompliance, for she was demoted and an edict was proclaimed to insure female subjection to their husbands.[92] Similarly, Esther must have changed course in her assessment of the situation arising from the threatened Jewish genocide, for she became an activist resister. Haman must have gravely blundered after Esther's accusation, for he was forthwith dispatched to his own gallows. And so on.

But the stress on the Jewishness of the heroes is what saves Esther from being merely an "adventure novel." For the narrated events ultimately belong to Israelite historiography, and the heroes' actions are encompassed within a much larger context than that of an episodic occurrence in the eastern diaspora. That it is not explicitly referred to in the book must be carefully taken under consideration (see below), for this void is not just for show. The story's emphasis on the Jewish people and their fate corresponds to the keen sense of history that characterizes Hebrew thinking. Barring generic ahistorical literature, such as wisdom literature and lyricism, biblical literature is saturated with a sense of time that we find again evident in Esther.

What this means is that, although God, YHWH, Israel, the *Heilsgeschichte,* and the Land are not mentioned in Esther, the book's place as part of Israelite (biblical) literature is self-evident. It is so because of the Jewishness of its heroes and the Judaization of the Persian festival, elsewhere called Fruraia, into Purim,[93] and because of the confrontation at the core of the story between Israel and Amalek, a sequel to the historic mutual hatred of the two nations.[94] Auerbach says of the Old Testament, that it is "obviously pieced together, but the various components all belong to one concept of universal history and its interpretation."[95] This applies as well to the book of Esther.

Space in Esther

If there is conformity with the "biblical" conception of time in the book of Esther, there is also, however, a new apprehension of space. As we saw above, it is probable that Esther was composed in the midst of the eastern Jewish diaspora in the third or second century B.C.E. But the ostensible chronotope is Persia in the fifth century B.C.E.—some three hundred years before the composition of the book, a fact that explains certain of its misrepresentations of the Persian Empire.[96]

Nonetheless, it is important to note that the action in the novella happens *outside* the (rather rigid) national framework, home of the epos. This monolithic, "withdrawn," world has been cracked open, as is also evident in other biblical stories, where one finds Joseph in Egypt, Jonah in Assyria, Daniel in Babylon.

This broadening of Israel's world vision evidently started with the sixth century B.C.E. exile in Babylonia. It grew even larger with the Jewish exposure to a succession of universal empires: Persia, Greece, and Rome. The mobility of the Jewish population (coerced or free) proved decisive to a deep axiological reassessment. From being somewhat confined to the purview of Israel's self-identity, Yahwism was confronted with "the world out there." Yahwism became universal, not only because of the Jewish dispersion (compare Esther 3:8), but because of a new interest among the Jews in the ambient world. A conspicuous sign of this is the mention of Persians professing themselves Jews in Esther 8:17. Thus one important factor favoring the book of Esther's entry into the Jewish canon of Scripture was this new Jewish interest in the external world.

The notion of space is omnipresent in the book. A quick look into the first chapters gives the following impressive result, a partial listing of scene changes that illustrate the text's versatility:

Banquet room in the royal palace (1:2)
Banquet in the palace garden (1:5)
Description of the site (1:6)
Banquet room in the palace (1:9)

Order of transfer from the second dining room to the first (1:10–11)
Letter sent to all the provinces (1:22; 3:13, 14)
Centripetal movement: gathering of young women to Susa (2:8)
Esther is brought into the best place of the harem (2:9)
Centripetal movement by women from the harem to the royal abode and centrifugally back to the harem (2:13–14)
Same movement by Esther (2:15–16)
"Banquet of Esther" organized by the king (no place specified) (2:18)
Mordecai sits at the king's gate (2:19, 21; compare 3:2, 3; 4:2a, 2b)
A gallows is erected for the conspirator (2:23)
The Jewish genocide is planned in the whole kingdom (3:6), in all the provinces (3:8; 4:3, 11)
In Susa (3:15; 4:1, 8)
In the city square in front of the king's gate (4:6)
In the palace (4:13)
"From another place" (4:14)
All the Jews in Susa are summoned (4:16)
And so on.

Clearly, space plays a major role in the story. In fact, no other biblical book emphasizes the spatial dimension as much. In Esther, it looks to be a quasi obsession of the writer. In Esther 5:1–2, for example, the description of space is stunning, to the point of topographical redundancy: "Esther . . . stood in the inner court of the king's palace, opposite the king's hall. The king was sitting on his royal throne inside the palace opposite the entrance of the palace. As soon as the king saw Queen Esther standing in the court . . ." (New Revised Standard Version; hereafter NRSV).

The localization of characters and events is not just a compositional method of zooming in on a variety of places; it also provides a kinetic dimension to the plot. The dramatic shift of chronotopes in Esther is striking. At one point, one can visualize the king sitting at Esther's table and then standing when he hears Esther's denunciation of Haman; he exits into the garden; he comes back into the dining room. Haman starts by coming into the banquet room; he sits down; he gets up; he prostrates himself before Esther; he is brought back to his feet; he is expelled to be hanged.

More impressive yet is the mobility of Esther herself. Initially in the tale she passes from her parental house, presumably in Jerusalem (see 2:6), to Mordecai's house in Susa, and then to the king's house (a rather frequent expression in the book), where she goes from a location meant for the common women to a better accommodation (2:9) and then to the king's bedroom (2:16). In what follows, she leaves her quarters at the palace to go to the king's audience chamber, then moves to various banquet rooms, and then returns to the palace, where she continues to assert her ubiquitous presence on all "fronts." In short, Esther is not conforming to the stereotype of the *femme au foyer*!

Despite a misconception on the part of biblical scholars setting out a too facile opposition between "time-oriented Israel" and the "space-oriented nations" of the ancient Near East, space has always been of keen interest to Israel. From the Garden of Eden to Mount Zion by way of the Oak of Mamre, Mount Moriah, the Nile Delta, the desert of Sinn, Mount Sinai, the land of the Canaanites, and so forth, space has always been of prime importance. The book of Esther just seems to be more acutely aware of space than were some prior documents in the biblical tradition.

But this does not mean that we should minimize the role of space in Esther. Although one cannot speak of a "discovery" of this notion here, it is clear that the consciousness of space has been sharpened by the Jewish diasporic experience of having been transplanted to foreign countries. As a result, we are faced with an increased maturity of a chronotope, reflecting the inseparability of space and time in human experience.[97]

In other words, the book of Esther affords us an amazingly mature work of literature for the second century B.C.E. Just as the time of Ahasuerus and Haman (see especially 3:7) was changed into the time of Esther and Mordecai (see especially chapter 9), so too space that began as being emphatically in the control of the king and his dependents, that is, a royal precinct, ends in the control of Esther and Mordecai (9:20–21, 30). At the end of the story, the vast spatial expanse of the empire shrinks under our eyes to the dimension of a single (Jewish) close-knit and restricted (homogeneous) community engaged in communal celebration and the exchange of gifts. Haman in chapter 3 had spoken of the Jews as "scattered" in the whole empire, but with Purim, all dispersion is transcended. True, there are town Jews and country Jews, but their celebration of common deliverance unites them into one eating, drinking, mourning, and reveling body. The contrast with the immensity of the Persian Empire cannot be starker. Eventually, the Great Vizier Mordecai and Queen Esther seem to reign over a nation reduced numerically to the size of the body of Jewish exiles. For the rest, what R. Bracht Branham says of Roman society appears to be applicable to that of Persia: it was "collapsing under the weight of an omnivorous empire."[98]

So Purim celebrates the reconquest of time *and space* by the Jewish diaspora. Esther is queen of Persia and Mordecai is second after the king, his sway felt over all the 127 provinces (9:30).

When all is said about this literary achievement, however, it behooves us still to measure the distance between the Esther novella and the chronotope typical of a Pentateuchal narrative, the sacrifice of Isaac in Genesis 22, for instance. The Genesis account contains no indication of time and hardly any of space. "Jeruel in the land of Moriah" remains vague. "Time and space are undefined and call for interpretation,"[99] and the story is "fraught with background."[100] This is much less the case with Esther, so that what Bakhtin hails as a novelistic progress, a fleshed-out chronotope, is perhaps not so much an improvement after all, when compared with the soberness and the "multilayeredness" of Genesis 22.[101] The result is that the demand the book of Esther makes on its readers is less one of interpretation than of analysis, while without interpretation, Genesis 22 means very little.

Speaking of literary attrition on the way from the patriarchal and matriarchal sagas to the Esther novella, another "loss" is, as we saw earlier, the stylization of its heroes. Esther and Mordecai are not "fraught with their own biographical past"[102] as are Abraham or David. On that score, Achilles and Odysseus never grow old, and neither do Esther and Mordecai.

Langue in the Book of Esther: An Exercise in Ambiguity

As is well known, Bakhtin was fascinated by the problem of language. One of his main categories of classification was the opposition between *monoglossia* and *polyglossia* or *heteroglossia*.[103] Esther happens to illustrate a perfect exemplar of empire monoglossia. When the king is not drunk and when his sayings are meaningful, his utterances are by state definition monosemic and unchangeable, even by himself. In fact, he may be drunk when he declares, "Vashti is never again to come before the king" (1:19), or, to Haman, "Do to them [the Jews] what seems good to you" (3:11), or again, to Esther, "What is your request, even to the half of my kingdom it shall be fulfilled" (7:2). He is infallible, and his words are the embodiment of the royal establishment and thus "inalterable." As a result, all the royal discourse is set on the same even level; such language is walled in, frozen, monoglossic.

Of prime importance in this respect is the reported language of the royal edicts. They represent such an extreme of monoglossia that they demand pure literalism of interpretation from the addressees. Their meaning is flat, plain, ironclad. It is "inalterable," like a theorem of geometry. It takes a second edict to contradict the first, without being able to replace it. As regards their effect, they are both appalling and ridiculous, tragic and comic.[104]

The monoglossia afflicting the Persian Empire could not invoke extenuating circumstances, for it was used in a polyglossic milieu par excellence. The text of Esther strongly insists on the multiple languages spoken in "the 127 provinces from India to Ethiopia" (1:1; 8:9; 9:20, 30). The monoglossic royal edicts allegedly must be chopped into pieces to be understood by so many diverse populations (3:12; 8:9–10)![105] Surely, by the way, in such a variegated world, there should be a place for the Jews! But, as we learn, anti-Semitism is the result of the sham assumption of the nation's homogeneity, which foreign bodies corrupt.

The worst enemy of monoglossia—on this Haman was not wrong, and the fact constitutes another intrinsic ambiguity of the narrative—is Jewish heteroglossia, which is about to "destroy the thick walls that had imprisoned consciousness within its own discourse, within its own language."[106]

Rather than being mutually exclusive, the fundamental conflict between monoglossia and polyglossia permeates literary genres in general. In the classic era of Athens, the trilogy of monoglossic tragedies was followed by an obligatory fourth drama open to ribald farce. This is a remarkable feature, but also one that keeps the two genres, the "high" and the "low," carefully separate.[107] It is remarkable, therefore, how the book of Esther mixes both genres, tragedy and iconoclastic parody. This mix in a second-century B.C.E. document is most remarkable. *Could it be perhaps a first in universal literature?*[108] Here, "weeping and laughter"[109] do not come in sequence but are concomitant. The sinister Haman is also a laughingstock, and the gallows he erects for Mordecai is preposterously huge.[110]

It should be noticed, furthermore, how the "establishment" is anxious to transform living discourse into written and frozen text.[111] The theme of writing runs throughout Esther. The royal dispositions are written down in the form of laws, and the king may delegate to some selected individuals this power of inscripturation, in the form of a seal (see 3:10; 8:10). Some scholars of the book of Esther have overlooked the parodic character of the story, and they condemn its ending for what they see as a sheer duplication of Persian rigidity. For them, the prescriptions about the Purim celebration are on a par with Ahasuerus's edicts.[112] But this critique, aimed in particular at Esther 9:25–28, is impertinent. The "irrevocable" disposition regarding Purim is the carnivalesque response in kind to the claimed absolute validity of the Persian law.

We can savor the thumbing of one's nose present in verse 9:27 ("as it was written and at the time appointed"). Purim itself, as we shall further see, is a parodic duplication of a Persian festival.[113]

The problem of language is central in Esther, its own language possessing tremendous attractiveness in its down-to-earth, prosaic discourse. The story is simply told without recourse to epic forms or mythic undertones. Even men obsessed by grandiosity, as are Ahasuerus and Haman, use hyperbole without pomposity. Mordecai and Esther keep their discourse at the level of ordinary speech.[114] It is in everyday existence, filled as it is with human interactions, and in taking account of circumstances, that appropriate and always variable (nonsystematic or normative) ethical decisions, with their inherent risks, are made.

Mordecai's decision not to honor Haman is a case in point.[115] What this rebellion hatches is only partially predictable and largely unforeseeable.[116] It is remarkable that Mordecai makes recourse to body language to express his contempt. Pressed by his peers to explain himself, he comes out with only the pithy and, in this context, enigmatic, "I am a Jew." This is enigmatic, but not cryptic. For, strikingly, neither at the outset of the drama, nor at the time of their final triumph, do the Jews adopt an idiosyncratic language of their own. The festival that celebrates the defeat of monoglossia is, fittingly, called by a "Persian" name, *Purim*—even though it is morphologically Hebraized—a just reciprocity balancing the self-Judaization of so many Persians, according to 8:17.

Mordecai's display of his Jewishness corresponds to the deep spirit of the whole tale. For the language in Esther, although carnivalesque in nature and exempt from religious jargon, is for all that fraught with ambiguous allusions to what can be called a theocratic understanding of Jewish destiny (see 4:14, where the presence of significant chronotopes is arresting: "another quarter"; "for such a time as this"). The Jews, it is here suggested, enjoy an uncanny protection. Such an authorial credo is a discreet but powerful justification of the Jewish diaspora.[117]

Other ambiguous religious markers appear elsewhere in the story. We are told, for example, that Mordecai, after learning about Haman's plan, dons sackcloth as tradition demands in cases of death (or the threat of death). He wails and leads a popular chorus, its members weeping, fasting, and lamenting, also attired in mourning garments (4:1–3). Later, Mordecai convinces Esther to intercede with the king, and here again mention is made of holding a fast (4:16).[118] On the other hand, in 8:15, we are told that Mordecai now dons royal garments, as he already had as an omen in 6:11, 13. In their material and colors these vestments—linen and blue, white, gold, and purple—recall those of the priesthood as described in the Torah (Exod. 28:6, 8, for example, which refers as well to blue, gold, and purple and to linen).[119] Bardtke is thus led to speak of Mordecai as a kind of secular priest.[120]

On the level of speech and gesture, the reader is brought in this way to the threshold of religious ritual. Furthermore, as already stressed above, at the core of the plot is the ancestral struggle between the Israelite and the Amalekite-Agagite and the conflicting worldviews they both represent. The events reported in Esther represent an ideological clash, and their respective conceptions of the Law unmistakably evoke the central position of the Torah in postexilic Judaism.

Let us mention here a further textual allusion in Esther to the religious tradition of Israel. It occurs in chapter 5. There, in verse 14, Haman's wife, Zeresh, advises him to erect a "tree" (so, literally) some seventy-five feet high, on which Mordecai should be "hanged." Now, hanging on a tree evokes the judicial system employed in Israel. The central text is found in Deuteronomy 21:23: for a crime punishable by death, the culprit is hanged on a "tree," and "anyone hung on a tree is under God's curse."[121] In short, we have in Esther the substitution of an Israelite punishment for a foreign one, because of its expected effect on a Jewish audience. The book of Esther, in fact, mentions hanging on a "tree" four times: in 2:23, the plotting eunuchs are hanged; in 5:14, Mordecai is to be hanged on the gallows; in 7:10, Haman himself is hanged; and in 9:14, so are Haman's ten sons.

Another characteristic of parodic literature is "to highlight certain elements while leaving others in the shade."[122] Clearly, at the crucial turn of the plot, when

Haman-"Agag" is squarely confronted, as well as at the very end, when a memorial of the salvation of the Jews is instituted, the author strikes a quasi-religious note. But the stroke is ever so light: the decisive term that would lift up the veil of ambiguity is delayed indefinitely. In short, the author plays with the reader's expectations. The text is gamelike:[123] "The 'normal' language"—as Bakhtin says[124]—is parodied brilliantly.[125] In the same vein, let us note the aberrant attribution of the gift of prophecy to Haman's wife, Zeresh (6:13)! This is doubtless meant to honor female intuition, but the polemical point will not be overlooked. Levenson sees the basis of Zeresh's prediction in texts that forecast Amalek's demise (for example, Num. 24:20).[126] But, here again, the text "does not identify the mysterious source of the deliverance of the Jews and the downfall of their foes."[127]

It is easy to imagine to what or to whom a traditional biblical text would attribute the Jewish salvation. With Esther, we are constantly verging on a theological pronouncement that is never expressed. This intended frustration of the reader's expectation belongs to the farcical mood of the story. And the irony extends to the social and political realms as well. A good example is offered by another ludicrous scene in Esther. It occurs in chapter 6, of which Levenson writes,

> Chapter 6 can be categorized equally well as a farce and as an omen. The farcical elements involve Haman's enormously foolish miscalculation as to the man whom the king would wish to honor (vv. 4–9) and the ensuing ludicrous scene in which the prime minister is compelled to serve as a herald for his archenemy, the lesser courtier, Mordecai the Jew (vv. 10–11).[128]

Another stylistic feature in Esther—present in all parodic literature—is its important dialogical dimension, already broached above. The contrast with the patriarchal and matriarchal sagas is strong, I said. But the tale here contributes to novelness with its inner dialogism, the dialogism of meanings, the dialogism of the local and the universal, of the anecdotal and the ever recurrent, of the new and the traditional, of the secular and the religious, of the moment and the *heilsgeschichtlich*, of the customary and the ritual.

The inner dialogism is compounded, of course, thanks to the tension between the book's time of composition and the reader's time; between "Persia" and the place in which the reading occurs; between the eastern Jewish diaspora and other Jewish contexts; or even between Jewish and Christian and secular viewpoints. For the religious realm is just sufficiently hinted at here to stir controversy. Esther *"donne à penser"* (is food for thought, as Ricoeur would say), if only because it disorients the reader.[129]

The narrative accent on the events rather than on the characters that we noticed earlier is, however, not strong enough to obliterate the latter's humanity completely. Thanks precisely to the speeches in the narrative, we feel, at least to a certain extent, Esther's terror (Esther chapter 4; in chapter 5, according to the Greek, she faints twice!) or Mordecai's steadfastness. Even Haman's yearnings and rage are made palpable and certainly audible (5:9–14; 6:13). The king's emptiness of mind and soul is evident, and his utterances contribute to verify the vacuum of his heart. True, the book presents no really successful character portraits, even though the tale is rich in reversals of fortune. But the author does allow the characters to interpret events for us from their own points of view, and their individual interpretations somehow contribute to the course of the events. Thus, although the characters are not here psychologized, we get some inklings of their psychology from the way they speak as much as from the way they act. Their speech is proactive. A modern attempt to analyze the psyche of Esther would perhaps be perilous but not out of the question, as is also the case regarding other biblical novelistic heroes—Jonah, for example.[130]

From the Pentateuchal sagas to the Second Temple period novellas, interest has shifted. According to the new zeitgeist, the focus is less on the overall thrust of history per se than on the historical experience of individuals whose interpretations of events and their significance conform or collide with one another. This new interest in individual experiences is illustrated too in contemporary Hellenistic literature. The Greek romance, for example, also features exceptional occurrences in which "the logic of chance is subordinated to another and higher logic."[131] Apuleius, for instance, focuses on his character Lucius's personal metamorphosis, "cut off from both the cosmic and the historical whole."[132]

But this, which is accurate of Apuleius's worldview, must be taken in another way when applied to the book of Esther. True, here too the story progresses thanks to peripeteia, but the "higher logic" in Esther is communal. The heroes in harm's way are the whole Jewish people, not just Esther and Mordecai, who probably could have escaped the common fate of destruction thanks to their eminent positions at the court (see 4:13; despite the contrary opinion of Mordecai).

This point is obviously of great importance. Inchoate individual psychology is here framed by a larger picture. Although *Israel* as a term never appears in the tale, it is Israel's fate from the point of view of diasporic Jews that is at stake. Eventually, this is acknowledged in the adoption of the feast of Purim in both Palestine and all Jewish communities.[133] Thus, Esther is no Greek romance. As Bakhtin says, the adventures in the Greek romance "constitute time sequences that are neither historical, quotidian, biographical, nor even biological and maturational."[134] The contrast with Esther is stark.

But Esther also is a *novel,* that is, a genre that Bakhtin held to be the most akin to everyday speech, one that is dialogical and relational in nature, with little recourse to artificiality, in short a "primary speech genre." As we saw, the very alloying of genres in Esther, corresponding to the variety of discourses, confirms that literary filiation. Esther displays the supreme Bakhtinian quality of *novelness* (*romannost*), the dialogical qualities of which contribute to the polydimensionality of the tale.

True, the focus is on a pair of Jewish heroes, but they cast a giant shadow, not just because of their personal intrinsic qualities, but because they embody an enormous surplus of meaning, a meaning not foreign to the ongoing dialogue of God with his people. This is not a small feat in a book that, deliberately, remained within the "confinement" of the secular. The far-reaching demonstration of this biblical book is that an absence of religious motifs may well speak louder than their textual presence. Counterbalancing the sacerdotal preeminence in the Second Temple, subversive narratives such as Ruth, Jonah, and Esther and poems such as Song of Songs have taken their distance from this with remarkable efficacy.

What is more, this new literary development is highly remarkable not just for shying away from stylistic religiosity, but for also shying away from all eschatological expectation. Not only are the narrated events stripped of all traditional paraphernalia, they find their full realization in the present rather than in the future. From a literary point of view, this can properly be called a major breakthrough. In Western literature, the only comparable parallel is found in the sixteenth-century Renaissance, with the triumph of humanism.

But let us say again that the book of Esther's areligious character does not mean it is "un-Israelite." Its protagonists are the Jew and the Amalekite, that is, good and evil, who also respectively represent polyglossia and monoglossia. The monoglossia of Persian totalitarianism clashes with the polyglossia of Israel's tradition, a polyglossia that has always thwarted systematization and dogmatism. While the Jewish heroes contribute to the "multilayeredness" of the tale, Ahasuerus and Haman proceed by edicts and utter generalizations. Even the license to overindulge with liquor is ordered by the king. (See 1:8, where the alleged inalterable Persian law is now the exemption from the law!)[135]

Similarly, Haman's description of the Jewish people as a "fifth column" in the empire is presented in terms of abusive abstractions. His discourse to the king (see 3:8) is characteristically vague and highly ambiguous. He describes the Jewish people as "unique" (the expression is often translated "a certain people," which hides the allusion), and the Jewish audience, of course, cannot but think: "unique as our God is unique" (see Deut. 6:4). They are "separated," continues Haman, and the audience would think: "Our separation belongs to our election [see Deut. 32:8], in the image of our God, who does not sit in any pantheon. And this is true also of our 'difference' and of our different laws [see Deut. 4:5–8]."

The reader will be accustomed by now to find the establishment employing a parody of parody, imitating the grotesque to attempt to neutralize the popular carnival. The wicked Haman turns what the people held in honor into shame and lawlessness. The dispersion of the Persian Jews ("scattered"), a painful predicament imposed by their enemies, is turned into a self-chosen, contemptible social and moral condition![136] No slanderous discourse could be more vicious, as it turns the best into the worst, the most honorable into the most abominable.

In a monoglossic world, the "others" do not really exist; they are but shadows.

Stalin once said, "The death of a man is tragic; the death of a million men is trivial." Esther and Mordecai, by contrast, are struggling for the acknowledgment and the integrity of the other. They impose on the king and his appointed vizier the *nomination*: those who were once anonymous and reduced to "nobodies" in Haman's discourse now face the king as concrete persons who cannot be ignored. One is the king's wife and the other a courtier, Esther and Mordecai, the queen and "the Jew" who saved the life of Ahasuerus. Even Haman is not anonymous here, because evil is no abstraction either. "Evil has a Face."[137] It carries a name and is therefore capable of being variously interpreted, despite its claim to monoglossia. It would be absolute only if Haman was nameless and soulless. But, with the advent of novelness in Esther, particularly from chapter 3 onward, "two myths perish simultaneously: the myth of a language that presumes to be the only language, and the myth of a language that presumes to be completely unified."[138]

The book of Esther is novelistic and not just a story. True, as Vladimir Propp would remind us, any folk-narrative always has a villain and a hero. But Esther is different from other comparable tales in that the villain here represents a construct, in fact, a worldview opposed to the Jewish worldview (see also 3:8).

In chapter 2 we shall address the topic of the dramatic confrontation of the two worlds: the world according to Haman and the world as interpreted by the Jewish people. These conflicting universes are the "surpluses of meaning" embodied by the narrative characters. They also constitute the all-encompassing struggle permeating human history from beginning to end.

2

The Book of Esther and the Powers That Be

Esther and Historicity

The book of Esther reports a set of events that never occurred. King Ahasuerus (Xerxes I, mentioned in Ezra 4:6) was not, in fact, the buffoon depicted in the tale. If there is any reality to his description in Esther, it is his known instability, sexual immorality, and violence. It would thus not be out of character for him callously to decide on the annihilation of a whole population of the kingdom. There never was a Jewish queen of Persia, however, nor was there a pogrom organized by the Persian establishment (the latter is recognized as having been unusually liberal). Nor was there a Haman the Agagite (3:1) or Haman the Macedonian (according to a Greek version, see LXX Add. E = Vulg. 16:1–24), and hence no in extremis salvation of the Jewish community in the East.

In fact, the inner chronology of the book indicates quite clearly that we are dealing with fiction. According to Esther 2:5–6, Mordecai was exiled to Babylon in 597 B.C.E., but he becomes vizier in "the twelfth year of the king," that is, in 473! Hence, his cousin Esther is some one hundred years younger than he, and Xerxes I (who reigned 605–562 B.C.E.) is made the direct successor of the Babylonian Nebuchadnezzar (who reigned 486–465 B.C.E.).

Are we then to conclude that Purim celebrates a fiction and that the story of Esther should be viewed as much ado about nothing? This would only be the case, if historicity were misconstrued as "historicality." For the book of Esther is truly *paradigmatic*. It mirrors the recurrent confrontation of Israel and Amalek (Esther 3:1 and 1 Sam. 15:8) and of Kish (father of King Saul) and Agag the Amalekite king (Esther 2:5 and 1 Sam. 9:1; 2 Sam. 16:5–8), points to which we shall return in chapter 5. The eventual triumph of Esther and Mordecai is the victory of the Angel Michael over the Dragon, of justice over injustice, of decency over obscenity, of good over evil.

The author of Esther probably wrote his or her stories in Mesopotamia (modern Iraq) or, more likely, in Iran, as reasons of language and realia argue for a Persian venue. If so, we must realize how much the Mesopotamian worldview influenced Persian mythology and religion. Ideologically speaking, no other place lent itself better to the conception of time as unfolding according to a predetermined cycle. We mentioned above the Babylonian New Year festival of the Akitu. Esther 3:7 is a clear reflection of it.[1] The god Marduk, after his victory over chaos (the goddess Tiamat), received from the other gods the power to decide the lots or destinies (*puru-um,* that is, *purim* in its Hebraized version) of all humans. It is certainly worth noting that the "anti-Marduk" Mordecai, after similarly struggling with destructive chaos, impersonated by the "wicked Haman," also has the power to make decisions for his people. This, however, he does *eph' hapax,* once and for all (9:20–23), not cyclically.

According to Esther 3 verses 7 and 12, Haman casts the *pur,* and the thirteenth day of the twelfth month (Adar) is designated for the genocide. This divine selection is proclaimed throughout the kingdom on the thirteenth day of the first month (Nisan); see verse 3:15. The date of the thirteenth day of the twelfth month (Adar) is repeated (and thus emphasized) in verse 13. All this is very precise and intentional.

Because the Babylonian Akitu, after merging with the New Year festival, was celebrated during the first eleven days of Nisan and "on the twelfth day Nabû and all the gods returned to their cities,"[2] the first twelve days of Nisan were out of the question for the invocation of the gods' blessing on the planned massacre. The first available day for casting the *pur* was the thirteenth of Nisan—which happens to be the eve of the Jewish Passover. This means that the edict of annihilation was signed as *the very first act* of the king after his restoration to the throne during the celebration of the New Year festival. Strikingly, too, the thirteenth of Adar is designated for the pogrom, that is, a date one month before the next Akitu or New Year ritual. Thus, the decision to kill the Jews, Passover, the Akitu, the Babylonian or Persian New Year, and even the actual slaughter are all combined into a single event that encompasses the entire year, from one New Year to the next.[3] The massacre becomes a prelude to the subsequent New Year festivities, a sort of blood orgy.[4]

What is furthermore remarkable about the annexation of the day on which Haman makes his decision to the main Babylonian (and now Persian) festival is that the destruction of the Jews is therefore tied to Marduk's victory over the forces of evil. The Persian purgation of its Jews will mark the beginning of a bright new era, corresponding to the advent of the new year. The feat deserves to be celebrated with some libation (3:15)—an uncanny blueprint for some modern demagogic propaganda.

In such a context, the planned pogrom is not an isolated event. It is integrated into the Persian religious calendar, and, therefore, it is easy to understand why the second royal edict, allowing the Jews to defend themselves, did not necessarily discourage an outpouring of anti-Semitism once the appointed day for the slaughter came along. After all, in the Babylonian or Persian myth, Marduk's foes were not "like a lamb that is led to the slaughter and like a sheep that before its shearers is silent" (Isaiah 53:7 [NRSV]). Perhaps, the Jew-haters thought that those of their own who would pay with their lives during the battle would be martyrs for a good cause and go straight to the abode of the gods?

At any rate, Haman's plan collapses, just like the walls of Jericho in Joshua's days. Or, at least, so says the book of Esther, the purpose of which, in parallel with the aim of the Purim festival, is, as it were, incantatory. Recounting the defeat of a seemingly invincible evil exercises an uncanny power of regeneration. Similarly, Bakhtin's book *Rabelais and His World,* written in the Soviet Union in the 1930s, proved to be a powerful regenerative instrument. Against the oppressive seriousness of the regime, Bakhtin brandished the supreme weapon: laughter.[5] The affinities of the book of Esther with the carnivalesque and satiric are unmistakable signs that it was written in a time of deep crisis.[6] The book's ostensibly historic setting is that of an impending genocidal threat.[7]

Paradoxically, the planned genocide is scheduled on the Persian religious calendar, while, in Esther, although the evil this time is external to the community (which is deemed an innocent victim, in contradistinction to Israel's prophetic denunciations of the people's own sinfulness), the traditional Israelite resource, the so-called help of religion, is dismissed as ineffectual. In Esther, the community looks not for divine intervention but for heroes, and the latter are not necessarily any more available to them than is God. The outlook is thus bleak, but the author expresses a firm belief that the "manifest destiny" of his or her people will meet the threat (4:14). True, the text does not completely dismiss religious tradition[8] and seems to credit fasting with a certain efficacy against evil (Esther 4:3, 16), but it clearly distances itself from *official* religion; in siding with the unconventional, its discourse becomes subversive.[9]

Now, several periods of Israel's history meet the conditions described in Esther. The Jews had a long history of persecution, and, furthermore, their official religion had been subjected to a constant strain of criticism. Other factors, however, help narrow the field, among them, the late cultivation of the novella genre. Other details in the text also indicate a date of composition in the late Second Temple period. The mention of the husband's language at home (1:22), for instance, which at first blush seems to make little sense, is in fact an interesting clue. Some readers have made recourse to a slight alteration of the Hebrew to mean "and [the husband should be able to] say whatever suits him," but such a "correction" is uncalled for. A simple comparison with Nehemiah 13:23–24 ("they [the former exiles in Babylon now back in Judah] could not speak the language of Judah, but spoke the language of various peoples," for "Jews had married women of Ashdod, Ammon, and Moab") shows in what context Esther 1:22 must be read and the era of its application. This and the state-organized genocide of the Jews during the Second Temple period, alleged by the book of Esther, leads us to assign the second century or, at the earliest, the third century B.C.E. for its (final) composition.

The book's fictional nature does not, of course, prevent it from occasionally echoing actual historical events. Even Rabelais's works contain accurate geographical names (the Abbey of Thélème, for example) and real historical allusions (such as the plague of 1552). The book of Esther displays a certain familiarity with Persia or, more broadly speaking, Mesopotamia. In short, chances are that the author was a Jew of the eastern diaspora deeply affected by the persecution of the Jews of Palestine and elsewhere under Antiochus IV Epiphanes (reigned 175–164 B.C.E.). But we have seen above how cautious one must be about drawing definitive conclusions from the exoticism of the setting of the book of Esther.[10]

Esther and the Empire

The book of Esther presents two worlds, the official world of the empire and the unofficial (and even secret) world of a community considered by Haman and thousands of anti-Semites to be "unruly," that is, to question the authority of the king:

> There is a certain people scattered abroad and dispersed among the peoples in all the provinces of your kingdom, and their laws are different from all people and they do not keep the laws of the king. It is not fitting that the king should leave them alone. (3:8)

As a corollary to this, Esther, as a mirror to her community, embodies the double Jewish response to the empire: assimilation and accession to government posts, on the one hand, but on the other a covert relativization of "the truth" claimed as timeless and absolute by the political authorities. Absolutism finds a fitting symbol in the book of Esther in the alleged immutability of the royal edicts, for absolutism consists in reducing all difference to conformity, in order to achieve a totalitarian (but nefarious) unity of the social body. By contrast, while Esther and Mordecai play by the rules, they know that the rules are transient and may unexpectedly become obsolete. A token of this can be inferred from Mordecai's indifference to the absence of the royal reward he should have received after uncovering the conspiracy against the king (6:1–3; see also 2:21–23). Esther and Mordecai are, in Johannine parlance, "in the world but not of the world" (John 15:19). An antipodal attitude is that of Haman, who believes in the "absolute truth" of the state and in himself as acceding endlessly to ever more power (3:1–2; 6:6–9; compare LXX, Add. E = Vulg. 16:1–24).

What the text of Esther seeks to convey with the (perhaps inaccurate) statement about the immutability of the Persian law is a certain conception of what it means to be human. It is a conception that clashes with Montesquieu's position, for instance, that humanity obeys a set of laws but is (and must be) nonetheless free to act.[11]

Dictatorial regimes, of course, deny this human liberty. They establish laws that claim to define what it is to be human and that are by definition immutable. This is the "historicity" we find in Esther and in Daniel's denunciation of the inflexibility of Persian law. What is more, the understanding of the state's ideology in Esther is not wrong.

Indeed, in order fully to savor the tale, it is important to understand the legal backdrop against which it unwinds. "In the political theology of the Persian kings," says David Bickerman,[12] the king himself is the law.[13] His person, and the unlimited legal power he represents, is the only decisive cohesive factor holding together his immense and motley empire. That is why the king's will is equated with truth and righteousness, the attributes of the supreme god, Ahura Mazda. Consequently, all insubordination must represent a lie and an injustice.[14] Biblical texts of that time show that Jews were deeply impressed with this conception of state law, however foreign it was to them. Both Daniel and Esther note with amazement the irrevocability of "the statutes of Persia and Media."[15] Despite some confirmation found in Diodorus Siculus XVII:30 (refer again to note 15, here), it is safer to construe this motif as belonging to folklore and as meant to emphasize the dramatic absence of any means of escape, first for Queen Vashti and then for the Jews.

The word used for *law* in Esther and some other biblical books is the Persian loanword *dat,* which in Hebrew came also to mean "religion." The Persian kings were not gods by nature, but there was little difference between the royal and the divine will—the king's unlimited power smothered itself and enslaved the lawgiver. The king cannot countermand his earlier decisions, whether to throw his friend Daniel to the lions or to allow the massacre of a whole population (Dan. 6:15–17; Esther 8:8).

The plot of Haman—"the enemy of the Jews," as he is repeatedly called[16]—takes its meaning from such a context. He describes an anonymous people unruly to the king and whose laws are not the king's dictates.[17] In such cases, Persian kings often had recourse to transplantation of entire populations. But the people in question are already scattered, Haman says; so, he urges, the only solution is the "final" one. They must be "destroyed, slain, and annihilated, all of them, young and old, children and women, in a single day . . . and their possessions plundered" (Esther 3:13).[18] To make the proposition more acceptable to the king, who might worry about the loss of so many taxpayers, Haman offers to pay ten thousand talents of silver to the state treasury, that is, by some estimates, about two-thirds of the annual income of the Persian empire (according to Herodotus 3.95, "the yearly tribute to Darius amounts to 14,560 talents"). Of course, Haman's offer must be put in a history-like context. Verisimilitude is respected here to the extent that Xerxes in the fifth century B.C.E. was hard-pressed for funds (but the amount of the bribe belongs to the author's comic strategy). Furthermore, Xerxes practiced a policy that favored the Persian population over other colonized peoples. Selling the destruction of an entire non-Persian community for cash (especially in this amount) is not entirely out of character.

This, by the way, allows us to understand better Esther's argument with the king in 7:4. She tells him, "We have been sold, me and my people, to be destroyed, slain and annihilated. Now, even if we had been sold into slavery, males and females, I would have said nothing about the fact that such an onslaught [*hatzar*] would not compensate [*showeh be*] the damage done to the king." The argument is purely economic. As David Daube writes, the book means to demonstrate "that a government has more to gain by orderly taxation than by giving over the Jews to massacre"[19]—truly, a minimalist reading of Esther!

In this respect, Esther's diplomacy is a model of wisdom. Her argument must deal a fatal blow to Haman without dragging the king into a scheme in which, in fact, Ahasuerus is himself deeply implicated. She exonerates him, however, by acknowledging that he, as the sovereign of Persia, had every right to reduce a community of his empire to thralldom. Were the matter just that, Esther would not even bother the king with a petition in favor of her people. But someone wicked has misled the king and replaced slavery (for an estimated benefit of ten thousand talents; see Esther 3:9) with annihilation pure and simple. Esther thus pretends to believe that the king initially had no intention to allow a pogrom but was manipulated by a deceitful vizier. She seems to say to her husband, "Of course, had you known that what you signed as law would cost the lives of my people, you would not have proceeded with the writ."

The king, now that he realizes that his queen belongs to the targeted people, rushes to seize the opportunity she offers and immediately looks for the "sole" culprit of the plot, whose identification will exculpate him: "Who is he and where is he?" (7:5)—a real Molière comedy! Some five centuries later, but in an obscene gesture that is a far cry from comedy, the Roman Pilate will symbolically wash his hands and declare himself innocent (Matt. 27:24).

As to the alleged compliance and glibness of Esther, let us realize that she had, at this point, only two options: either to pit power against itself—which is what she actually does—or to attempt to behead Ahasuerus her husband and his vizier with a sword, à la Judith. (In this, the story of Judith offers an alternative to the story of Esther.)[20] But Esther's tale is not about a coup d'état, which, by the way, would have been a suicidal folly providing full justification to the Jew-haters for their pogrom. What proved productive in the case of Judith "at home" would have been totally counterproductive in the case of Esther abroad.

In presenting his indictment of the unruly people he wants to annihilate, Haman has carefully avoided specifying exactly about whom he was speaking. Now Esther turns the scheme against its author and suggests that the king was kept in the dark and signed the first edict on the basis of a different interpretation than that intended by Haman. The spotlight has thus shifted back to Haman's discourse in Esther 3, duplicating its innuendo but now providing a motive as to why "it is not in the king's interest to let [the ones flouting of the king's laws] rest" (see 3:8). We shall follow that lead. Linguistically speaking, Haman's conspiracy represents, as says Bakhtin, who knew what he was talking about,[21] the gloomy "seriousness" of "a truth already established,"[22] a "truth" that expresses itself in "violence, intimidation, threats, prohibitions."[23]

Haman's "already established" truth, behind which he hides and on which he builds his lethal scheme, is the inalterability of Persian law. Consequently, what he deems unbearable, not only personally but also for the entire empire[24]—on the model of the unacceptability of not only Vashti's but all women's disobedience in chapter 1—is that there should be any other conception of the law than that shared by all non-Jews (3:8).

Thus, the book of Esther recounts the clash between two laws and, beyond that, between two worldviews. We could define the problem as a contest between two concepts of inviolability. The dénouement of the story will show that, in reality, it is the Jewish people who are inviolable, not any such abstraction as "Persian law" (6:13; compare 4:14). When ideology prevails over humanity, the machine indiscriminately crushes both friend and foe. It is up to satire to show that the first victim of such legal inflexibility is neither a Jew nor an outlaw. Summoned by her godlike husband to appear at the royal banquet at Susa, Queen Vashti refuses and is summarily put aside, to the chagrin of everyone involved. The king has indeed become a laughingstock for, when his claim to status is denied—by Vashti—he "becomes mere vanity [and] an object of ridicule or contempt."[25]

The Powers That Be

The book of Esther contains neither ideology nor mysticism: no Jewish isolationism and no flag-waving. The Jews in Persia do not constitute a separate entity by their location, for they are "dispersed and scattered among the peoples in all the kingdom's provinces" (3:8). They are not troublemakers, for their fidelity toward the host nation and its governing body is in truth flawless (2:21–22; 6:2). Their "otherness" is not in and of itself subversive, for some of their eminent representatives have justly acceded to high positions in the government of Persia. Notwithstanding this, the point put into relief by their foes is not their contribution to the welfare of the state[26] but their *difference:* they have "different laws from those of all nations," as Haman says (3:8).

This chief accusation, let us note, is all the more paradoxical and even ludicrous as some half a century earlier the Persian king Darius had promoted the "Jewish" law to the rank of state law in Judea, so that much of the actual Pentateuchal legislation found formal expression and official validation under the Persian administration. Xerxes' successor, Artaxerxes I, continued Persian backing for Jewish law and appointed Ezra to enforce it (see Ezra 7:26).

Jewish alterity is what Haman and the empire cannot tolerate because, for them, another truth beside the "absolute truth" is inconceivable. "Another law," by state definition, must be disobedient to the king's laws, just as no sanity but that declared by the state can be so. Haman in Esther 3:8 lays bare the very foundations of dictatorial regimes. All dissidents are to be "destroyed, killed, and slaughtered," whether "young or old, children and women," and "in one day" (3:13). In Bakhtin's time, they were sent to gulags or to psychiatric institutions or worse.

Within this sociopolitical context, the most interesting aspect of carnival is the *epochè* (state of doubt) it initiates as regards all the powers that be. In this "*monde à l'envers*"[27] instituted by carnival, all social inequalities are leveled; all hierarchical differences are erased for a time. The "absolute truth" of the establishment is shown to be relative after all. Carnival inflicts a mortal blow to totalitarianism. This is what Bakhtin had in mind in so unconditionally praising laughter and the grotesque. A counterexample to this insight is provided by the modern unhappy examples of dictatorial systems such as Nazi Germany, Italian and Japanese fascism, Stalinist communism, or the North Korean burlesque: they all had or have recourse to huge popular "spontaneous" mass manifestations of support for their enslavement systems. I have called these manifestations a "parody of parody," because their aim is to prevent the free expression of the carnivalesque spirit by channeling and manipulating it into its antipodal opposite.

Now, it is true that the author of Esther seems to invite criticism on this score, considering that, at the end of the story, two aspects are combined that look mutually contradictory. On the one hand, the dénouement purports to show Mordecai and Esther endowed with a redeeming authority in Persia. They change the course of events for the better; they institute the festival of Purim and decide its perennial celebration. But, on the other hand, if left this way, the new situation under the sign of another dictated solution could be construed as the replacement of one (oppressive) power by another (benign) power, that is, in sum, an anticarnival that would defeat the general purpose of the book. Accordingly, the whole passage of Esther 9:27–32 containing the commandment to observe Purim has been regarded by critics with great suspicion as to its authenticity.[28] An official ordinance is ill-suited to the unofficial and merely tolerated nature of popular carnival. Laughter no more than love can be commanded!

And yet, Jesus for one repeats the Leviticus command to love one's neighbor (to which the Nazarene added the order to love even one's enemy). Love thus can be ordered to defeat hatred—and laughter can be ordered to defeat fear. For laughter frees us from fear. This is its main function; "laughter is essentially not an external but an internal form of truth."[29]

Esther and Mordecai are, of course, totally incapable of making the people laugh on command, but they can and they must command the people to choose laughter over fear. They order them to commemorate their salvation from historical determinism (that is, to enact a presentment of the past), and this is highly paradoxical in a book that so far had been all but historically amnesic, as we saw above. Against this, we are meant to understand that the institution of the festival of Purim is an anamnesis: "do this in remembrance." One readily thinks then of Hans-Georg Gadamer's exhortation to rescue memory from being just a psychological faculty. "Memory must be formed, for memory is not memory for anything and everything."[30]

All the same, Esther and Mordecai have adopted a stance of authority toward the people (as Jesus later will do in his command to love). Now, although the line of demarcation between power and authority may at times be blurred, the distinction between them must be stressed. There is no authority without a foundation of power, but the problem is always what kind of power shores up a claim of authority (parental authority, for instance). As for King Ahasuerus, he wields an abusive and preposterous authority based on a despotic and unquestioned power, the Persian "immutable law," and Haman cannot tolerate that this kind of absolute power might not wield authority over Mordecai, for obviously a power without authority is a "clanging cymbal" (1 Cor. 13:1).

Regarding Esther and Mordecai, the question raised in the last chapters of the book, therefore, is what kind of power they represent that endows them with authority in the eyes of their people. Of course, we could invoke their eminent positions at the royal court. Esther is queen, and Mordecai is vizier. But then their authority would not be any more legitimate than the ridiculed one of the king or the nefarious one of Haman.

Hence, the author faces an ambivalent situation: the Jewish heroes must be described as wielding authority, even a quasi-supreme authority, but not in the name of an oppressive, unquestioned power. Because of this, the style in chapters 9 and 10 of Esther becomes convoluted. Queen Esther is said to be "daughter of Avihail" and the Vizier Mordecai is, as usual, "the Jew,"[31] both of them representing a two-sided figure combining aristocracy and populism (9:29). The order of their names in the text is interchangeable: "Mordecai the Jew and Esther the Queen" (9:31). They institute the feast first "for themselves" (9:31) before extending it to others. Furthermore, the ingredient of fasting and mourning (9:31) sets a mood far distant from carefree reveling on the model of the royal banquets (especially as depicted in Esther). Significantly, in the following verse (9:32), Esther is deprived of all her titles. And as for Mordecai, although he is "second in power in the kingdom after Ahasuerus," he continues, as just mentioned, to be designated as "Mordecai the Jew."[32] This awesomely powerful man[33] appears to his people as simply "a great man, beloved by the multitude of his brethren" (10:3).

Vis-à-vis the Persians in general, Esther and Mordecai exert a power that stands very much in parallel with Joseph's rule over the Egyptians in Genesis 49. Vis-à-vis their own people, however, Esther and Mordecai are just primi inter pares. In summary, in the utopia found in the book of Esther, the powers have not altogether disappeared, but they have been shaped to serve democracy rather than their own absolutist claim.

The story of Esther is truly about the clash between two worlds, the powers that be versus utopia.[34] No other biblical book is more poignantly "modern" after Auschwitz. Even geography contributes to the universality of the tale. The immensity of the Persian Empire—a fact stressed in Esther—makes the chronotope appropriate to the story cosmic. Banquets in the book involve thousands of people and last for months. Space and time are sketched on an enormous scale. They provide a context of excess for the evil hatched by Haman and for the no less "excessive" defeat of that evil by Esther and Mordecai.[35] The festival of Purim that concludes the story confirms the universal dimensions of a local incident in the eastern Jewish diaspora. The voluntary Judaization of non-Jews follows naturally (Esther 8:17).

But evil is not only hatched around a few bottles of wine (see 3:15). Evil translates into cunning and violence. I shall broach these terrible ingredients in the book of Esther in chapter 5.

3

The Secularism of the Book of Esther

A Nonreligious Document in the Bible

As the Song of Songs scoffed at certain sclerotic customs (such as the *mohar*) in contemporary Israel,[1] Esther scoffs at the foreign culture of the Persian (or any other) empire. In the persons of Ahasuerus and Haman, the empire has become mad. In opposition to this, but deprived of any semblance of power (even Esther is powerless; see. 4:11, where she is among "all alike"), the people's only recourse is carnival. Now, carnival is essentially parodic[2] and devoid of the sacred and of official piety, both of which are sometimes satirized. Esther does not go that far, but it all but ignores the sacred. That is why the Greek versions of the tale that reintroduce the sacred utterly miss the point, despite their good intentions (see chapter 7 for more on the Greek versions). It is impossible that any of the Greek versions of the book can be more "original" than the Masoretic text.[3] For a narrative of this kind to have any authenticity, it must be areligious. Carnival is no procession of the Holy Sacrament. The absence of piety is voluntarily subversive. Implied is a critique of the official religiosity as incapable of helping a community under threat of annihilation and as therefore obsolete for all practical purposes. The reader must be sensitive to the scandal of a story purporting to recount the salvation of the Jewish people without divine intervention, when no other circumstances could more imperatively demand the acknowledgment of Providence. The reader's expectation is utterly frustrated. On the eve of the Persian "final solution," in Esther 4, Mordecai expresses his conviction of Jewish survival, but it will not be thanks to God's protection. There is thus a dramatic shift from God's care for his people to a popular quality of resilience (see chapter 8 on Esther as Judeo-centric). Esther is an expression of folk culture.

Let us note that Mordecai's discourse to Esther in chapter 4 is what Bakhtin calls "innerly persuasive," that is, the discourse is "half-ours and half-someone else's."[4] It is evident that Mordecai's words are rich in background and that they are not his creation; but their orchestration—as Morson and Emerson say[5]—is his. Finally, the persuasiveness of his discourse is a product of both what it assimilates from others' speech—here Israel's socioreligious tradition—and how it "reaccentuates the word" by giving to it a new meaning.[6]

Had the author struck an unambiguously religious note in the narrative, the story's philosophy would have been utterly altered. Esther subverts any monoglossic absolutism, not in the name of dedication to another expressed chronotope (for instance the *Heilsgeschichte,* or Zion), but out of conviction that absolute truth kills.

An example of Esther's ambiguous vocabulary is provided by Laniak in his monograph *Shame and Honor in the Book of Esther.* He calls attention to the description of the king's volatile reaction to Vashti's disobedience. The verb "to be angry" in Hebrew is most of the time attributed to God. The same lexical contamination was also true as regards the king's glory earlier in the chapter, Laniak says, and the description of the royal palace in Esther 1 makes one think of Israel's Temple.[7] Beside the fact that these elements reveal the author's familiarity with Israel's traditions and literature, there is without a doubt a parodic style here. The king's hubris almost amounts to a claim to divinity. The "divine" Ahasuerus, however, covers himself with ridicule in the ensuing scenes. Vashti is banned just as Israel was exiled for disobeying God, says Laniak. But, here again, all this is said in Esther with tongue in cheek.

The book of Esther is thus areligious, but it is not pagan. In chapter 1 above, I have discussed several examples in which the author harps on quasi-religious themes. The author toys with the reader's expectations; the text is gamelike, we said. In the already mentioned episode of Haman's consultation of fate, let us note an interesting detail that once again contrasts with traditional biblical literature. In a parodic move that recalls the Israelite recourse to the *"urim and thumim"* (compare Exod. 28:30; Num. 27:21; Ezra 2:63 = Neh. 7:65), Haman casts the *pur* to request the support of the numinal for his lethal project. In a stark contrast to this, the Jews have no corresponding resource in our story, although they confront a whole complex of vicious individuals, state machinery,[8] and demonic spirits. Against all these odds, nevertheless, charismatic Esther and Mordecai triumph with their "bare hands," so to speak, and the victory is celebrated in a festival ironically called *Purim.*[9]

For an important element of the "Jewishness" of the book of Esther is the implicit understanding that history is not the product of any kind of determinism. The actions of Esther and Mordecai do make a difference; so much so that they actually change the course of history. According to Ahasuerus and Haman, history is predetermined; it is programmed and cast indelibly in writing. On the thirteenth of Adar, some eleven to twelve months after Haman cast the *pur,* "all the Jews . . . throughout the whole kingdom" will be destroyed (3:3, 6). Even when the king feels sorry for his earlier command, he cannot change it, something that would actually relativize the absolute determination of history (1:19; 8:8; see Dan. 6:9, 14–18). Against this, the pivot on which the book of Esther turns is precisely the change of fortune that allows the community to pass from death to life.

The delay between the casting of the *pur* and the actual date of the genocide has often intrigued commentators, who see no sense in this "unnecessary" feature of the text. But, in fact, the delay of eleven months shows a sadistic trait in Haman's plot. He is like a cat playing with a mouse before eating it. The agony of the prey is protracted in the knowledge that it has no escape. Pragmatically, the retardation of events allows the department of state propaganda ample time to incite anti-Semitic feelings among the empire's other populations. The latter are informed that the gods have determined there will be an extermination and when it will inexorably take place. The delay, therefore, is not "inexplicable" (so Paton, followed by many scholars): it is sheer viciousness.

The story sets up an uncanny correspondence between, on the one hand, the twelve-month preparation of the maidens before being summoned by the king (2:12), and, on the other hand, the Jewish genocide that is to happen on "the thirteenth of the twelfth month" (3:13). True, the author is fond of such coincidences, but the purported parallel looks incongruous. Later we shall deal with the common fate of women and Jews in the story's "Persia." Suffice it for now to notice that the authorial device of retardation emphasizes the king's indecisiveness and whimsicality, both in his private life and in politics. There is also a comic contrast between the haste in gathering the young maidens, or in publicizing a royal edict of extermination, and the sluggishness of the result. In one case, twelve months of preparation precede one night with the king; in the other case, eleven to twelve months of threatened danger hang over the Jews before the planned massacre will commence "on one day, the thirteenth of the twelfth month" (3:13).

The story is not shy about stating with precision when the various events take place. The delay between Haman's casting of the *pur* and the actual genocide must be meaningful. The same is also true when earlier in the story four years elapse between the selection of beautiful virgins for the king's pleasure and Esther's summons to the palace (see Esther 1:3 and 2:16). Now the second writ of the king is dated "the twenty-third day of the third month [Sivan]" (8:9), and Clines perceptively notes that seventy days have passed since the casting of the lots.[10] The number *seventy* is highly symbolic as a multiple of two figures that point to completeness: seven and ten. When Jeremiah 25 forecasts a symbolic seventy-year duration for the exile in Babylon, his prophecy is nevertheless taken literally by subsequent generations, although it is inaccurate chronologically speaking (the exile's duration was less than half that figure). Daniel 9, to cite an example, is also built on that assumption (see there, verse 2). *Seventy* has become the cipher of exile. When "seventy" years are over, the time of restoration starts.

The allusion in Esther 8 to the time of the exile and its eventuation into the time of restoration is a subtle but very consequent mimicry. Both exile *and restoration* are now happening in Persia. The return to Zion after 538 had given increased meaning to Passover; but in Esther, there is no return to Jerusalem and no Passover; there is an entirely new celebration, Purim, a celebration of the happy[11] Jewish implantation in the land of their "exile." The *people* has been substituted for land, Temple, and cult; its leaders are not priests—as were the high priest Joshua or the priest Ezra—but sages fully involved in the host country's affairs and politics. Indeed, the book of Esther is the exultant acknowledgment of diaspora Judaism.

Pursuing our investigation into the quasi but not quite religious nature of our tale, let us recall the principle of extravagance, encountered earlier, that permeates the book of Esther. Terms such as "grotesque" or "parody" have been used. The rapprochement with the same worldview in the Gospels is uncanny. One thinks, for instance, of the overabundance that characterizes the Kingdom of God, according to Jesus. Most of his parables are about it: selling everything one has in order to buy the precious pearl (Matt. 13); the Kingdom of God being a seed of mustard becoming a tall tree (ibid.); the woman sweeping all her house floors to retrieve a lost coin (Luke 15); giving up one's life to earn life (Matt. 16); presenting the other cheek when slapped in the face (Matt. 5); leaving the dead to bury their dead (Matt. 8); the lavishness of the widow's perfume as an ointment for Jesus' feet (Luke 7); judging according to the principle of amplification dictated by love (John 8); and so forth. Extravagance is certainly a central concept in Jesus' teaching. Finding it so amply developed in Esther is remarkable. Of course, not all extravagance is to be applauded as such, but when it is at the service of loving commitment and of liberation from the shackles of petrified religion, it amounts to a rebirth.

Esther sets itself at a distance from what Bakhtin calls the "high, proclamatory genres—of priests, prophets, preachers, judges, leaders, patriarchal fathers, and so forth."[12] The book's secularism demanded that much. True, the "biblical" narrative genre in general—the main literary genre in Bible literature—has provided the author of Esther with a compositional style, but what is remarkable is the resulting avoidance of the proclamatory tone of voice. The contrast is made even starker when set against the Greek versions, which adjoin long citations of petitions to the divinity for its intervention in favor of the people, things purposely left unexpressed in the Hebrew text.

From a generic point of view, nothing prevented the Esther novella from making use, as discreetly as one might wish, of, say, the prophetic proclamations so characteristic of the earlier biblical narratives. As a matter of fact, the Hebrew Esther contains a "prophecy" of sorts, set ironically in the mouth of Haman's wife, Zeresh (see below in chapter 4). Even Mordecai's firm conviction in Esther 4 that "salvation will come from another corner" (verse 4:14) can be equally construed as prophetic. But those clues are exceptionally understated and ambiguous. The Bakhtinian distinction between *first line* and *second line* in the history of novelistic literature applies here. In short, the distinction between the two lies in how a particular novel "exploit[s] the resources of heteroglossia to create dialogized 'images of languages,'" as Morson and Emerson say.[13] The first (stylistic) line "merely approximates [a] true novel," as we find it only in the second-line novels (of Dostoevsky, for instance) with their full heteroglossia. First-line novels are stamped by their authors to such an extent that the characters are more or less stereotyped and act, so to speak, by remote control.[14] Second-line novels allow their characters much more freedom of opinion: they express themselves more or less independently of authorial control. The author is in dialogue with his or her characters in a second-line novel, while in first-line novels the author is from the outset omniscient and thus engaged in a monologue that uses alternate voices. This division of the material is in part chronological, Esther belonging to the first line, while Dostoevsky's work, for instance, is clearly second line. I shall return later to this point.[15] But, beyond the chronological, they are also separated by an ideological divide. According to Bakhtin, it is a characteristic of the first-line novellas to include quotes from conventional discourse, such as letters or legal texts; hence, we may infer that some kind of oracle would not be out of place in the Hebrew Esther, which could, therefore, have cited such discourse. It is evidently with the purpose of remaining extra sober in tone that the author refrained from doing so. When we turn to the Greek versions, it is remarkable that the "double-voiced" proclamatory quotes of edicts, discourses, prayers, exhortations, and so on, are detachable from the whole and are therefore marked as disposable; their absence from the Hebrew text contributes to the same conclusion, of course.[16]

We have seen in chapter 1 above that the literary genre of Esther is not epos, tragedy, history, or lyric poetry. It rather recalls the antique Greek *spoudageloion* (seriocomic) configuration. Characteristic is the absence of recourse to tradition (including religious tradition), which is treated—if at all—with mistrust or even cynicism. It is, Bakhtin says, a whole revolution in the history of the literary picture.[17] Another characteristic is the mix of the elevated and the vulgar and the parody of quoted dialogues or pronouncements (edicts, for example).[18]

Thus, Esther is a very "modern" document emanating from a freethinking writer clearly influenced by folklore (although it is not itself a piece of oral literature). Rather than speculate, however, about the "folk" origin of the story, we must credit the author with a high degree of creativity and a skill for ironic composition, "expunging the sacred and authoritarian word in general, with its indisputability, unconditionality, and unequivocality."[19] It is a trait of carnival literature to deal with existential questions in a nonphilosophical, nonreligious, and nondogmatic way. Thus is verified Bakhtin's assessment of the "carnival-grotesque" as,

> liberat[ing] from the prevailing point of view of the world, from conventions and established truths, from clichés, from all that is humdrum and universally accepted. This carnival spirit offers the chance to have a new outlook on the world, to realize the relative nature of all that exists, and to enter a completely new order of things.[20]

The absence of the customary ingredients of historic Israel's religious thought (such as Land, Zion, Temple, ancestral history, Mosaic Law, and so on) allows the author to remain utterly focused on the microcosmic dimension of the events as narrated. One finds in Esther the basic theatrical unity of place, time, and plot. It is only when everything has been said and done, when the plot has reached its dénouement, that the book dovetails to include all generations and all places (9:28).[21] And this it should do, lest the story remain at the level of a parenthetical and tragically common incident in the Jewish diaspora.

Interestingly enough, the microcosmic concentration of the tale in Susa helps create a world the coherence of which is enhanced by precise allusions to the Persian court and regime and by its anchorage in history.[22] At those points, the author differentiates the story from the "legendary" and makes clear that it develops a powerful image of actual anti-Semitism and even of a specific threatened pogrom. The author may have in mind contemporary events in Jerusalem or Alexandria, but he or she clearly knows the eastern diaspora better and thus sets the drama in Susa, although "this individualized picture is presented in wider dimensions,"[23] to include all the Jews everywhere as well as the non-Jews who join them.

This latter group (see 9:27) are called the *nilwim* (joiners), a word that later designated converts to Judaism.[24] The term *nilwim,* however, is semantically the same as the word for Levites (*lewiim*). In Esther, those who "join" are gentile subjects of King Ahasuerus, but the reversal of situation that occurs at this juncture of the narrative is so radical that those gentiles appear to fulfill the prophecy of (Third) Isaiah 66:21: "And I will also take some of [the gentiles] as priests and as Levites, says YHWH."

In this total turning of the tables, by which it becomes preferable in the empire to be Jewish rather than "goyish," there is a roaring laughter—and a blatant wishful thinking, of course. Would it not be hilarious if the non-Jews, instead of considering Jewishness as a liability, queued up at the synagogues to be circumcised and become Jews? This is the amusing element in 8:17. The habitual "rabbits" are now killing the "hunters." Wisely, says the text, some of the latter pass into the ranks of the former: an idealistic conception.

All the same, this conjunction of particularism and universalism is remarkable. The book of Esther has been frequently condemned in Christian milieus as nationalistic and exclusionary. But the carnivalesque genre represented here is antipodal to "privatism." As we saw above, elitism and exclusionism do not apply here, but they do apply to the Persian institutions and official ceremonies. These are a parody of carnival because they are meant to back up authoritarianism as a fait accompli. On the contrary, questioning the powers cannot be individualistic and bigoted. The feast of Purim is an open invitation to all, as behooves carnival.[25] As Bakhtin insists, carnival is not meant to be a show for the pleasure of spectators. Carnival demands that onlookers become participants.[26] This feature is much stressed in Esther. The effect of the royal decision to massacre the Jews throws the city of Susa into pandemonium (3:15); when fortune turns and the Jews are saved from annihilation, the city of Susa "cries out in joy" (8:15). Thus, although the anti-Semites in Persia were not few in number (seventy-five thousand of them are killed), the populace in general did not remain passive; they were not "watching through the drawn curtains of their windows," as happened so often in twentieth-century Europe, when "the folktale turned into a horror story."[27] The isolation of Ahasuerus and Haman in the story (3:15) is a very effective literary device underscoring the falsity of the administration's claim to speak for the people. The exercise of power, indeed, isolates.[28]

In short, the result of the royal decisions is not the one expected. While Ahasuerus and Haman drink and make merry, the populace—that is those capable of mounting a carnival—are on the contrary "thrown into confusion."[29] This information is highly significant; it shows that Persian anti-Semitism was circumscribed to people in power or to those avid to accede to power. This clear distinction between the authorities and the populace had already been stressed long before in Exodus 12:36 (the Israelites found favor in the sight of the Egyptians), a motif, by the way, ironically repeated in Esther 5:2 (Esther finds grace with Ahasuerus). A comparison of these two texts, however, indicates the vast distance from "Egypt" to "Persia" and from epic to novella. The Jews in Egypt found grace with the populace despite the administration's rage; in Esther 5:2, grace is found with the king of Persia, for the populace had already been won over. Be that as it may, a chasm separates those in power—who believe everything is under control—from the populace, who feel estranged and ignored. Royal authority flirts dangerously with popular unrest. Some day, many Persians will openly side with the Jews and join their ranks (see Esther 8:17).

Let us repeat that it is a misapprehension to classify the book of Esther as chauvinistic. There is nothing chauvinistic in describing the crumbling of an absolutist regime (similar to the crumbling twenty-two centuries later of the Berlin wall), neither is there chauvinism in stressing an uncanny Jewish assimilation into Persian society and even the accession of Jews to the highest positions of government.[30]

Yet Jewish particularism is not an anti-Semitic invention. Those supporting a more narrowly defined Jewishness have always been offended by the laxity of Esther, connubial with a pagan king, commensal with him and even with the wicked Haman, and secretive as regards her Jewish origins. (This was on the recommendation, it is true, of "Mordecai-the-Jew," who in the story represents another kind of Jew, one much more scrupulously attached to his or her ethnicity.)[31] In fact, Esther does not contribute to what we might call a kind of Jewish solipsism. On the contrary, evoking circumstances that would have been best suited to a Jewish withdrawal from their secular environment and neighbors, the book speaks of Jewish courtiers, of a Jewish queen, of a Jew foiling a plotted regicide, and of popular manifestations of sympathy with the Jews.

Even the names of the Jewish characters are strangely "worldly." One is Mordecai (that is to say Marduk, or an adept of the god Marduk), the other is Esther (Ishtar or her adept).[32] Now, generally speaking, children were not given the names of gods and goddesses without further ado. Names were phrases: Tutmosis, "son of Tot"; Yeshayah [Isaiah], "Yah[weh] is saving"; and so on. In Mesopotamia, the divine names of Marduk and Ishtar would be used for mortals in incantatory forms: Marduk-be-merciful or Ishtar-queen-of-heaven. These actual names shed light on the rationale for calling the Jewish heroes of the tale by Babylonian designations. If Ishtar is "queen of heaven," the Jewess Esther becomes queen of Persia. If Marduk is compassionate, then Mordecai embodies compassion toward his people.

Irony? Certainly. Those masks on their faces suit the ambiguous roles the heroes play and indeed the whole grotesque character of the narrative.[33] Without their masks, that is, outside the masquerade, Esther is Hadassah and Mordecai is Kish (2:6–7).[34] The duality of their names corresponds to the duality of their identities or personae. More for Esther than for Mordecai this establishes an inner dialogism in parallel with the general dialogism in the story.

Now, a tenet of Bakhtin's philosophical anthropology and linguistics is that carnival's praise and blame are "divided among *private* voices, *but in the voice of the whole they are fused into an ambivalent unity.*"[35] In its stress on inner dialogism, this reflects one of Bakhtin's central convictions,[36] strikingly exemplified in the book of Esther, as I will show in chapter 4.

4

A Trio of Women: Vashti, Esther, Zeresh

Vashti

Vashti represents the first movement of resistance to the oppressive imperial regime. The text emphasizes this from the outset by stating she was fetched from her banquet for women by seven eunuchs (1:10). Seven! Why not the whole army? Is Vashti a prisoner? Is she expected to come with manacles on her wrists? At any rate, the guard of honor appears to display a baleful aspect, especially since Vashti knows she will be treated as an object on exhibit (1:11).

The queen's refusal is courageous, but it fails. She is demoted and falls into oblivion. So another kind of resistance will be necessary, one more subtle, more tongue-in-cheek, more indirect—the resistance Bakhtin will adopt in other circumstances. Just as Vashti refused to obey the king, Mordecai refuses to bow, but Mordecai's refusal is to a prime minister, while paying allegiance to the king (2:23; 6:2). Vashti's part is that of an offended maiden, but she is a fool. Mordecai's part is that of a fool, but he is cunning. And so too is Esther when she undertakes to fight on behalf of her people: she acts foolish, but she is wise. As smoothly as Vashti's refusal to obey had been abrupt, Esther ensnares the king and Haman in chapter 5.[1] In 5:4, displaying the legendary prudence of the serpent, she invites the two men to a banquet of her own. The architectonic structure of the tale demanded that what had been hatched by Ahasuerus and Haman during a drinking bout (3:15) should also be deconstructed during a banquet.

It would be wrong, however, to consider the Vashti episode as self-contained. It is not merely an introduction to a story that could as well remain integral without it. The Vashti episode sets up the carnivalesque mood of the whole story, thereby opening a subplot that will eventually arrive at closure with Queen Esther's triumph.

Vashti's insubordination provokes the creation of a new law in the kingdom (see 1:20). The whole scene is funny, but it also displays a frightful grimace: the new law increases the repressive character of the regime and further entrenches its inherent misogynic paranoia, which will now all the more effectively oppress 50 percent of its population in the persons of its women.[2] In no uncertain terms, the royal adviser Memucan states that women must be repressed in the manner of insubordinate slaves (1:17), who respect their masters only from fear. He therefore suggests dealing with the women with an iron fist (1:18–19, 21), the official misogyny as usual initiating a spiral of violence. The first writ directed against the female population is soon followed by a second edict, this time dealing with the Jewish ethnos condemned for their "strange" laws. Consistent with the sick logic of the repressive system, these new victims will not be merely subjugated but annihilated. The chiasmus has reached its nadir.

A third writ is meant to control the damage occasioned by the second.[3] And thus, the "liberationist" Jewish laws (see Deut. 17:14–20, for example) prevail. Finally, the fourth application of the law in the book is a triumphant one. A woman, Esther, accedes to supreme authority in Persia, and thus the first Persian "new law," directed against women, is cancelled by default. Vashti, humiliated by Esther's election, is now victorious through Esther's initiative.[4] What had been felt in need of redress by a king was an alleged affront to *all* men (1:16–18). What is ultimately redressed by a queen is the affront to *all* women (9:29). Haman and his ten male offspring are hanged on the gallows (9:25), and Ahasuerus, the chauvinist king, is completely eliminated, reduced to the shadow he always was. If Vashti stood for all the defeated women of the kingdom, Mordecai for all the threatened Jews, and Haman for the whole brood of scoundrels, Esther, we may conclude, stands both for all the Jews and for all the women of Persia, as she is both Jewish and female.

Esther

There are clearly "two Esthers" in the narrative. The first one starts by being a kind of pinup and sex toy for the pleasure of the king; she hides her ethnic and religious origins and, accordingly, behaves like a goy. When the moment of crisis comes and she is challenged to stick out her neck for her people, she erects a barrier of excuses and must be shamed by her cousin, Mordecai, to bring out the "surplus" of her personality.[5] She evolves, however, because the "abiding mystery in character as biblical writers conceive it . . . [is] a center of surprise."[6] The second Esther is a heroine, risking her life and entirely determined to turn the tables against Haman for the salvation of the Jewish community. Clearly, the Esther figure has gone through a dramatic transformation: from a coy harem inmate to a wise, independent, and prudent woman.

Thus, each manifestation of the persona Esther displays only a partial aspect of her identity. Only the narrator has a global view of who she is and of how she builds a "signifying whole," as Bakhtin says, "a necessary whole."[7] In other words, the hero of the tale is dialogized, as I said above, and the author disposes of a "surplus of vision"[8] that allows the storied Esther to be this and also that, to be the queen of

Persia and also the servant of her people.[9] The author is evidently in dialogue with the heroine, and chances are that the first Esther and the second Esther represent the personal evolution of the diasporic Jew(ess) who wrote the tale.

The evolution starts by showing Esther's deference to the advice of the eunuch Hegai (2:15; compare 2:9), a humble attitude that compounds her obedience to Mordecai (2:10). In the first part of the tale, Esther is presented as coy and as malleable by others who, however, happen to be wise and reliable, and this reflects positively on Esther's own wisdom. The least one can say is that she is not impulsive and empty-headed—perhaps an authorial hint that her natural beauty does not conceal stupidity; she is not a "dumb blonde." This is a welcome indication indeed at a time when the crowning of Esther with the diadem stripped from Vashti when she refused to appear before the king (1:11; 2:17) makes the Jewess look to be no more than a sex object.

Although according to the text the two women never meet, they are in an obvious mutual rivalry. Some commentators feel sorry that Esther did not refuse to play that remote-controlled game—as if indeed she were free to resist it. But had she done so, she would then have missed something of importance relating to an ancestor's blunder, whose lesson she would not have been willing to neglect. As a matter of fact, there is an uncanny correspondence between Vashti and King Saul. As we saw above and shall see again later, the text of 1 Samuel 15 is constantly in the background of our narrative. A parallel between a character in Esther and King Saul in 1 Samuel is therefore far from trivial. Levenson has called attention to the linguistic similarity of Esther 1:19 ("Let the king give her royal position to another who is better than she") and 1 Samuel 15:28 ("[YHWH] has given it [the kingdom] to another who is better than you").[10] This, of course, sheds a different light on what is really going when "one who is better" is substituted for one who is found wanting (as King Saul was replaced through the office of the prophet Samuel).

Esther's representativeness is made clear as soon as she lets herself be persuaded by Mordecai in chapter 4 to act on behalf of her people. Her "conversion," or at least her change of mind, her *metanoia,* takes place when she identifies herself with the Jews[11] (as Moses did in Exodus 2:11) and when she corrals, so to speak, other women to her cause (4:16: "I and my maids will also fast as you do" [NRSV]). The new resistance movement (after the abrupt disobedience of Vashti) is first of all a harem "uprising." This powerless and will-less milieu par excellence becomes the headquarters of the insurrection (4:16–17). From being a commodity, Esther passes to being in command.

Earlier on, replacing Vashti had not been a onetime feat for Esther. The king was renewing the population of his harems (2:19), and Esther had to have been in constant competition with others for the favor of the royal bed (4:11).[12] This will prove important to understanding her action in entering the throne room uninvited (5:1).[13] The instability of her situation is demonstrated by her earlier unawareness of the plot against her own people (Esther 4). That is, she is unaware of palace intrigues and kept ignorant of inside schemes. This, of course, is unexpected and contributes to the literary aspect of the tale as a comedy. In accord with the blurred vision characteristic of characters in comedy, the king initially ignores Mordecai, who thwarted the regicide, and favors the wicked Haman, who, according to a Greek version, is a traitor, a "Macedonian" infiltrating the Persian court (see Text A:17–18).[14] The king is blind to his true friends and suicidal in allying himself with his sworn enemies (see 3:1 in contrast with 2:23). According to the Greek versions, the plot against the king was instigated by Haman.

The "coy" Esther will not remain timidly marginal while events take their course. True, inasmuch as she personifies the eastern Jewish diaspora, the temptation not to make waves is alluring. At first, Esther shows a strong reluctance to commit herself to muzzling the monster that threatens to devour her people. History has shown hundreds of times how seductive it is to imitate the ostrich: the threat will soon evaporate; the status quo ante will be reinstated; there is no need for "overreacting." To face down this response, Mordecai, the other aspect of the Jewish diaspora, must become brutally clairvoyant and denounce such dangerous wishful thinking (4:13–14).[15]

Mordecai's "surplus of vision" is evident when he urges his niece (or cousin) to lead the resistance to the king's edict: he sees the "fulfilled form of the other one," to which he prompts Esther to conform. This necessary role—in which the *I* enters into dialogue with a *Thou*—is the very foundation of being human according to Martin Buber and Mikhail Bakhtin. In a vein deeply reminiscent of Buber, Bakhtin writes, "There would be no individuality if another did not create it."[16]

Esther and Mordecai's Masterstroke

Esther's seizure of power occurs at the end of the story, namely, in chapters 8 and 9 of the book, after the defeat and death of wicked Haman and the vindication of Esther and Mordecai in the eyes of King Ahasuerus.

True, it must be conceded, with many commentators on Esther, that chapters 8 and 9 are written in a less satisfying style than the rest. Furthermore, they seem to merely reiterate what readers already know about the reversal of the Jewish fortune. But once this is said, we must also realize that the execution of Haman and his ten sons in Esther 7 took care only of the tip of the iceberg. Nothing up to that point has been said about the Jewish fate, which continues to be determined by the first royal mandate. Since the king has already so generously rid Esther and Mordecai of their main enemy, however, these beneficiaries are, understandably, treading a bumpy road in their determination to save also their people (see 8:7). Their petition could easily be construed as overstepping the limits of decency.

Esther's intercession in chapter 8 thus becomes tenser. For the first time she weeps; she uses terms of appeasement and endearment in her speech to the king (see 8:5–6). We understand her desperation when given the royal reply (8:7): he has done his part; he has hanged Haman and his sons; and he gave the wicked vizier's house to Esther. If there is more to do at this point it must be done by her with Mordecai's help. On the king's part, of course, this is almost a cop-out, but it is understandable, given that what needs to be done is, in reality, changing the unchangeable.[17] It is truly an impossible task—one that only people with a sense of "going beyond" the law are capable of accomplishing.

"Now, you yourselves write," says the king (8:8), because, on the one hand, he is incapable of imagining what to write himself, and, on the other hand, it would be moral and political suicide for him to initiate a reversal of the "irrevocable law" of the Persians. The whole empire is founded on this deterministic inalterability. Only a Jew is capable of untying this Gordian knot.

And so it is done. The king's first command has irreparably opened the dike to the rush of bloodthirsty anti-Semites. It is understood that the designated victims of that command have no right to contravene the royal order by their resistance. They are "like a lamb that is led to the slaughter" (Isa. 53:7). But now, the second decree reverses, not what has been written in the first, but what was *not* written there. The Jews of Persia will defend themselves with the approval and aid of the authorities (who previously were supposed to back up the anti-Semites [9:3]). The Jews may carry arms and prepare their resistance. The planned massacre becomes a pitched battle. The genocide is no longer admitted and even commanded. Those who decide to try their luck against the Jews know they are now themselves at risk. This is announced all over the empire with the same fanfare as was the first edict. From now on, the game will be played by different rules.

Whether or not the last chapters of the book are a literary "bumpy road" due to a lack of compositional skill, they are felicitously descriptive of the urgency with which the two heroes face a desperate situation. There is a back-and-forth of activity between them, the credit going at times to one and at times to the other, and an interchangeability of effort and thought that corresponds to my earlier suggestion that Esther and Mordecai are the two faces of one personality (see also below). There has been a certain tension between the two all along, especially in chapter 3. But now they have become "one flesh" with a dual role: Esther is the queen and she acts as such. Mordecai is the prime minister, and his actions accord with his functions. There is no need to attribute the lack of stylistic smoothness to a possible merger of two original stories, one about Esther and one about Mordecai, later woven together into the Hebrew book of Esther.[18]

Through their dual intervention, the reversal of fortune initiated in chapter 7 of the book comes to its full completion. After its ophidian head, the body of the murderous mob is also crushed, not a trifling task. The hydra Haman had ten extra grimacing heads; the body of the monster is also enormous—evil is the ruler of the world, says the Gospel of John. The tale of Esther reports that the charge of "the sons of light" into the ranks of their foes was devastating: seventy-five thousand anti-Semites died. To use another metaphor, introduced above, the "lamb" kills over seventy-five thousand of its would-be slaughterers! The author even insists on having a second day of battle rather than just one (9:13). We are smack in the middle of carnival. The military power of the supremacists' militia is in a complete rout. All bets are by now lost. David has killed his Goliath. And the feat will be repeated time and time again, every year on the appointed days, because it is an open-ended event announcing the dawn of what Bakhtin calls the "homecoming festival."[19] Esther 8 and 9 feature a Passover-like hurried preparation for the utopia. Esther 10 is the premise of that utopia.

Dualities

The heroine has two names, in accordance with the pairing of elements with which the whole story is built. Hadassah, Esther's Jewish name, is barely mentioned in the tale. Her official civil name, Esther, is the name by which she is known to her contemporaries and to tradition. Daniel and his companions likewise have dual names, but in the book of Daniel the balance tips the other way, with the accent definitely falling on maintaining a Jewish identity in a potentially adverse foreign situation, indeed in a situation that had become, at the time of the book's composition in the second century B.C.E., a full-fledged Antiochan persecution of the Jews. Esther's tale shows the face of the Jew that is turned toward the world. Figuratively speaking, Esther at the "synagogue" is Hadassah. But the tale bypasses this aspect of her life. She is depicted from start to finish in her role at the royal court of Ahasuerus, where she is known as Esther. Her other face remains veiled, sometimes concealed and sometimes revealed. This is not to say Esther's personality would be split, but, in the diaspora, her "Esther" aspect gives substance to her "Hadassah" aspect. "Who knows," says Mordecai at the hinge point of the story, "if it is not for a time like this that you reached royalty?" (See 4:14.)

The duality of names and of themes corresponds to the almost perfect symmetry between the two parts of the story, a pattern strongly emphasized by Sandra Berg,[20] for example, and from which Joyce G. Baldwin infers the story's unity, based on role reversal (from triumph to defeat or from elevation to downfall in the case of Vashti, Haman, and the Jews' enemies; from humiliation to victory in the case of Esther, Mordecai, and the Jewish community).[21]

The truth is that the Jewish confrontation with Haman-the-Wicked (and the systemic evil of absolutist Persia) is much less the feat of "Esther" and "Mordecai" than of Hadassah and Kish disguised as Esther and Mordecai, two names that, in the Mesopotamian context, give a false impression of "being part of the furniture." Together these two pretenders or tricksters crush the Dragon, as did St. George, another carnivalesque hero.

As a matter of fact, Esther and Mordecai can be classified among those, such as the young Joseph in Genesis, whom Susan Niditch calls *underdogs.*[22] Popular folklore is fond of those "heroes" who, facing impossible odds, somehow succeed in fulfilling great designs. In a way, this is a feature that "runs in the family," for what is true with Mordecai and his cousin Esther was already true with Joseph and his father Jacob. They all climb the social ladder, "from rags to riches," to the delight of their people. But the parallel between the heroes in Genesis and heroes in Esther goes only so far. "The trickster," wrote Niditch, "sees God face to face, whereas the wisdom hero receives his messages through symbolic dreams."[23] This difference, as a matter of fact, already had created a chasm between father and son in Genesis. Jacob is a trickster, facing God directly, but Joseph is only a dreamer. And, although the Greek versions of Esther begin by leveling off the story to attain the old structure of popular tales, presenting Mordecai as having had a premonitory dream, in the Hebrew text neither Mordecai nor Esther see "God face to face" or are graced with "symbolic dreams."

In short, Esther's story is highlighted not only by what it shares in common with the old "legends of wise heroes and heroines,"[24] but also by what distinguishes it from them. Seizing power implies highly different moves. The striving of Jacob and Joseph or of Joseph and his brothers to fulfill their ambitions is vastly different from what the heroes in our story undertake to do. Invariably, however, acceding to high positions amounts to becoming the favorite of a central power figure: father, slave master, Pharaoh, or Persian emperor. As to the means to satisfy such ambitions, they span a whole gamut of possibilities, from sometimes undisclosable callousness to feminine wiles, wisdom, determination, and steadfastness.

Joseph was never graced with a theophany we said; to him God was more or less present, more or less absent, as befits a man who himself is rather lukewarm and without any trace of extravagance in his behavior—all of his extravagance is exhausted in telling his dreams to his father and brothers. With Esther and Mordecai, the author takes a further step in the evolution toward total secularism. Here, extravagance is far from absent, starting with Mordecai's shunning of the great vizier of the king and continuing with Esther's bravura. This was one more reason why the Greek versions of the book of Esther could not comprehend the immense theological gap of the Hebrew story, since traditionally such human courage is condoned and rewarded by divine intervention, at least indirectly.

Dreams are one favorite means by which the divinity inspires, prompts, or forewarns the potential hero in the old folkloric tales. Their absence in the Hebrew Esther is all the more conspicuous. It is true that during the time that elapsed between the composition and the appearance of the book of Esther confidence in the mantic value of dreams, let alone in direct divine dialogue with human beings, had been submitted to strong skeptical questioning (see Deut. 13:2; Zech. 10:2; Sir. 34:1–8). At any rate, the oneiric medium, when at all credited, was deemed in need of an authorized interpretation, as shown, for example, by Daniel 2:24–45 and Esther 11:5, in Greek.

There is no such direct or indirect divine communication in the Hebrew Esther, where the two Jewish heroes seem able to count only on themselves and on good fortune to have "the downtrodden turn the tables on would-be oppressors—a common wish-fulfilling message of traditional narrative."[25]

Esther and Mordecai are the two faces of one reality, but they are not the sheer duplication of one another. They build a contrasted parallel in regard to their sexes, their ages, their alternate relationships of guidance and obedience, their statuses in the Persian administration, and their attitudes regarding integration without compromise into both Persian society and their Jewish identity. The author presents a *dédoublement* (in German, *Verspaltung*) of his or her hero in order to strengthen even further the dialogical dimension of the tale at all levels. The dialogic dimension occurs at the intersecting point of their two consciousnesses, the voices of which are "unmerged," for each of them holds on to his or her *outsideness*. It is, of course, not by chance that Mordecai and Esther are unified-separated as ostensible-Jew versus crypto-Jew, marginal versus official, and so on. It is their dialogue, however, that brings about the people's salvation. Now, it so happens that this feature of *Verspaltung* strikingly corresponds to an often invoked figure in Bakhtin's works, namely, the Janus figure. He writes, "An act of our actual experiencing is like a two-faced Janus. It looks in two opposite directions: it looks at the objective unity of a domain of culture and at the never-repeatable uniqueness of actual lived and experienced life."[26] And, elsewhere, he writes of "unity not as an innate one-and-only, but as a dialogic *concordance* of unmerged twos or multiples."[27] True, it is difficult to designate among the dyadic heroes of Esther[28] the one who stands for "the objective unity of a domain of culture" (more so Mordecai than Esther) and the one who stands for "the never-repeatable uniqueness of actual lived and experienced life" (more so Esther than Mordecai), but the dialectical reality of the pair should be underlined.

In contrast, the pair Ahasuerus–Haman is not of the same nature (for they only parody the dialectic relation of Esther–Mordecai). They are not in dialogue but are, rather, interchangeable. This pair lacks what Bakhtin calls *transgredience* (*transgradientsvo*) or *extralocality* (*vnenakhodimost*, also translated as "outsideness").[29] Haman's dream is to be dressed in the king's clothes, to be crowned with the king's crown, and to ride on the king's horse. That Mordecai is eventually invested with such honors and holds the king's seal (8:8, 10) is a source of popular laughter. Mordecai is a king *pour rire*. Through Haman, the alter ego of the king, all the powers that be are derided. Haman plays the role of the "king for a day," i.e., Mordecai's buffoon.[30]

Outsideness

Seen from a distance that allows the reader to embrace the totality of the plot, Mordecai's provocation of Haman is astoundingly daring; we could even say that it looks irresponsible. His scheme had started with his command to Esther not to reveal her origins. Had Haman known that the queen was Jewish, he certainly would have thought twice before organizing the Jewish genocide. There can be no doubt that "Mordecai-the-Jew" puts the whole Jewry of Persia in harm's way. But the Bakhtinian concept of transgredience is at work here. It corresponds to a surplus of seeing that obtains when the *whole* existence of the other is contemplated from outside. True, Bakhtin rightly insists that such a total vision is, in fact, impossible, and Mordecai's capacity to judge Haman with such a "surplus" is no exception. But we must remember that Haman is not merely an individual bearing that name. Haman is Agag, he is Amalek, he is an embodiment of the Jew-hater omnipresent in Jewish history, as much so as Jim Crow is of modern racism. Mordecai's perception is historically grounded and teleologically accurate. It remains, however, that such a perfect transgredience is only feasible in a work of fiction, in which the characters are typified. From this perspective, it is also true that, conversely, Haman is not mistaken when he selectively chooses Mordecai as the odd man out. Mordecai is "the Jew": he is Jewishness incarnate. He and Haman face each other like the serpent and the mongoose.

One of the decisive meetings of the book occurs in Esther 3 between Haman and Mordecai. It is marked with the mutual recognition of mortal enemies, a recognition with deep historical roots, beginning with King Saul and King Agag, Israel and Amalek. Their (renewed) meeting opens the dike, releasing a torrential (but muted) flow of history. We are at a far cry from the private heroes of Greek romance who find themselves isolated in a strange world with no calling to a task that must be accomplished.[31]

It must be said that the typification of its characters is, from another point of view, a flaw in the book of Esther as fiction. This is true because of the relative depth (or lack thereof) of the heroes taken individually. We are, of course, at quite a distance from Dostoevskyan protagonists. As we saw above, the actors in Esther are "superficially drawn."[32] To recall, the phenomenon belongs to what Bakhtin calls the "first stylistic line," by contrast with the "second stylistic line" favored by Bakhtin for its fuller, richer exploitation of the genre's "potential."[33]

The book of Esther belongs to the first line, as do ancient novellas in general. But what the tale of Esther loses on that score it recuperates to some extent at the level of plot. The accent is here on the unfolding plot, in which the central "hero" is neither Esther nor Mordecai but peripeteia. Or, to see it from another angle, what is central to Esther is the collective dimension of its heroes, who are "fraught with background."[34]

This last point allows us to reassess the stereotypes of Mordecai and Esther by creating a most interesting tension between, on the one hand, the centrality of both characters in the tale, and, on the other hand, their self-effacement to the benefit of their people. Their figures are simultaneously individual and typical. There is thus a constant oscillation between front scene and back scene, between the heroes' assertiveness and their humility. This oscillation underlines the inner dialogism of the story. It also exemplifies the Bakhtinian necessity of "distance," not only on the part of each protagonist but also of the reader, whose view comprehends both the characters' individual self-effacement and centrality and who must, therefore, make sense of such tensive dialectics.

A case in point is obviously Esther's decision to keep her Jewishness secret on Mordecai's recommendation. I will return to this surprising feature, if only because the secret is for some but not for all, for a time but not forever. This *vnenakhodimost* of sorts may be set in parallel with the donning of masks in carnival: "happy negation of uniformity and similarity; it rejects conformity to one's self."[35] As we shall see below, Esther removes this token of ambiguity at a crucial moment in the drama. She reveals her true identity, but not before putting something like a second mask on her face. Playing to the hilt the role of a Persian princess, she organizes a series of two banquets, corresponding to the two banquets earlier thrown by her kingly husband. Now, banqueting belongs, of course, to the carnivalesque. "Under the influence," the king offers Esther half his kingdom. Everything becomes disproportionate, distorted, out of focus. Esther's parody of the king's powers wins the day. She could ask anything from the king-buffoon.[36] Unknown to themselves, the king and Haman become carnivalesque characters; they "successfully" play the fools. Even the misconstrued move of Haman when begging Esther for his life shares in this character.

Esther thus personifies *irony,* for irony basically plays on the distance between appearance and reality. As the *eiron* is flanked by the *alazon,* so Esther is tied to a king blinded by his groundless grandiosity. On this score, the information given in Esther 4:4 is highly ironic: "Esther's maids and her eunuchs came and told her [about the royal decree for the destruction of all the Jews]." As in the commedia dell'arte, the relationship of Esther to Mordecai is an open secret to her maidens. Similarly, everyone seems to know about the planned course of events except the principal character, the Jewish queen (4:5). Clearly, the relations between husband and wife are strictly sexual. Eventually, that shallow relationship will be credited with bringing about the salutary reversal of the Jews' fortune. Just as displeasure with one person, Mordecai, provoked a deadly ire aimed at destroying a whole people, so pleasure with another person, Esther, brings about the reversal of fortune that saves the nation. In this way the irony of history as a whole is underscored: had Mordecai not been in Haman's way, or had Esther been a few years older, "there would be no plot at all."[37] The "locomotive of history" is not necessarily a big event (Soviet missiles in Cuba, for example); it may be an apparently insignificant incident (the simultaneous presence of two homonymous Attas in Prague in 2001).

Secrecy in the story is uniformly attached to the theme of Jewish identity. Esther's silence about her Jewish origins finds an uncanny ironic echo in chapter 3, when Haman fails to disclose the name of the ethnic group he wants to see destroyed. Another surprising repetition of the theme occurs in chapter 7, when Esther speaks to the king of herself and her people (verse 3) without stating that she is a Jewess. She intercedes for those she calls, somewhat mysteriously, "my people" (7:3–4). This recurring silence contributes to the aura of mystery surrounding the Jewish people.

In fact, there are no fewer than five occurrences of the motif. Beside those already mentioned, in chapter 6 the king wants to honor someone he does not name. Haman, thinking he is that man, recommends a fantastic ceremony involving the services of "one of the king's most noble princes" (6:9). This vague designation, however, ends up placing Haman himself in the servant's role.

We may see in this cultivation of mystery a literary device meant to inculcate suspense. The author winks, as it were, at the audience, sharing with them the secret and thus establishing with readers a thrilling complicity. As in a French comedy of the seventeenth century, the self-centered Ahasuerus is deaf and blind; he does not know or understand anything. But not so the recipients of the story, who are invited to feel savvy and good about themselves.[38]

Moreover, at another level of understanding, secrecy befits the abovementioned use of masks, which characterizes so well carnival revelers, who are never who they pretend to be. A major dimension of carnival is the temporary disguise of one's identity—a very effective way to avoid responsibility for one's actions. In Esther, the masks do not conceal undisclosable acts, but they are an effective defensive device. As they are "unarmed," the designated victims of the pogrom must, as much as is feasible, fade away into the general population.[39]

The last occurrence of the theme of secrecy comes at the point when all the masks must fall; thus Esther's silence is paradoxical in 7:3 when she identifies the future victims of Haman only as "my people."[40] In fact, the veil has changed its significance, for Esther now renders transparent the veil that had covered the Jews, openly calling them "my people." They are not yet fully "unmasked," but secrecy has shifted to the ultimate revelation of identity in the eyes of Ahasuerus: whoever those people are, they are the queen's people! In other words, Esther makes him understand that he had been about to kill none other than his beloved wife and her community. Put in more trivial terms, the king had been poised to saw off the very branch on which he was sitting. Suddenly, he realizes that the Other is kin so close as to be inseparable from the self—a potent lesson to the haters of foreigners of all times.

But, when all is said, it remains that Esther's concealment of her identity is arguably the most surprising and unexpected feature of the book. Certainly unconventional and "unorthodox," the motif marks the distance separating the author from the official Judaism of the time. The most arresting aspect of this disguise, to boot, is that it is recommended by Mordecai who, as we saw, represents a more conservative and steadfast face of the hero as compared at least to early Esther. Mordecai clearly has a hidden agenda. His recommendation aims at a future purpose from which a sense of the confrontation with Haman the Agagite is far from absent.[41] In view of the subsequent tragic events, it is true, Mordecai's advice may also be construed as a premonition[42] and as protective of his niece. She will not wear the "yellow star"—but he will: all along he is identified as "Mordecai-the-Jew."

The bifacial hero of the book of Esther is thus simultaneously non-Jewish and Jewish (up to but not including the time at which the non-Jewish aspect would become betrayal; see 4:14). With this conjunction, the author displays great daring. Were it not for the appalling events hatched by the wicked Haman, Esther would never have been known as Hadassah. In fact, this dialectical equilibrium between two seemingly contradictory terms is made evident in the contrast between Esther 2:10 and 2:20, where Mordecai recommends to his adopted daughter that she conceal her Jewishness, and Esther 4:14, where Mordecai prompts Esther to remain silent no longer in the developing circumstances. There is clearly a time not to speak and a time to break the silence. This kind of maneuvering reflects the diasporic world. Circumstances constantly change, demanding constant adaptation from the Jews.

Mordecai's initial move regarding his niece doubtlessly deserves more reflection. Let us turn again to Bakhtin's expansion on carnival. He applauds the characters' "right to be 'other' in this world, the right not to make common cause with any single one of the existing categories that life makes available. None of these categories quite suits them; they see the underside and the falseness of every situation. Therefore they can exploit any position they choose, but only as a mask."[43]

There is, I think, no more fitting epithet to describe this "right" than *subversive*. Esther subverts the conventionality of Jewishness. But, as James Sanders rightly says, "All texts have some built-in constraints which work against complete subversion of a text."[44] Here, the constraints are paradoxically stronger than is their parody. Esther, queen of Persia, is merely a *mask*. Her non-Jewishness is a veil concealing her true identity. The veil can remain before her face for only so long. It represents a second world. The difficulty for the masked person is to know when to remove the cover-up, unavoidably felt to be hiding one's nakedness. It may happen that the mask fits so well and becomes so habitual and comfortable that the person eventually shares society's expectations, and "the face behind the mask become[s] the mask itself."[45]

That is why Mordecai, who himself had put the mask over Esther's face, must now help her to remove it and to retrieve her own face. As far as she is concerned, the story really starts at that very point. The "submissive" Esther was a sham; now a rebellious Esther emerges who will change the course of history. At the literary level, the false carnival, false because of its artificiality, is replaced by the true carnival: derision of potentates and their systemic grandiosity. Like a Trojan horse, Esther has infiltrated the royal court, and now no longer the alleged sex object, she readily manipulates the powers that be to her (and others') advantage.

The irony is that unmasked Esther must now appear "naked" at the royal court, when Vashti had refused to do so and been dismissed.[46] Vashti's refusal of self-exhibitionism was entirely a manifestation of her self-respect. Esther's willingness to be exposed, by contrast, is a manifestation of her self-oblivion. Where is reverence, where is ridicule?[47] As regards Vashti, the reverence has turned to ridicule; as regards Esther, the ridicule (of being unveiled and utterly vulnerable) turns out to be worthy of reverence. She could ask for half of the kingdom—and indeed she becomes, through her brinkmanship, for all practical purposes the ruler of Persia.

An example of the "chronotope of the threshold," where both reverence and ridicule meet, as we saw in chapter 1, is provided by the mention of fasting (see 4:3, 16; 9:31) as if, *by itself*, the refusal of food could influence the course of history. Here again, the tale comes within a hairbreadth of becoming religious, and this teasing device cannot but frustrate the reader's expectation—an effective way to whet the reader's interest, of course. The same religious impasse may be said to apply to the institution of Purim, with which the story ends. For one thing, there is not even a hint here of expressing gratitude to God. The fasts and laments commanded by Mordecai and Esther in 9:31 remain as though suspended in air. To whom are the laments addressed? What is the meaning of a fast at this particular point? Are we to believe that the ritual has become self-referring and the liturgy a form without content, simply a vestige of what it meant in the past to be Jewish?[48] As a matter of fact, it may very well be that fasts in the book of Esther are deprived of *religious* content. The glaring absence of a reference to God in Esther 4 is nothing short of shocking. In similar circumstances and with similar manifestations of mourning, even the pagan Ninevites in Jonah 3 "cry mightily to God" (Jon. 3:8). All attempts on the part of critics to circumvent the areligiosity of the book of Esther shortchange the most remarkable characteristic of the book.[49] I maintain that the readers of Esther are confronted with the following alternative: either the book of Esther is out of place in Israel's sacred literature or it is parodic, subversive, carnivalesque—and reforming.[50] For Esther's injunction to the Jews to fast with her is not without any sort of content, as we shall now see.

I suggest that Esther here gives form and order to the Jews' chaotic initial response to the king's lethal decree. She acts with the people as a mother with her children; she organizes their feelings and determines their new identity qua threatened community. But now she does this *"from the outside,"* as Bakhtin says. Esther's words "come to meet the dark chaos of [the] inner sensation of [themselves]: these [words] name, direct, satisfy, and connect it with the outside world. . . .[51] And as a result, they give, as it were, a plastic form to this boundless, 'stirring chaos' of need and dissatisfaction in which . . . is dissolved and drowned the future dyad of [their] persons confronting the outside world."[52]

Esther's words are, as they must be, *familiar, Jewish,* and hence *reassuring.* The recipients will be associated with her action. In fact, they will *do* something to change their predicament. They will act on their fear, shifting it from panic or terror to resolve and, perhaps as Bakhtin wishes, to laughter at their dread. The fast in Esther 3 is cut of the same cloth as the silence of the throngs in Madrid after 3/11/2004. It is incoherence transformed into coherence.

Linguistically speaking, the intervention into the everyday discourse of some kind of religious language (even emptied of substantial content) provides a case in point of Bakhtin's "dialogized heteroglossia," that is, of languages "interanimating" each other through their mutual dialogue. This process is always present in live discourse, but it is particularly remarkable here in a narrative that seems to exclude systematically religious jargon. When this happens, we encounter the phenomenon of "one language (and the verbal world corresponding to it) [seen] through the eyes of another language,"[53] or, to use another expression favored by Bakhtin, a "double-voiced word."[54]

Zeresh

Zeresh is a shadowy female figure, as was Vashti before her. Zeresh's part in the tale is bifocal. She advises her husband, Haman, to erect the gallows to hang Mordecai (5:14), and she also predicts Haman's impending doom (6:13). She is an ambiguous figure and a very ambivalent one. Haman's most trusted ally and counselor (5:10), she suddenly turns against him, and he loses her before losing his life.[55] Is she some manner of Talleyrand or a female Balaam? Is she a mirror of feminine versatility or of someone who comes to her senses when she realizes that Mordecai is—despite his name—a Jew? Rather than a female Balaam, she resembles Rahab and, like Rahab, she saves herself by acknowledging the Jews' extraordinary destiny (see Josh. 2:9–11; Isa. 2:1–4; 45:14–23; 60:1–18). She also joins ranks with Abigail, the wife of Nabal ("The Fool") in 1 Samuel 25 (see 1 Sam. 25:25). Nabal had eyes but did not see; Abigail was not blind as he was, and she became the wife of King David (2 Sam. 2:2). As Linda Day writes, "Zeresh proposes to her husband the following: Instead of waiting the many months for the edict about the non-Jews attacking Jews to be enacted, Haman should get rid of his enemy immediately: erect a gallows and have Mordecai hanged or impaled upon it."[56] We may, however, infer from such a potential elimination of Mordecai that it would invalidate the royal edict to save the people of the Jews, as anyway for Zeresh they are invincible. At any rate, Zeresh fits the dark humor of the story, and Haman becomes a tragic figure after having wielded an awesome power of destructive omnipotence in the kingdom.

Literarily speaking, Zeresh is a secondary character. But, ideologically, she contributes to the tale's insistence on the decisive feminine role of liberation. Later we shall reflect on the uncanny association in the story of women and Jews. Misogyny and anti-Semitism are placed here on the same footing. Zeresh's acerbic rebuke of her husband in Esther 6:13 acquires all of its importance from the perspective, clear from the outset of the tale, that any feminine expression of independence evokes male anxiety. The book of Esther is the story of a dramatic reversal of fortune, not just to the benefit of the empire's Jews, but also of its women. I refer the reader to chapter 8 of this volume.

5

In the Background: Israel versus Amalek

The Ideological Background of the Story's Protagonists

As happens so often in history, entire periods of time are stamped with the effigy of a tyrant, be it Antiochus IV Epiphanes in the second century B.C.E., Ivan the Terrible in the sixteenth century C.E., Stalin in the twentieth, or any number of others. In the ostensible time of Esther's story, namely, the fifth century B.C.E., the despot is Haman-the-Wicked. He represents, almost to the point of caricature, the "official seriousness" of which Bakhtin speaks so disparagingly. Such seriousness, Bakhtin says, is bad because it intimidates. In contrast, the "unofficial seriousness," so clearly exemplified by the figures of Esther and Mordecai, "is fully positive, expressed in human compassion for suffering and weakness."[1] As a foil, the narcissistic Haman has no feeling whatsoever other than to wish for his own aggrandizement. When, in the tale, he is described as beset with what is misconstrued by the king as an erotic feeling for the queen, he in fact becomes involved in the scandalous scene while abjectly begging the queen for his miserable life (7:8). As Bakhtin says, speaking of "authoritative discourse"—obviously Haman's mode of utterance—if it were not for such discourse, people would fully "coincide with themselves."[2] This, the Russian philosopher goes on to say, is sheer illusion.

Haman "coinciding with himself" is still no better than a puppet, with which he shares a total absence of feeling and imagination. His designs are uniformly egregious and paradoxically self-destructive. His hatred of otherness is in reality self-loathing.

"All who take the sword will perish by the sword," Jesus said.[3] When it comes to literary fiction or to eidetic representation, this truth is nowhere better demonstrated than in ironic modes. Regarding Haman's destiny, the development in Esther is true to the literary genre that Bakhtin calls *Menippean* in the famous chapter 4 of his revised edition of *Dostoevsky's Poetics*.[4] The outcome for Haman is tragic, but not before achieving a comic impropriety worthy of Molière: Haman is hanged on the gallows he himself erected for someone else.

The core of the plot is the conflict between the "Kishite" Mordecai and the

"Agagite" Haman, and it becomes increasingly clear in the Masoretic text, and even more so in the Greek versions of Esther, that the clash between the two is caused not just by their incompatible temperaments but by their conflicting worldviews. In fact, the story of Esther is the redemptive sequence of the unfinished business reported in 1 Samuel 15.[5] There we are told that King Saul spared the Amalekite Agag and plundered the Amalekite property, instead of fulfilling the divine command to kill Agag and to put the spoils "off limits," that is, literally, under ban (*ḥerem*). Saul's disobedience became the grounds for his rejection as king and was the beginning of his fall.

Mordecai, we recall, is introduced in Esther 2:5 as a Benjaminite, a descendant of Kish, the father of Saul.[6] He refuses to bow before Haman, and rather than being presented as a display of arrogance in flagrant violation of the king's orders, Mordecai's refusal receives an "explanation" of sorts in the text with the statement that he is a Jew. The witnesses to Mordecai's insubordination, we are told, waited "to see whether Mordecai's words would stand, as he had told them that he was a Jew" (3:4). This statement would remain rather cryptic were it not for our having learned that Haman is "the son of Hamdatha the Agagite" (3:1) and thus a descendant of Agag the Amalekite king spared by the ancestor of Mordecai! The two archenemies are face-to-face once more: Saul and Agag, Israel and Amalek.

But the story of Esther, while resurrecting the conflict between Israel and Amalek, characteristically distances itself from the ideology of holy war, so patent in 1 Samuel 15. In the clash between Mordecai and Haman, the author does not even hint at the participation of Israel's God (as was to be expected—Laniak is right—after 1 Samuel 17:43, 45, for example).[7] Thus, the central meeting scene in Esther is the hostile confrontation between a descendant of an Amalekite king, Agag, and a descendant of the Israelite king, Saul.

This development of the tale, we said, might be thought of as retrospectively indicative of why Mordecai commanded his niece not to reveal her Jewishness in the first place. An untimely proclamation by Esther of her origins would short-circuit Haman's plan, when Mordecai, on the contrary, intends to challenge Haman to devise his "final solution of the Jewish problem." For a long while in the story it looks as if Haman has the power of life and death over Mordecai and the Jewish people, but the truth is that he is himself manipulated by his intended victim. Mordecai in this case would have counted on the hostile and murderous instinct of the Amalekite, knowing that Haman's thirst for Jewish blood would push him to extremes and at one point or another would drive him out into the open where he would be exposed. If this holds, both the elements of secrecy and of civil disobedience on the part of Mordecai belong to a master plan that risks an enormous wager, namely, the very lives of the diaspora Jews, including Esther and himself, in order to triumphantly overcome the enemy. The Jew is waiting with a sling of his own, capable of killing another Goliath.[8]

Haman must feel free to vent his rage against the Jews and thus to meet his doomed destiny, lest he beget another generation of "Amalekites" to torment and slay Israel. That the planned disaster was reversed (*nehphakh*, says Esther 9:22) and Haman and his nest of serpents were destroyed by Mordecai's scheme deserves to be celebrated "by every single generation" (9:28). As the story of Esther demonstrates, Amalek is the symbol of the perennial presence of evil in the world, of the enemy present wherever Israel moves.[9]

Yet this is not the only possible reading of the text. Mordecai's decision not to bow before Haman may serve as a touchstone for another of Bakhtin's main quests. Bakhtin, as a matter of fact, struggled all his life with the question of the dynamic process of creativity or "authorship." He successively rejected three possibilities. The first was that an author's oeuvre should be considered as "Platonic," that is, a teleological development of "the life course of one seeking true knowledge."[10] In this case, Mordecai's challenge to Haman would, indeed, be oriented toward the ultimate purpose of killing Haman. In contrast, we could also think in terms of *energeia*, that is, the unfolding of some given purpose.[11] Then Mordecai is moved from the outset by the conviction that he must, as a descendant of Kish, finish off Amalek in the person of Haman. A third possibility would be the so-called analytic biography, in which time becomes irrelevant. In this case, Mordecai's refusal to bow before Haman is already the destruction of Haman, which subsequent events will only confirm.

Bakhtin rejects each of these models as inadequate. He wants, rather, to affirm the dialogic interaction of characters and of thoughts and to take seriously the influence of the environment on all decision making at any time. In this case, Mordecai's seminal breach of protocol initiates a *history*, which Mordecai does not foresee in detail or in its punctual effects but which is, however, oriented and set within a specific context and chronotope. Mordecai's insubordination initiates a poetics with a purpose.[12]

That is why we have characterized the book of Esther as a novella, that is, as the tale of a dramatic flow of events, of "live events," unified into a "plot," which is itself "one of many possible plots and is consequently in the final analysis merely accidental for a given hero,"[13] as it could potentially have led elsewhere, for instance to Haman's repentance, or at least to his relenting.

But Esther displays a dimension of the tragic implacability that characterizes "Persian" absolutism. Haman is caught in the unswerving, "inalterable" stream leading to his destruction. This monologic steamroller actually crushes any possibility of relenting. Haman is by choice no more than a quasi automaton and, finally, a monster. He is "finalizable."[14]

We must also keep in mind concerning Haman that all of the characters in the tale are, as we saw, in the words of C. A. Moore,[15] "superficially drawn," a declaration that must be taken *cum grano salis*, for, comparatively speaking, the Homeric protagonists, for instance, are much more homogenized.[16] But it remains that Haman is less an individual than a stereotype of his nation, Amalek.[17] Through him, the whole of his race is scorned in Esther 6 and destroyed in Esther 7; he is "hanged on the same gallows that he had erected for Mordecai" (7:10).[18]

Although Esther is intrinsically more monologic than Bakhtin would wish, with a plot "overpowering" the characters' unfinalizability, the launching event of the plot, namely, Haman's catastrophic genocidal scheme, pushes all of the characters toward their behavioral threshold. This is of great importance, for the story is built in such a way as to force every character to reach his or her ultimate identity. Vashti, Haman, Mordecai, Esther, Zeresh—all become their quintessential selves.[19]

In this sense, the intertextual relation of Esther and 1 Samuel 15 comes to a climax, that is, the events in Esther find their counterpart in 1 Samuel 15; but in neither text does this exhaust all possible meaning. This is what King Saul had missed at the time of his clash with Agag. The fight described in 1 Samuel was not a mere episode in the history of Saul and his people. Saul overlooked the real dimension of the encounter with King Agag. The war was eschatological, so to speak. It was endowed with a finality that Saul aborts by being casual and finally irresponsible about carrying out the divine command. By sparing the life of the Amalekite and plundering his belongings Saul indicated a reductionist interpretation of the Israelite vocation of eradicating evil wherever it is found. Hence the fury of the prophet Samuel. By relativizing evil, Saul has also, as a result, relativized his own anointment (his "messiahship" in its etymological meaning). An all-pervasive evil demands to be countered with a total dedication on the part of Israel, but Saul has been "lukewarm."[20]

In short, the most important feature of 1 Samuel 15 was the representative role of its characters: Saul, king of Israel, and Agag, king of Amalek. In Esther, these are replaced by Esther and Mordecai as the Janus-face of diaspora Jewishness, with Haman as the latest monologic avatar of (Amalekite) wickedness. Mordecai would have been remiss in duplicating the half measures of his ancestor in dealing with Haman. Death had to be the outcome, whether of Captain Ahab or of Moby Dick. *Tertium non datur:* there is no third term. And death indeed is horribly present at the end. Mordecai was meant to die with all of his people; Haman dies, not only with his ten sons but also with seventy-five thousand of his supporters.[21] For evil is a monster with many heads and many faces, and the "Amalekites" must be subjected to *ḥerem* (ban, total destruction).

Therefore, Purim is much less a celebration of V-Day over more than seventy-five thousand anti-Semites than over Haman and his descendants. The killing of the seventy-five thousand is a mopping-up operation following the hanging of *Agag redivivus*. Haman, dead, has uttered his ultimate word. As for Esther and Mordecai, after remaining silent for a long time (Mordecai's silence when glorified with the king's accoutrement in chapter 6 is typical), they become prolix at the end and utter their penultimate word.

At the end, all the characters have totally become what they potentially were from the beginning. The author dramatizes this becoming by first showing Esther wavering between noncommitment and risk, or again between exhorting her cousin and mentor Mordecai to give up his fight against evil and then jumping herself into the fray of resistance. Even the hanged Haman fulfills the badge of death he was carrying all along, as his wife Zeresh intuited (6:13) and as is signified by the placement of a blinding shroud over his face (7:8). The Jew-hater is psychologically suicidal; what he hates is to discover his own humanity magnified in the Jew. For, if the human is the image of God, the Jew to boot is the image of the human.

Thus, the book of Esther is more than the unwinding of a plot; it is no epic. But Esther is not entirely dialogical either. Haman's voice, for instance, is choked off by the authorial voice. A polyphonic writer like Dostoevsky would have allowed every character of the story to have his or her own voice to defend his or her own truth, almost independently from the author's truth. Haman's "truth" is never heard but disparagingly. Haman is the "wicked Haman," the "Jew-hater," the "foe and enemy" (7:6), the traitor (Greek Esther): Haman's voice is unworthy of being given a hearing. He has a name but no voice, in contradistinction to "So-and-so" in the book of Ruth, who has a voice but no name (see Ruth 4), or to the Egyptian killed by Moses, who had no name, no voice, and no humanity (*lo ʾish*, says Exodus 2:12). Allowing Haman to plead his case in the story would anachronistically place Esther among the second line of novelness,[22] a development that occurred only much later in the history of literature.[23]

Yes, the characters in *The Possessed* or *The Brothers Karamazov* are psychologically richer than are Haman, Mordecai, and Esther. Dostoevsky's new chronotope leads to the stormy debates Raskolnikov has with himself regarding the violent elimination of the old widow he eventually murders. Nothing of the kind is found in Esther regarding the killing of the "seventy-five thousand," for instance. Esther's chronotope is entirely different. But this is not the end of the matter. For in Esther the Jews emphatically refrain from plundering their victims.[24] Clearly, we are not dealing with an epic such as the *Iliad*. Whatever may be the motive for the Jews' restraint—which I shall explore below—it is the outcome of an inner debate. The Esther Jews were not led by fury and excess, but by deliberation, in both senses of the word. They did not proceed to the desecration of their victims; they did not trample their tombs.

In fact, the author found herself or himself in a sort of quandary. On one hand, the author found it necessary to stress that the Jews abstained from pillaging their enemies' goods (despite the royal writ allowing such pillage, on the model of Haman's edict in Esther 3:13).[25] It was essential that they avoid and atone Saul's fatal blunder in 1 Samuel 15. But, on the other hand, poetic justice demanded that those who planned to expropriate Jewish possessions be themselves dispossessed. The author solved the dilemma by transferring Haman's property through Esther to Mordecai (8:1–2). The comedic slapstick of the biter bit is thus presented for the reader's pleasure.

In the midst of extravagance, a characteristic in the book of Esther, this peculiar restraint is not psychologized. Rather, it is understated, itself a notable trait of the Hebrew narrative. The reader must divine the rationale behind the act, as it is not naked and self-sufficient. The chronotope in Esther is a composite of Israelite history (and the ongoing war with Amalek), of biblical tradition (and its consciousness of historical continuity), of Jewish adaptation to the eastern diasporic land (along with the issues such a topographical situation entails), of reaction to Antiochus's persecutions in Palestine (and the baleful clouds that thus gathered above all Jewries elsewhere), and of the quest for a genuine Jewish identity (in a time-space marked by foreignness). All this places the narrative accent on the communal rather than the individual (Esther and Mordecai *are* their people) and on events rather than on one-to-one dialogism.

The Dialogism of Esther and Mordecai

The relative "monologism" of the book of Esther as regards Haman is purposeful. It corresponds to the monologism of Haman's discourse. Haman is indeed unidimensional and monologic. It is not, therefore, necessarily a flaw in the narrative, in the same way that the anonymity of "So-and-so" is not a flaw in the book of Ruth.[26] But now, what is true of Haman in terms of his representative role is also true of the Jewish characters in the story. Esther and Mordecai represent the collectivity of the Jewish diaspora of the East. As we saw earlier, despite their high positions at the Persian court, they "have come to regard [those] as loss"[27] for the sake of their people. Monologism, however, does not apply to them.

To illustrate this, let us note the inevitability that the reader of any work of fiction will suspect that its author shares a certain affinity with one or some of his or her heroes. This feeling easily leads readers so far as to speculate about a possible authorial identification. In my recent study on the book of Ruth, for example, I ventured the thought that the (probably female) author of the story finds a reflection of herself in the figure of Naomi.[28] But, regarding Esther, the problem is much more difficult and aporetic. If I had to arrive at a conclusion from the little we can infer about Esther's author, I would say that she or he is to be identified with the double-faced composite of Esther-Mordecai. Precisely this double-gendered identification makes it impossible to decide if the author was male or female.

This aporia of sorts is certainly implied by the author. I would say that it corresponds to Esther's secrecy about her origins, in the sense that the aura of mystery surrounding Esther as well as the tale's author is meant to steer the course of events. Secrecy in both cases is not an end but a means. It is what identifies the author and Esther: they both are secretive, because both of them are hiding an "arsenal" of historic (and, in Israel, historically tested) potentiality. It assuredly emphasizes the Bakhtinian unfinalizability of any human being, a central characteristic in Esther, which does not propose one (or more) of its heroes as the holder of the whole truth.[29] The reason for this is to be found in the heroes' representative roles. Esther and Mordecai commit with themselves a whole historic community; both heroes are thus individually and collectively dialogical.

The author shows little interest in describing these exceptional Jews.[30] At the end of the tale, the reader hardly knows much more about Esther and Mordecai qua personalities than at the beginning. True, for the sake of verisimilitude and of faithfulness to folkloric tales in general, we are made privy to superficial things such as Esther's beauty (2:7) and Mordecai's older age (2:7). We also learn that Esther fears for her own life in appearing uninvited before her awesome husband (4:11), a psychological touch but one so understated here that the Greek versions felt it necessary to elaborate the scene by having Esther faint twice in the audience room.[31] Undeniably, the Greek text overdoes it here to some extent, but, on the other hand, it is not superfluous to alert us that Esther's act voluntarily puts her on "death row" (even twice; see Esther 4:11, 16, and 7:3) and that it is as the recipient of a "governor's grace" that she lives ever after. We may also add another piece to the psychological dossier of Queen Esther. Further along in the narrative, we find Esther guilty of a callous duplicity in remaining silent when Ahasuerus misinterprets Haman's prostration (7:8). But, when all is said, the harvest is rather meager.

As to Mordecai, we know still less about him, and perhaps this is a hint as to the authorship of the book, as I shall develop below. He is wise, daring, obstinate, somewhat indifferent to honors (see 6:3), determined to crush "the head of the serpent." What else? Mordecai is "the Jew," and, following his model and his objurgation, Esther reclaims her own Jewishness. Mordecai is an image, an exemplar of what it means to be a Jew in the wide world.

Now, interestingly enough, on the basis of the text of Esther 9:20 ("Mordecai recorded these things . . ."), Rashi (writing in the eleventh century) makes of him the author of the book.[32] Why not? If so, it adds to our impression of the man as humble indeed (remember Esther 6:3 and his demeanor in chapter 6 as a whole and his description in the final chapter, chapter 10).[33] Mordecai—a pen name, perhaps—would have written a book to the glory of Esther, not to his own, thus bowing down to Esther, not to Haman! This hypothesis sheds some light on the awkwardness of the double letter in Esther 9:29 and the "coda" of chapter 10, in which Mordecai clearly keeps a low profile. Is it because he is the author of Esther that 2 Maccabees calls Purim the "Day of Mordecai" (16:36)?[34] After all, it is also on the basis of its "coda" that the fourth Gospel is attributed to John, who tantalizingly puts himself on the stage, although always mysteriously (John 21:20, 24).

At any rate, Mordecai is the demonstration that Israel's history has bifurcated and is now unwinding as much in Susa as in Jerusalem, a decisive development that profoundly transformed Israel's religion forever. In fact, according to the tale of Esther, the historic confrontation between Saul and Agag, that is, between Israel and Amalek and, at greater depth, between good and evil, oddly enough continues and comes to its fulfillment in the Persian diaspora. Hence, the apparent rigidity of Mordecai's persona and the corresponding temporary veiling of Esther's face are merely facades covering the multidimensionality of their personalities and the polyglossia of their discourse.

Earlier, I mentioned the purposefulness of Esther's areligiosity. It is also true that the author had a further excuse for shying away from all "history of salvation" material. Because of the intrinsic polysemy embodied by the two Jewish heroes, the author may have deemed it unnecessary to mention the obvious—and in general unavoidably trivialized—ingredients of a "biblical" tale, namely, God, Zion, the Torah, the Temple, and the Prophets. All those things are intrinsically constitutive of our protagonists' Jewishness. The Jew's voice echoes a multitude of voices: ancient, present, and future. Esther is related to Mordecai, who is Kish, descendant of King Saul, and Haman is related to Agag, king of the Amalekites. A whole world, a whole chronotope, lies in their background and in their foreground. Although we are facing characters that are less "fleshed out" than those of Dostoevsky, we are after all, here as there, dealing with a dialogical literature.[35]

If we were, instead, to accept the nonidentification of the author with one or another of the two main Jewish characters, I should say that, in a way, this nonidentity underscores the author's creativity. The tale of Esther is not narrated from the point of view of Esther, for example, or even of Mordecai, but from that of an omniscient "witness" who, among other things, knows what is happening in the royal harems and in Haman's household and who can at will take readers from Susa to the provinces or from Esther's environment to Ahasuerus's audience hall.[36] The author thus demands our trust. It is clear that the reader may totally or partially refuse to grant credit to the author's version of events and his or her judgment thereon. Similarly, the reader may feel revulsion at the author's evident satisfaction with the great number of anti-Semites slaughtered in place of the intended genocide victims. When this happens, however, the reader must realize that the tale is deeply affected in the process and may, eventually, fail to survive such distrust.

These hypothetical negative cases show at any rate the dynamism implicit in the process of reading, that is, the ongoing participation of readers in the very elaboration of the story and the dialogic nature of apprehending a text. The author is the creator, and the readers play their "role in *renewing* the work of art," says Bakhtin.[37]

What is most important in the book of Esther is not the persons of Esther and

Mordecai; it is what happens *in the space* that lies between them and the other protagonists and between them and their readers.

In summary, contrary to what happens in the Greek romance, for instance, where everything is expressed without allusion to a background (for example, in Apuleius and Petronius), the clash between Mordecai and Haman transparently refers to a deeper historic hatred between the nations they represent. So Mordecai's refusal to bow before Haman certainly cannot be construed as passive (any more than pacifism can be so construed in politics). Mordecai's attitude is clearly confrontational and provocative. On this score also the novella takes its distance from the Greek romance. There, the characters are "completely *passive*," says Bakhtin,[38] who adds, "Fate and the gods hold all the initiative in their hands, and they merely inform people of their will."[39] On the contrary, in the Hebrew Esther, as we have stressed all along, the fulcrum of the story is not theocentric but ethnocentric.[40] Fate lies not in the *pur* thrown by Haman, but in the hands of the diaspora. Esther and Mordecai propel history to a happy conclusion.

In the Greek romance, time is insubstantial;[41] it is essential in the book of Esther. Here, time is split into a period preceding Haman's (failed) pogrom and a period succeeding it, as Israel's history is divided by the watershed of the exile in Babylon into a preexilic and a postexilic period.[42] In both cases, nothing in the *after* resembles anything in the *before*.

More on Haman the Agagite

In parallel with Nebuchadnezzar, the egregious destroyer of Jerusalem and its Temple, "the wicked Haman" is the initiator of the deadly watershed (on a much smaller scale, it is true), and his concocted cataclysm is all the more baleful for echoing the Babylonian curse intentionally relegated by many Jews to oblivion. Haman is repeatedly called "the enemy of the Jews." This again is another way to typify his character. In the book of Esther as a folkloric tale, Haman is monstrously egomaniacal and full of rage. As mentioned earlier, postmodern critics feel dissatisfied with such brazen characterization. Contemporary scholarship tends to psychologize. In this process, much today is both gained and lost through a skeptical—at times forthrightly cynical—stance, which tries to adopt the viewpoint of those figures marginalized or vilified in their texts,[43] among them Orpah of the book of Ruth and Vashti and Haman in Esther. Some wonder, for instance, whether Orpah wasn't more "authentic" in her reclamation of her Moabite roots than was Ruth, who cut all her natural moorings to follow Naomi. There is, of course, no difficulty in extolling Vashti's resistance at the expense of Esther's peevish compliance. About the latter point, however, it is wise to remember Shemaryahu Talmon's warning: "Wisdom teaching considers lack of wit not a regrettable inborn deficiency, but a punishable defect. . . . There is no room for the idealistic dreamer in the world of wisdom. . . . [Vashti's] behavior can be attributed only to sheer foolhardiness which makes Vashti a suitable companion for Ahasuerus."[44]

Nevertheless, it is legitimate to question Haman's portrait in Esther. After all, a human monster is in general an unalloyed brute with a single purpose in life and unaffected by the multitude of pleading voices past and present. But Haman shows signs of worry. He asks for the opinion of others (6:13), and when confronted with his own turpitude he loses his head figuratively before losing it physically (7:6). So, despite the dearth of information provided by the story, we can perhaps adopt the terminology of Michael André Bernstein and see Haman as a Célinian "abject hero."[45]

The discussion of whether Haman is the monster that the tale describes or, rather, the "abject hero" that modern sensitivity prefers would make a lot more sense, of course, if Esther were a historical document. As a work of fiction, however, the wicked, Jew-hating Haman is what he is for the sake of the story's integrity. Any psychological mitigation of his viciousness will not fundamentally alter his anti-Semitic bloodthirstiness. As we saw above, Haman carries with him a "surplus of meaning": he actualizes the presence of Amalek.[46]

Characteristically, Haman directs his attacks against the Jews at their most sensitive spot: they are a people with strange laws. Because of their difference, says Haman, with an astounding superficiality, they should not be tolerated (3:8). Their laws make them scofflaws![47] Haman is thus a propaganda machine. Erich Auerbach has written an unforgettable page on propaganda; I quote here a few words:

> It might be called the searchlight device. It consists in overilluminating one small part of an extensive complex, while everything else which might explain, derive, and possibly counterbalance the thing emphasized is left in the dark; so that apparently the truth is stated; for what is said cannot be denied, and yet everything is falsified, for truth requires the whole truth and the proper interrelation of its elements.[48]

Haman's bloodthirsty rage is indicated by an accumulation of such terms as "destroy, slay, and exterminate all of them, young and old, children and women, in a single day . . . and their possessions plundered" (3:13), the descriptive quality of which evokes a reliable image of the predicament of those deprived of royal protection. They are stripped of all rights and become nonentities.[49] They may be abused, plundered, and slain with impunity.

What should not be missed by modern scholars is that the very identity of the designated victims makes the event of their condemnation ipso facto a "religious" affair.[50] At any rate, the Septuagint shows that the story of Esther was right away understood or reinterpreted as conveying a politico-religious message. The book's allusions to the historic confrontation of Israel and Amalek were readily picked up and amplified: but with a twist. In the LXX of 9:24, as well as in its Addition to 8:12 (16:10), Haman is called a *Makedon*. He was "a Macedonian, an alien in fact" who, verse 14 says, plotted "to transfer to the Macedonians the sovereignty now held by the Persians." By contrast, the Jews are there called by the king, "our loyal Persians" (verse 23).

One finds other indications in the LXX text that Haman was a stranger in Persia. In 3:1, 8:3, 5, and 9:10, 24, he is an Agagite (that is, Amalekite) but also, by a possible play of words in the Greek with Agag, he is a Gogite (that is, one coming from the cursed city of Gog; see Ezek. 38–39). More puzzling is the Codex Sinaiticus revised by its Corrector at Esther 9:24. There, Haman is an *Ebugaios*, a term that remains unexplained but is assonant—with a Greek ending—with "Agag."

It is clear from those multiple designations that Haman may be seen as belonging to any nation or group that happens to be inimical to the Jews at any given time. As just said, that is likely the implicit meaning of *Ebugaios*; "Gogite," on the other hand, is certainly symbolic and goes beyond a mere update. It eschatologizes the notion. This decisive step was first taken by the Greek translator of Esther. It is the first evidence we have of a well-established tradition that sees the presence of Amalek in every generation, until the eschatological Gogite is destroyed and the Kingdom of God dawns. For the rabbis of old, Amalek is the epitome of evil on earth. It has remained so until today; the commandment to blot out its memory is still read annually in all Jewish congregations on the Sabbath before Purim (see Sanhedrin 20b). Amalek, according to Midrash Shoher Tob 9:10, is the last roadblock before the triumph of God.

As we saw above, one of the most frightening ingredients in Haman's denunciation of the Jews to the king in Esther 3 is that he does not even specify the people of whom he is speaking, and the king does not bother to ask for the identity of those alleged scofflaws Haman wants to massacre. This is not an oversight of the text for, later on, in the hilarious chapter 6, Ahasuerus charges Haman to honor "Mordecai the Jew" (6:22), thus demonstrating his failure to connect him with those people he has ordered annihilated. Practically speaking, this means that Ahasuerus has signed the writ without even reading its contents, for it had evidently stipulated the identity of the "rebels" within the Persian populace. The warrant "was written in the name [only] of King Ahasuerus and sealed with the king's ring" (3:12b), but the text was "according to all that Haman commanded" (3:12a).

It is Haman's blind rage that allows Esther, or her substitute, Mordecai, to take control of the situation almost from the beginning and to keep the beast at bay as the situation progresses.[51] We find here an ironic situation that the Midrashic reading of the story emphasizes still further. The Midrash not only stresses the guile of Esther (in chapter 5, for instance), it also amplifies the scene in Esther 6 to mean that, during his insomnia, the king realizes that Haman is out to kill him, as well as Mordecai, his loyal subject. He therefore decides to have Haman honor Mordecai, his archenemy. In the same vein, the king affects to be angry with Haman when he sees him bent over the couch on which Esther is lying. Furthermore, Megillah 16a sees irony in the last term of Esther 6:4: "[the gallows that he had prepared] for him." The context demands that we understand that the gallows was prepared "for Mordecai," but as it will, in fact, be Haman who hangs there, "for him" must then mean "for himself."[52]

It so happens that, without divine intervention, without any prodigy or any external hardening of anyone's heart, without any other such heavenly push or shove,[53] Haman provokes his own destruction. His wife and friends had predicted that much to him (6:13). The story is full of acts of manipulation, but not by a deus ex machina. Mordecai and Esther display mastery in bringing the enemy to bay but, in so doing, they do not take advantage of any kind of immunity or transcendental protection. It is precisely the main ideological contribution of Esther that it stages a series of events in which Jews face seemingly insurmountable obstacles on their own.

Yes, Haman in the book of Esther is not far from being stereotyped as a monster "who utters monstrous words."[54] That he is, however, a history-like figure in the tale, one belonging to a genealogical line identifying him as an "Agagite" and an Amalekite, contributes powerfully to the book's alleged historicity and to its hidden participation in the free flow of *Heilsgeschichte.* By the same token, in that this new chapter in the "history of salvation" displays peculiarities so divergent from traditional developments, the historicization of Haman and of his conspiracy has also a decisive bearing on the "new theology"—or on the absence thereof. As Gillis Gerleman says pointedly, Esther brings about "a consciously consequent desacralization and detheologization of a central salvation history tradition."[55]

In fact, if there is in the story a possible discrepancy between the gloom of part one (the threat) and the succession of serendipitous events in part two (the deliverance), it is not due to an ideological midcourse change in the plot, but to the necessities imposed by the parallel, central to the entire story, between the Persian events and those in the Saul versus Agag episode. This parallel runs deep and is detectable even in details common to both Esther and 1 Samuel 15. As Agag and Saul's confrontation implied whole armies clashing, so too in Esther must Haman have an army of his own that meets defeat by Israel (here, the Jews) as Agag's did by the forces under Saul. The fight reported in 1 Samuel 15 occurred between two kings; so too is it necessary in Esther that Haman and Mordecai be invested with royal authority: the Persian king gives his signet ring first to Haman (3:10) and then to Mordecai (8:8). Similarly, after Haman is elevated to the position of personal representative of the king (3:1–2), Mordecai appears as kingly in 6:8–11 (proleptically) and in 8:15 (definitively).

Some critics have stumbled over the point that the Jews of Persia refrained from despoiling their foes of their goods, iterated three times (Esther 9:10, 15–16). Indeed, that the text explicitly mentions this raises problems. King Ahasuerus had given the Jews permission to plunder (8:11). Furthermore, if the parallel with 1 Samuel 15 holds, the Jewish restraint in the time of Esther must be reconciled with the divine command to Saul to put the Amalekite property under ban, that is, to destroy it utterly. McKane is gravely mistaken when he interprets the Jews' restraint in Esther as a lack of interest in the concept of the ban. He also sees the extermination of Haman's house as an "uncomplicated and untheological [motif] of revenge," on the grounds that the author of Esther believed in the "intrinsic superiority of the Jews over the Gentiles."[56]

Nothing is farther from the truth. First of all, it is clear that the royal permission to plunder ran counter to the divine commandment to Saul in 1 Samuel to destroy utterly his enemies' property. In Esther's time, the Jews did not repeat the sin of their forebears. They would not even touch their enemies' property (Esther 9:10, 15–16), for the enemies' goods are of two provenances: some are Haman's (Agag's), and some are Persian. The ban on either one was not recommended. Indeed, it was much wiser to let the spoils go to the royal treasuries (so Rashi, Ibn Ezra, and so on). Greed, we may recall, had been an incentive to the Jews' enemies in the earlier edict of Ahasuerus (see Esther 3:9), and it had been conducive to Saul's blunder centuries earlier. It was expedient to demonstrate to the king that he did not lose any income by rescinding the effects of his first edict permitting the "contract murder" of all the Jews in his empire (see 3:9; 7:4) and to demonstrate to all concerned that the Jews had no mercenary interest, in contrast to those who attacked them.[57] Although allowed by the king to enjoy the spoils, the Jews renounced them, a gesture that, without the background of 1 Samuel 15, would be mere anecdote. The king gave Haman's property to Esther (8:1, 7), and who is the fool who would destroy a royal present? Esther was no fool. She put Mordecai, the descendant of Saul, in charge of the estate of Haman the Agagite (see 8:2). The verisimilitude of the tale demanded that conclusion.

Second, a distinction must be made between, on the one hand, Haman and his sons, and, on the other hand, those who attacked the Jews in Persia, thus taking advantage of the first royal edict. While Haman is "Amalek," the seventy-five thousand slaughtered by the Jews, defending themselves according to the permission given in the second royal edict, are not necessarily "Amalekites." To mark that distinction, Haman is called by an Elamite name (see chapter 6, note 93, in this volume), and the LXX, as we saw, calls him a Macedonian, a spy for the Greeks, a parasite in Persia, a man whose claim of fidelity to the king is a cover for his ill intentions. This contrasts with the Jews, who in reality are "loyal Persians."

Haman's purpose—to annihilate the Jews of Persia—is expressed with unabashed ferocity in Esther 3:13. The mention of "young and old, women and children" is horrible and belongs to an authorial depiction of the villain as particularly vicious. But psychology does not exhaust the meaning of the motif. Haman is Amalek, and Amalek personifies cowardice. Deuteronomy 25:18 tells us that the Amalekites threw themselves at Refidim on the rear of the wandering Israelites on their way to the Promised Land, that is, on the weaklings, the women and the children: "[Amalek] struck down all who lagged behind." Then YHWH promised to blot out the memory of Amalek, and Moses commented, "As a hand was raised against the throne of the Lord, YHWH will have war with Amalek in all generations" (Exod. 17:8–16).

Such a context sheds light on the true purpose of Haman in 3:8–9: he wants to deal to the Jews the very ban (*ḥerem*) that they had vowed against Amalek (Deut. 25:17–19; see Ps. 83:8). Another text says that Amalek is "the prime of nations" in terms of perversity (*re'shith ha-goyim,* says Numbers 24:20), the quintessence of barbarism. As behind Esther and Mordecai one finds the collectivity of Israel, so behind Haman are the Amalekite hordes, always lying in wait to swoop down on their victims.

When Haman dies, his death "has solved nothing, relieved nothing. He himself may be dead, but his evil is very much alive. And it lives on under the banner of unalterable Persian law."[58] For Clines, the author of these lines, this failure to completely eliminate evil through the destruction of Haman means that the motif here is irrelevant and "inauthentic,"[59] likely added later to an original story that can be found more or less intact in the so-called A-Text in Greek, which ends with the simple revocation of the king's edict (the end of Esther 8). But not only does this indicate a misunderstanding of the A-Text,[60] it also shows an amazing insensitivity to the "persistence of evil" that has marred human history since the world's creation, and does so still, even after the hanging of all Eichmann incarnations. "Nothing is solved" or "relieved," of course, after Haman's death. The Esther author entertains no illusion about that. As the Sages of the Talmudic times said, Amalek is born again from ashes. They identified it, for instance, with Rome after 70 C.E. But Mordecai is also perennial. What carries the story of Esther beyond its chronological boundaries is what is proclaimed by Esther 10:3. In fact, an ironic tale ends with an ironic absence of true closure.

Clearly, irony is also built into the book's structure, the remarkable balance of which has been particularly well demonstrated by Sandra B. Berg. The author of Esther, for instance, repeatedly uses the root *gdl* (great) to emphasize the comic paradox of Haman elevated (becoming great) by action of the king, until he is "elevated," physically this time, on the gallows he erected for Mordecai (7:9–10).[61] After presenting numerous illustrations of Haman's attempts to climb the social ladder (see 3:1; 5:11), the text shifts focus, and all the occurrences of the root *gdl* apply to Mordecai. He goes from being threatened, tormented, and humiliated to acceding to the highest elevation within the court. In Esther 8:15, he receives a high diadem, and his subsequent promotions are punctuated with the adjective "great" in 9:4

(twice), 10:2 (twice), and 10:3. Immediately after the description in 2:21–23 of how Mordecai's loyalty saved the king's life, the verse following abruptly reports the promotion, not of the faithful Mordecai, but of Haman. The promotion of Haman by the king is thus paradoxical. Such crisscrossing situations delicately indicate that Haman's glory is usurpation, while that of Mordecai is justice.

A Carnivalesque Closure to an Ancient Historical Flop

In conclusion, Kish / Mordecai is the reincarnation of sorts of his ancestor Saul, son of the first Kish. In Esther 3:1–6, Mordecai refuses to bow down to Haman, and the reason for this is never spelled out in the book. It is not forbidden for a Jew to bow before a human being (see, for example, Gen. 23:7; 27:29; and 1 Kings 1:31), despite the claims in Addition C in the LXX = Vulg. 13:8–18;[62] the explanation must be sought elsewhere. As we saw earlier, there remains no other alternative but to look for what Haman *represents* as a persona in Mordecai's eyes. Were he anyone else, Mordecai would bow without hesitation. Indeed, it is likely that there were other high dignitaries at the court, not to mention the king himself, before whom Mordecai had to prostrate. But Haman is *Agag redivivus,* and the descendants of Kish / Saul do not honor the descendants of Amalek. There is thus no room for speculation about Haman's alleged demand for divine honors.[63] Even King Ahasuerus did not utter such a claim for himself.

It is, once more, against the backdrop of the book of Samuel that one should consider the later prostration of Haman before Esther when he begs her for his life (7:8). Haman is Agag, whom Saul spared, and in doing so lost his kingship (1 Sam. 15:23). Had Esther spared Haman in Esther 7, she would have repeated Saul's "sin" (1 Sam. 15:30). Furthermore, in the book of Samuel, Saul-the-sinner begs Samuel to forgive him and to allow him to prostrate before God (verse 25; see also verses 30 and 31). He seizes Samuel's coat and tears it, a feature that looks like a model for Haman's contact with Queen Esther on her couch!

It is also within this context that Mordecai's edict in 8:11 repeats the terms of the first edict (inspired by Haman and issued by the king), including the allowance given to the Jews to kill the women and the children of the attackers (see 3:13). In the background is the commandment given by God to Saul to kill the women and children of the Amalekites (by *ḥerem* [ban], 1 Sam. 15:3; see also Deut. 3:6).[64] Missing this intertextual back-and-forth relationship, the motif would simply be abhorrent. Retrospectively, Esther 8:11 confirms Haman's intent (in 3:13) to submit the Jews to the *ḥerem,* thus reversing the (botched) *ḥerem* of Amalek in 1 Samuel 15.

The second decree, signed by Mordecai, contradicts the effect of the earlier kingly writ, which it dialogizes or decenters, in Bakhtin's terms. This was an important condition for the success of the tale, for no language can remain undialogized.

Questioning absoluteness already initiates destruction of the absolute—which by definition stands beyond agreement or disagreement. In Esther, monologism is forcibly dialogized, and an element refractory to dialogue, such as the legal language of edicts, is absorbed into the dialogical genre of the novella.

Earlier, several references to Exodus were made. Now, reference is made to 1 Samuel 15. These citations should not surprise us, for the multiple authors of the Bible conceived it intertextually—Bakhtin speaks of *metalinguistics*. Furthermore, Bakhtin is certainly right when he insists that no one—except for Adam in Genesis[65]—is ever the first to talk about any topic whatsoever. "In a sense," say Morson and Emerson, "all speech is reported speech."[66] This point, which is true generally, is truer still as regards what is commonly and rightly recognized as "biblical tradition," that is, an *oriented*, multivoiced testimony to what was felt to be transcendent Truth.[67]

This phenomenon is of the utmost importance, for it illustrates a fundamental principle of hermeneutics *within* the Bible, namely, the open-endedness of its traditions. As these biblical traditions were embedded in texts that later became canonized, they offer a flanking position to misinterpretations that regard the texts as "frozen" and self-contained. The principle of reaccentuation, however, is essential to the New Testament authors as well as to the entire Jewish postbiblical tradition—especially to the so-called Qumran covenanters of the Dead Sea Scrolls. They refer to the ancient texts as "potentials" that are "these days" more fully accomplished. So, the texts are submitted to a *lecture infinie*, as we said above, or, as Bakhtin is fond of saying, they are unfinalized.[68]

6

Banqueting and Festivities

Banqueting in the Book of Esther: A Theme in Chiaroscuro

The five sets of banquets or drinking bouts in Esther (ten in total) make one think of the feasts and food consumption in Rabelais's work. True, Esther is a tense drama edging toward tragedy, but this notwithstanding, it is punctuated with revels. In this way, much of the ambivalent atmosphere of the book is artistically woven into the plot. Tears and laughter, fasting and eating, fear and exhilaration alternate—even Purim is not exempt from mourning—and the main motor of the story is peripeteia, reversal of fortune (see 9:1: "there happened a reversal of situation.")[1] This is especially highlighted in the book's central chapter, chapter 6, in which we see Mordecai shed his sackcloth and don royal vestments to parade through Susa, the Persian capital, while Haman rushes home to mourn his dwindling powers.[2]

The element of mourning is important because all Israelite / Jewish celebration includes tears of remembrance of a not-so-merry past, just as all lament includes an element of mirth: lament is not allowed to have the last word. Furthermore, the weeping motif during Purim reminds us that celebration can occur "in spite of something that has happened," as Cox says.[3]

This theme of mourning in the description of Purim is all the same highly surprising; it even looks at first blush to be out of place. Purim is carnival; Purim is unrestrained reveling. Striking the note of weeping in the midst of laughter (see 9:22), however, makes Purim at this point a chronotope of the threshold. Why is there such a dampening motif here?

From its beginning, the story as told has been under the shadow of death. Death in Esther has become for the whole community a specter of the horrible, an unbearable *tremendum*. It would indeed bring an utter dissolution, annihilation—as Haman or Hitler had planned—were it not also a revelation: the revelation of its indissolubility from reality. As soon as death is called down on the "scattered and separated" people of the Jews, the community, with Queen Esther at its head, coalesces under the signifier of a communal fast clearly belonging to mourning rites. Death is not denied. Death is assumed to be the other face of life. In the double-faced reality of life and death, one aspect mourns the persistence of finality, the other celebrates renascence. By acknowledging the two aspects' indissolubility, the amorphous "people scattered and separated among the peoples of all the provinces" (Esther 3:8) has found form and content.[4] One thinks of Kierkegaard's reflections about the intrinsic failure of persecution.[5]

Hence, the joyful dénouement of the Esther story was not permitted to become a denial of death. The people's resurrection could not negate the people's ordeal. Easter cannot shed the cross like a dead skin. The triumph of life over death that Purim celebrates paradoxically integrates death into the celebration—one of the favorite tenets of Bakhtin's thought.[6]

True, death, whether in Haman's morbid projection or as an ingredient of reality in the Purim festival, is the same death. It is its interpretation that changes in passing from the former to the latter, that is, from annihilation (reduction to nonreality) to a state of pregnancy with new life, of striving toward the "homecoming festival" hailed by Bakhtin.[7]

Thus Purim celebrates life *and* death, laughter *and* weeping, triumph *and* apprehension before the future, because life is double-faced, and utopia—a term I have used in this essay—is drastically relativized. Associated figuratively with the comic, Purim is seriocomic (*spoudageloion*), a tempered rejoicing.

Something similar may be said of the book's contrasting pair *elevation* versus *downfall*. The Hebrew verb *naphal* (to fall), for example, occurs four times in the first half of the book (in 3:7, where the expression *casting of lots* is, literally, "making the lots to fall," and three times in 6:13), and it is a marker of Haman's demotion from his former high elevation. This carnivalesque motif of enthronement / dethronement is difficult to miss.[8] The apex of reversibility is reached when the story's exaggerations spill over, so to speak, and show the "terrorists" being themselves terrorized by their designated victims: "the fear of the Jews had fallen upon them" (8:17), a wishful motif with the same verb *naphal* reiterated in 9:2–3 around the figure of Mordecai.[9] Other comic contrasts in the narrative may be mentioned, for instance between the litany-like list of officials invited to the royal banquets and the apparition on the scene of the young orphan refugee Esther.

So, let us return to the strikingly numerous banquets in the book. This multiplicity points in several narrative directions. First, the abundance of food is stressed. Obviously, the empire's problems are not economic. According to the authorities, nobody in Persia, or at least in the capital, Susa, goes hungry. But in truth the royal banquets are above all for officials and ministers, nobles and governors, and they afford the occasion to "display the great wealth of the kingdom" (1:4).[10] It is true that the royal invitation in Esther 1:5 extends to all inhabitants of Susa, "from great to small." The text, however, continues with a description of the lavish setting, adds that the drinks were "served in golden vessels," and so on. In short, the visiting rich are slumming. Their purpose is more to impress than to help.

Second, and more important, the banquets set the narrative stage on an earthy level. This is congruent with the secular character of the tale, which contains little that can be called "spiritual." *Bodies* have come back to biblical literature with a vengeance.[11] The axis of the book is entirely horizontal. The king in particular and the Persians in general, thanks to the immensity of the empire and to its awesome power, feel no threat and eat and drink unguardedly. Their enjoyment of the world's possessions constitutes the surest sign of their domination. The Persians give themselves over to consumerism because they feel that they wield the strongest political and military power in the world.

From the standpoint of carnival, the role of the body and bodies in Esther is striking. In the parody of parody with which the book starts, the king and his court are ravenously gobbling things up. The king for one is intoxicated, and, after Vashti's refusal to expose herself to the voyeurs among her husband's guests, he repudiates her and organizes a procession of feminine beauties to garnish his harem.[12] We learn that Esther is the best bedmate and that she wins the royal preference, something that will prove decisive for the rest of the story.[13]

Then in the second part of the tale, it is a question of fasting, of gallows erected, of kingly accoutrements, of processions, of banquets again, of the queen's couch, and then of a pogrom, massacres, and reveling. This emphasis on things of the body in the Judaism of the Second Temple is significant. It is also illustrated in another document of the same era, namely the Song of Songs. This beautiful poem cannot be classified as carnivalesque, and its distance from Esther is vast, but one thing is common to both books: a subversive aesthetics of the human body. They are both subversive because the Judaism or Judaisms of the Second Temple period were oriented toward an ethics of the mind and an aesthetics of learning. As for human flesh, it was strictly regulated by the authorities. In reaction to this, some documents during the Persian era promote the body to a place of honor. Animals, for instance, are suddenly regarded as "bodies" participating in human destiny as a "topocosm," as says Theodor Gaster.[14] In Jonah, for instance, salvation embraces humans and beasts alike (3:7–8, 4:11).

Esther as a Social Pamphlet

When the Persian Jews realize the extent of their weakness, they have recourse to fasting, unaware that their fast will eventually serve as a preparation for Purim. Fasting, we saw, belongs to the external rites of mourning, such as tearing one's clothes and throwing ashes—the dust of death—on one's head. These are clearly signs of the cessation of all activity and are generally accompanied by sexual abstinence (as was the case for medieval Christians during Lent). Procreation ceases along with all other expressions of joie de vivre. In fact, by instituting a collective fast, the Jews under threat of annihilation already taste the death bearing down on them. The mourning comes to an end when fasting is replaced by banqueting at the end of the story: eating is a privileged marker of life's triumph over death.

In contrast, Ahasuerus's overindulgence is not justified by any escape from death. His devouring is gratuitous and groundless; it is a parody of liberation and corrupts freedom into sheer license. Death here is simply denied. Present as well in the reader's mind is the sense that it is illusory to think that abundance prevails generally; it must be shared with the poor. One could say that the Jewish mix of sorrow and of joy, of abundance and of sharing with the deprived—whose predicament is no longer denied but recognized (see 9:22)—signals a discreet reentry of the sacred into the narrative.[15] But, corresponding to the general atmosphere of the tale, the sacramental communion with the poor is, as it were, secularized sacredness. In this story, exempt from all forms of religiosity, sending gifts to the poor has replaced sending sacrificial animals and other offerings to the Temple (see Exod. 25:1–8; 35:21; 2 Chron.15:18; Ezra 2:68). In opposition to the "display of the great wealth of the empire," the Jews at Purim redistribute this wealth, an act that the rabbis of old called *gemiluth ḥasadim,* the fulfillment of charity, the acme of goodness. Whether pious words are added to it—as the Greek versions of the book would prefer—goodness is goodness. Besides, the poor are not fed with edifying discourses.

Purim contrasts with the royal festivities on another level as well. While the "display of the great wealth" clearly points to the past (of which the present is the outcome) and ordains its perpetuity—all historical empires have vowed to last for millennia—the Jewish feast looks toward the future (9:27–28) with a vivid concern for the community's integrity. The empire celebrates the status quo; the Jewish community rejoices in breaking the status quo. Purim is subversive. Forever and ever it will recall to mind that all claims to absolute truth fail. The lesson is socially, politically, ethically, and religiously of the utmost importance. When it is not heeded, hell breaks loose on earth. Systemic absolutism and individual arrogance are plagues on human society. In the book of Esther, they are strikingly described as bound together (chapter 3). Haman's *superbia* cannot admit any relativizing of state power. He bribes the king and requests the annihilation of a whole nation that could cast umbrage on the king's name (3:8–9). Then, the "absolute" monarch (see 4:11; 5:1–2) orders the massacre without giving it a second thought, after which he and his vizier "sat down to drink" (3:15).[16]

"One of the themes of the book of Esther is the contrast between wise and foolish joy," says Levenson.[17] To describe "foolish joy," the text of Esther twice uses the rare expression *tob leb,* "feeling good" (1:10 for the king; 5:9 for Haman; and in 1 Samuel 25:36, Nabal the fool also feels good). The story in Esther clearly conveys the sentiment that the only occupation of the rich is to eat, drink, and make merry. The sheer emptiness of such *far niente* does not even occur to them, because they think that their power grants them the right to a parasitic existence.

Mordecai's refusal to bow before Haman is, among other things, a token of his nonacknowledgment of this, a radical questioning of the concept of authority and its alleged privileges. For the book of Esther is also a social pamphlet. It befits Mordecai at the end of the story to order that food and presents be shared with neighbors, because the purpose of acceding to a high position is not to claim exceptional privileges (among which, we may infer, is immunity, despite Esther 4:14), but to grant joy and merriment to others (10:3; 8:16): joy and also *rest,* as verses 9:17–18 and 22 emphasize. It is within this context that we can assess Purim as another way of banqueting.

Purim's Place in the Book of Esther

After a groundbreaking article by J. Lewy on the topic,[18] it is now clear that the Hebrew loanword *purim* comes from the Old Assyrian *puru-um* or *purum.* The word *puru* means "lot" and, secondarily, "fate." It is, however, by popular derivation that Esther 3:7 and 9:24 focus on an alleged singular Hebrew form *pur,* thus taking *purim* to be a plural form. This gives way to a later abstraction foreign to the intent of the text: *purim* would be taken as recalling the double fate decreed for the Jews by Haman and by God (see the verb *haphakh* in 9:1, 22, "the reverse happened"). In reality, *purim* is a Hebrew transliteration of the Assyrian *purum,* and originally had no plural connotation. The Hebrew text refers to casting "a lot" (not "lots"). But, because there is in the tale a striking symmetry among its parts, *purim,* which looks morphologically like a word in the masculine plural in Hebrew, was seen by ancient commentators as divided, so to speak, into two parts or two *pur,* a linguistically hybrid formation.

Ideologically, however, the artificial creation in the Esther text proved a very effective Hebraization of a foreign word, *and of a festival.*[19] It seems established, as a matter of fact, that *purim* in Esther refers to the reversal of destinies, although they had been determined during the New Year Akitu by a casting of lots (in the plural) in Babylon in the last month of the year (Adar). What the Babylonians celebrated in that most important season of the year, the veritable acme of their religious life, had its very own *hieros logos* (that is, the legend or myth of *Enuma elish*), which in turn came to constitute the seed of the legend underlying the Jewish festival.

Purim thus belongs generically to a preexistent folk culture and is no *creatio ex nihilo.* Furthermore, its origins are pagan. In the Greek versions, where the different manuscripts give the festival various names, the main designations are the following: in the LXX, *phrourai,* and in diverse manuscripts of the A-Text, *phourdaia, phourdia, phourmaia,* and *pharaia.* In view of this, I suggest the following reconstruction of the term *purim:*

a. The ending *-ai, -ia,* or *-aia* in the Greek is characteristic of the idiom (see the statement in LXX about *phrourai:* "in their language").

b. The stem is apparently *ph / r / m* (sometimes, *ph / r / d*). (*Pharaia*, we can assume, is a corrupt form devised for ease of pronunciation.). As no Hebrew word can start with the sound *ph*, the consonant is pronounced *p*, and the stem becomes *p / r / m*.
c. It seems established that, "in their language," the first syllable was pronounced *phu*; hence, the vowel *u* remained in the Hebraized form, **purm*.
d. The second syllable so far is not vocalized; the missing vowel is naturally provided by adding a short *e* or a short *i* sound, hence: *purim*.

What we learn from this reinforces the admission in the Hebrew and Greek versions that *purim* is a foreign word and in no way a Hebrew formation. It betrays, therefore, the foreign origin of the Jewish festival carrying that name, whose hoary existence, needless to say, thus predates the tale of Esther and was not created for the purpose of the book.

Purim's place on the calendar, in close vicinity to Passover, contributes to another sense of vicinity, namely, to religion—despite the latter's conspicuous absence from the Esther text. In fact, due to the festival of Purim, one may view the salvation history tradition as being a watermark on the Esther story. Haman, for example, defiantly casts lots on the thirteenth of Nisan, immediately before Passover, which falls on the fourteenth or fifteenth of Nisan, that is, in the first month of the year. The cast designates the thirteenth of Adar, the last month of the year—just one month before the following Passover—for the fateful massacre of the Jews, but nowhere in Esther is this Jewish celebration mentioned.

Similarly, when Esther orders a popular fast in Esther 4, it is in direct conflict with the meal commanded for Passover (see Exod. 12:18; 34:18; Lev. 23:5–6; Num. 28:16–17; Deut. 16:1, 3, 8; this was already noted in EstR 9:2 and Megillah 15a).[20] Clearly, such an unexpected absence is not accidental. This seems especially true given that the problem in Esther is so close in nature to that depicted in Exodus, namely, salvation from death. In both documents, the pattern of events is similar and resembles that recurrent in the book of Judges: life threat, deliverance, vengeance on the enemy, triumph. The texts of both Esther and Exodus add a commemorative festival as well.[21] It is evident that Purim, falling on the fourteenth and fifteenth of Adar (the last month; 9:17–18),[22] corresponds to Passover, falling on the fifteenth of Nisan (the first month). Both are said to be kept "forever" (Exod. 12:24–27; Esther 9:19). Furthermore, both celebrate the slaying of the enemies of the people and the liberation of Israel from oppression in a foreign land.

Liberation and rest: in the institution of the festival, the term *to rest* is used several times (Esther 9:16, 17, and 18 with a similar verbal form and 9:22 with a different one). Remarkably, each tradition—the exodus from Egypt or the rescue from Haman—provides a reprieve. Exodus 33:14 reads, "My presence will go with you [says God], and I will give you rest" (NRSV). Deuteronomy 3:20 confirms the theme:

"When YHWH gives rest to your brethren like unto you." Just as the Sabbath day is a respite from the week's work, Purim is a recess from pain and oppression.[23]

Now, the irony is that in Esther 3.8 Haman used the verb *lehaniḥam* (to give them rest) negatively. Do not allow *them* to rest, said Haman; yet, the narrative concludes, the Jews enjoyed a complete rest after defeating the anti-Semites. The author certainly chose the term *rest* deliberately, for it is attached to a tradition no Israelite could overlook. In the book of Joshua, the notion of rest plays an important role in the description of the fulfilled conquest of Canaan. At that point, Israel finds rest. True, the term *šqt* occurs in Joshua 1:23, but elsewhere the verbal root *nuaḥ* is preferred, as we find also in Esther (see, for instance, Josh. 21:44; 22:4; 23:1). In Joshua, however, YHWH is the one who gives rest to his people; in Esther "the Jews *gained* rest from their enemies"!

Resting here is not just relief but, as it were, a nonhistorical time necessary for time to pulsate and thus be "alive."[24] Remembrance occurs during the resting caesura: the contents of time are celebrated (in mourning or in gladness or in both concurrently), but without the caesura, time itself would be sheer ongoing terror.[25] That is why, as the text of Esther tells us, the Jews of Persia bound themselves by oath to celebrate Purim annually (9:27–28; see also verses 21, 23); this declaration is a performative act of remembering that *shalom* is always fragile and, hence, always miraculous. Purim represents a conception of history that cannot be called either pessimistic or optimistic. History is seen as totally unpredictable and (at times) as providential. In the latter case, the book of Esther calls history a "turn of fortune" (see 9:1).

Purim introduces utopia, that is, it deconstructs history and gives the imagination free rein to conjure a different world. The "real world" is that of Haman and Ahasuerus; the utopian world is that of mirth, freedom, and rest. Fantasy or utopia, says Cox, "can inspire new civilizations and bring empires to their knees."[26] This is what makes Purim subversive. The glee occasioned by Purim is exactly what Bakhtin, living in the Stalinist era, sought and hailed as liberation.

In fact, the carnivalesque ending of the book of Esther allows us to reassess the figure of Mordecai retrospectively. This can be done at this point using "intratextual" analysis of references to Mordecai throughout the text and what Purim reveals about him at the end.[27] Is he really the stern, single-minded, stubborn character he is generally imagined to be, or is he the real "clown" of the story? Earlier, I spoke of Haman as a false clown, and Mordecai is clearly a foil to him. His very name, for one thing, cast in the mold of the deity called Marduk, is parodic. Second, when we first meet him, he appears as Esther's avuncular, benign relative. All we expect from him is that he will be debonair and nonaggressive. But, on the contrary, he "catches fire" at the news of the first royal edict. Strikingly, he puts on sackcloth, which, to be sure, is habitual mourning attire, but, on the part of a courtier, it becomes a Hamlet-like gesture, one even interpretable as somewhat harlequinesque. Mordecai's act in donning a sack is certainly disruptive, for Esther "becomes very frightened," and she presses her cousin to put on "normal" clothes (4:4). Furthermore, he starts behaving as if demented, "going out through the city and crying a loud and bitter cry" (4:1). Mordecai, of course, is free to express his despair in private, but what is felt to be embarrassing is that he makes it public. As his functions are performed at the king's gate (2:19, 21), it is also to the king's gate, that is, the liminal area bordering the royal palace, that Mordecai brings his unseemly rags, tears, ashes, and screams (4:1–2), not unlike another famous victim, Tamar, violated by her half brother Amnon (2 Sam. 13:19). Not only is such behavior on the part of a nobleman shocking, but it is contagious to boot (4:3). Furthermore, Samuel Pagán is probably right when he sees in Mordecai's cries, "not a funeral lamentation," but "a shout of protest."[28] Yet, a "funeral lamentation" can also be a "shout of protest." So in a gesture imitated by many a modern protester, Mordecai brings his protest to the "king's gate," that is, to the gates of the powerhouse from which the edict came in the first place. He cannot go any farther, not only because of the intrinsic quality of his cry, but because he is not dressed to enter the royal palace. Esther, therefore, sends him proper attire, as if the wearing of a "tie" would solve any problem! (Esther 4:4).

It is to be noted how the progression of the story is marked by the inner transformation of the chronotope. Mordecai begins, indeed, by sitting at the gate of the palace, and his liminality[29] falls in parallel with Esther's equally off-center situation in the king's harem. Eventually, both heroes are shown to proceed from a spatial as well as a social threshold to the heart of the palace, the center of power. So, the initial centrifugal movement, on the model of the Jews' reversal of fortune, undergoes an about-face of sorts that renders it centripetal.

In a contrasted parallel with Esther 4:1, the famous chapter 6 of Esther displays as a foretaste a first triumph of the clown: Mordecai accedes to high honors—by the hand of Haman himself. The grotesque mourning sackcloth is replaced by royal robes, and Mordecai rides on a royal mount. He no longer shouts in the streets and squares of Susa; he no longer wears torn clothes and ashes on his head. He now wears royal accoutrements. His attitude at this point is amazingly uncanny. The text reports his total passivity; the Pagliaccio of yore is now silent, his face inscrutable, while someone else publicly proclaims his glory. What conclusion are we to draw? Is Mordecai not adopting here the part of the silent mime? His assumption of such a role would make much sense, especially if we remember, as a background to the scene, the Akitu festival observed in Babylon and elsewhere in the ancient Near East, with its jesting substitute "king," fleetingly seated on the throne. (Akitu is discussed further below.)[30] At any rate, the transformation of Mordecai is metamorphotic, and "irony borders on slapstick."[31]

With this, his role as "clown" comes to an end. True to the prevailing chiasmic structure of the story as told, Mordecai returns to being the avuncular and debonair figure he was in the beginning.[32]

But, before all this occurs, Mordecai seems to play the part of the royal buffoon. Ordered to pay homage, he refuses to bow before the appointed prime minister of Ahasuerus. Does he do this with a stern face, or is he jesting? Who knows? He gives as an excuse that he is a Jew (3:4), temptingly using the term as a possible synonym for bumpkin: what else can you expect from a clown? Haman, of course, is infuriated (3:5) but "thought it beneath him to lay hands on Mordecai alone" (3:6). Why? Is it because dealing with a fool is foolish?

The end of the tale, with the institution of Purim, ricochets back on the preceding story. We have just tried to trace this motion as regards Mordecai. Other characters also appear at the end in a somewhat modified light: Vashti, for instance, whose "rebellion" is vindicated, as are also "all the women" (see 1:17) of the Persian kingdom.

As far as Mordecai and Esther are concerned, the distance they have covered since the outset is immense. No longer mere subjects of the empire, they are now in positions of authority, roles concretized in their ordinance regarding Purim. According to the ricochet principle just enunciated, we can now recognize that the coy Esther and the humble Mordecai, initially disregarded by the authorities, were wearing masks. Within their personalities lay powerful capacities for leadership, even statesmanship. Their feigned passivity was only anticipation of the moment, the *kairos*, we could say. Those who today criticize young Esther are sinning by impatience. Esther is and has always been "Esther Regina." When the masks fall, the Jewish pair come forward with an edict of their own—an "epiphany" of sorts that is fraught with its own problem.

For, within the folk cultural context, free expression is generally highly critical of officialdom, making it somewhat surprising to see Mordecai and Esther, the prime minister and the queen, taking it on themselves to order a feast. We have already stumbled on this unexpected development above.[33] But such sanction by official entities, it must be realized, is the commandment that prevents Purim from being a naturalistic celebration (of cyclical destinies or horoscopes, of blood, of *Volk und Vaterland*). Purim is a performance, and as such it generates a new language, both verbally and concretely embodied. Such a creative act is attributed to individual Jews, who become the "playwrights," while the people (of all generations) become the actors of the drama. The text emphasizes the creativity of Esther and Mordecai in this matter because "the carnival is not a given of nature . . . it must be officially sanctioned and temporally circumscribed."[34] Esther 9:27 confirms this; it reads, "The Jews established and accepted as a custom . . . that without fail they would continue to observe" Purim.

The performance of Purim is ritualistic. The ritual is a way to give or acknowledge meaning in what would otherwise appear to be a meaningless discontinuity. The ritual *organizes* the disparate and *re-members* the dismembered. Contrary to a persistent opinion that the development of Purim in the book of Esther appeared in a later-added appendix to the narrative, Esther without Purim is a crippled assemblage of discontinuous parts, gathered under the sign of *pur* as chance. Purim elevates chance and transitoriness to the level of destiny and legacy.[35]

Hence, if the Jewish ritualization at the end of the tale indeed raises a problem, one must remember that it is *laughter* that is institutionalized. Laughter becomes calendarial on the model, also chiasmic in structure, of the Persian festival at the core of Purim. Thus, the calendar of officialdom opens itself up to utopia; it allows the usual victims to daydream. Utopia is an important part of carnival. Wishful thinking (or what Cox calls "fantasy—the faculty for envisioning radically alternative life situations")[36] defeats the powers that be and expects to celebrate its own "victory" over official realism.[37] It is not just poetic license; utopia belongs to the compensatory imagination of the powerless. The oppressed never miss the recourse of imagining their oppressors seized by a more or less supernatural fear of their victims, or by what their victims represent, be it innocence, justice, or a divinely appointed destiny. Then, of course, "no one can stand before them, for the fear of them fell upon all people" (9:2).[38]

But wishful thinking does not mean that imagination is given an absolutely free rein. In a traditional society, more so than in an uprooted one such as ours, collective memory shapes imagination. The little Jewess who becomes queen of Persia resembles the Hebrew slave Joseph who became the alter ego of Pharaoh. Mordecai is a descendant of King Saul, and Haman a descendant of Agag. So, all of the characters are intended to fulfil their respective roles. When the drama eventually unfolds, "Agag" is killed by "Saul," and history at last, having long been disoriented, is reoriented. Each participant has received his or her lot. All have met their destiny. The celebration can begin.

Did Purim Replace "Mosaic" Passover in the Eastern Diaspora?

Esther, as we know, shows no concern for or interest in the Temple or the cultic activity in Jerusalem. She makes no attempt to get advice, much less approval, from the Judean authorities.[39] Here, the diaspora community appears to be self-contained and independent. To a certain extent, the *mysterium tremendum* attached to the person of God in biblical literature shifts in Esther to the Jewish people. The saying of Mordecai to Esther in 4:14 indicates that much ("relief and deliverance will rise for the Jews from another quarter"). It is true that it has been recently suggested that Mordecai's words should be read as an interrogative clause (expecting a negative answer): "If you do not rescue your people, will relief and deliverance come from somewhere else? [If you think so] then you and your father's house will be destroyed."[40] In other words, all depends on Esther's attitude, for no alternative salvation can be expected from anywhere else.

At any rate, "another quarter" is no substitute for God, for it would then indicate that the person of Esther is one "place" and God another, "meaning that they are on the same plane . . . and that is not conceivable."[41] Furthermore, Mordecai's rhetorical question, "Who knows?" is much too vague to draw from it a theological conclusion (on the basis of texts such as 2 Samuel 12:22; Joel 2:14; or Jonah 3:9). But it remains that Mordecai's direct speech to Esther deliberately edges toward religious rhetoric. Similarly, in her response to Mordecai, Esther calls for a fast (4:16), and in the majority of cases, a fast in the biblical texts points to a religious practice (see, for example, Isaiah 58:3, 4a, 4b; Zechariah 7:5 [three times]; 8:19 [four times]; and so on). While we cannot really speak of parody here, the text certainly comes close to it, although in a serious mode.[42]

That the narrative accent falls on the Jewish people as such is confirmed later by a female "Balaam" of sorts,[43] in the person of Zeresh, wife of Haman (6:13). It then reaches an amazing climax in chapter 8, where we learn that "people of the land," that is, the non-Jews in Persia, went through a self-Judaizing process (verse 17; the same situation arises in the book of Judith).[44] In a nonutopian world, of course, the reverse situation obtains. Many Jews, starting with Esther herself, have tried with more or less success to pass for non-Jews, when the fear of the gentiles fell upon them. To imagine a situation in which the cats cave in from fear of the mice is comic—it has often been exploited by cartoonists. Esther 8:17 is a cartoon; it could share the famous title "The Mouse That Roared." Such an about-face belongs to the general reversal of situation and of history at the center of the book of Esther. As Bakhtin so powerfully said, to the tragedy of "the real world," the people oppose their laughter; this tradition has continued in the Jewish shtetl ever since Esther (or Jonah or even since Jacob and before), in the form of what is universally known as Jewish humor.

But Esther 8:17 contains a deeper level of irony. The text says that gentiles in great number "Judaized," for the *paḥad* of the Jews had fallen (*naphal*) on them. Note that, according to Joshua 2:9, the fear of the Israelites fell upon the Canaanites during the conquest; the transposition in Esther is telling (see Esther 8:17; 9:2–4). The vocabulary is significant, for biblical literature in general reserves the word *paḥad* to indicate the correct human attitude before YHWH! A number of texts say that "fear [before YHWH] is falling upon" a collectivity. Thus, in 1 Samuel 11:7, the fear of YHWH falls upon the people; see also 2 Chronicles 14:13; 19:7. The following references are perhaps still more interesting because they speak of the fear of YHWH being upon Israel's enemies: in Psalms 105:38, upon the Egyptians; and in 2 Chronicles 17:10, upon all neighbors of Israel: "and the fear of YHWH was on all the kingdoms of the lands around Judah" (in the days of King Jehoshafat). Another interesting parallel can be drawn from 1 Chronicles 14:17, for, as Esther 9:3 replaces the fear of YHWH or of the Jews by the fear of Mordecai (9:2 and 3), so the text of Chronicles speaks of the fear of David falling upon all nations.

The secularization process in Esther is here again manifest.[45] Among the texts in the background of Esther 9:2–3, there is perhaps most especially Exodus 15:14–16, which describes the divinely inspired fear of the Israelites among all nations ("fear and dread shall fall upon them"). Gerleman judiciously sets this text in its natural context of holy war (compare Deut. 11:25). The fear spoken of here is the inordinate kind inspired by the numinous. In Esther, however, the one inspiring fear is no longer YHWH, as it was in Exodus 15:16, but the people of the Jews, without any recourse to the numinous. As we know, Gerleman concludes that the holy war motif is here "desacralized" (*entsakralisiert*).[46] The parodic nature of the shift from *YHWH* to *the Jews* is unmistakable. The mystique of the *people* fills a space generally reserved in the Second Temple period for the mystique of the Law or of the Temple.[47] This is not necessarily a sign of antireligiosity, as we said previously, but certainly a sign of some kind of retreat from the customary attachment to rituals and festivals as detailed in the Pentateuch. There is thus no justification for "assuming" divine intervention[48] in a context that systematically avoids such assumption. The readers' surprise, evidently, will make them think.

At any rate, a considerable distance lies between Exodus 15, with its praise of YHWH-the-Liberator in Egypt, and Esther 9, with its focus on the wisdom and courage of Esther and Mordecai. In Esther the community is endowed with numinous immunity, and the wise courtier replaces the inspired leader or prophet. Consequently, the diaspora Jews do not feel under any compulsion to go as pilgrims to a center of divine power, such as the Temple, as they themselves have become, so to speak, that very powerhouse.

Hence, while Passover was the grandiose launch of an entire people en route to finding the theophanic axis of the universe, Purim, falling exactly one month before Passover, embodies the people's consciousness of being themselves endowed with a mysterious power, call it birthright or election, that distinguishes them wherever they are, carrying, so to speak, Zion on the soles of their shoes.[49]

Does the apparent ignorance of Passover in Esther point to a diasporic rejection of the old festival and its replacement by Purim, as Gerleman believes?[50] The silence about Passover in the book of Esther is more likely to be on a par with Mordecai's order to Esther not to reveal her Jewish origins. As we saw, even God is not mentioned in the book; nor is any traditional Jewish festival of any kind. There is no allusion or reference to the land of Israel—a fact without parallel in the Bible and the Apocrypha.[51] This does not mean that the author of Esther was agnostic or unattached to the ancestral country. But it certainly means that the diaspora faced new issues, the main one of which was to survive in the host country.[52] Passover and the Exodus were assuredly not forgotten at Susa. A stronger imperative for Persian Jews, however, was to keep their identity as Jews while finding a modus vivendi with their non-Jewish compatriots, although, to a certain extent, their singularity made them strangers in a strange land. As Mordecai makes clear to his niece, the queen, her ascension (that is, Jewish assimilation) is not the goal but only the beginning of a development that may indeed lead either to death or to a Jewish presence in Persia without loss of identity.

So, while Passover represents "jumping over" (*pasaḥ*) and departing in haste, Purim decisively entails striking always deeper roots in alien soil, even if this implies changing by their mere presence the significance that their non-Jewish compatriots attached to the "lots," the times, the rules, the laws, and the norms.[53] This had proved impossible in Egypt at the time of the Exodus; it became reality in the Persia of Esther and Mordecai. The aims of the two festivals are thus at cross-purposes.[54]

That is why breaking all rules during Purim, the Jewish carnival, is of utmost importance.[55] The breaking of rules relativizes not only the alleged absolute truth of the autocratic Persia but also, by implication, the absolute claim of the "doctors of the law" within the Jewish people. Purim, lacking explicit reference to all the Torah holds dear (the Land, Zion, the Temple, the sacrifices, the laws and prohibitions, the High Holidays)—with the exception of the People—prevents the Torah from becoming an idol, some kind of "inalterable law," à la Persian (according to Esther 1:19; 8:8; Dan. 6:9, 13, 18). The Commandment "suspends" the Law; the commandment to save another's life or one's own is an example; the commandment of compassion and charity; the commandment of Purim. The absolute truth is God's truth. This has been particularly well understood by Dostoevsky and his disciple Bakhtin. Bakhtin writes that in every utterance there is a "'superaddressee' [*nadadresat*] . . . whose absolutely just responsive understanding is presumed."[56] Sometimes Bakhtin calls this "third one—a possible someone who evaluates"[57]—Christ[58] or anyone or thing referred to in "various ideological expressions (God, absolute truth, the court of dispassionate human conscience, the people, the court of history, science, and so forth),"[59] at any rate, "an invisibly present third party who stands above all the participants in the dialogue."[60]

Thanks to Purim, or alternatively to a Talmudic principle such as the one that invites us to go "beyond the dictates of the law,"[61] Israel's law is a law of freedom. Its sole but polyvalent aim is to promote love, trust, justice, hope, thanksgiving. "If I do not have love, I am nothing" (1 Cor. 13:2).

Thus the Jewish law is inclusive, not exclusive, as it is often misunderstood to be. All humans are called to practice love, trust, justice, hope, thanksgiving. There cannot be any exclusivity here. That is why our tale says that the whole "city of Susa shouted for happiness" (8:15b);[62] it also says that many a gentile "Judaized" and that Purim is also for "all who join them" (see Esther 9:27).

It is within this perspective that one can understand the amazing displacement of Passover by Purim. Passover is a celebration of birth; Purim is a celebration of rebirth or of resurrection. The latter festival reflects a phenomenon of metamorphosis: the people who were dead, for all practical purposes, now are alive and well. Passover celebrated the beginning; Purim celebrates the fulfillment.[63]

Thus, rather than a replacement for Passover, we may see Purim as bringing Passover to its ultimate accomplishment—even if, for its demonstration, the novella chooses a genre and a tone contrasting starkly with the Exodus epos. For Esther is more a parody of Exodus than its "stylization," to use a Bakhtinian distinction. The "fulfillment" here *subverts* rather than corroborates. It is "centrifugal." We should, however, stop short of considering the "voices" thus represented as "clash[ing] hostilely with [the] primordial host and forc[ing] [it] to serve directly opposing aims."[64]

As Passover originates from a spring apotropaic pagan rite, so the book of Esther substitutes a Jewish legend for the much older Babylonian *hieros logos* of the New Year festival. This had been adopted in the Persian version of the ritual, and Esther now transforms it into a Jewish commemoration. The New Year shift from winter to spring, and from a death threat hanging over gods and humans to prosperity determined by the casting of lots, leaves room in Esther for an accumulation of historical coincidences, to the point, it is true, of implausibility.

One night, says Esther 6, the king had insomnia and had someone read to him. The document that was taken from the shelves happened to be the annals of the empire, apparently the best sleeping pill of the time. The "book" was opened at random, and the passage read to the king happened to be the one about Mordecai's report to the king of a conspiracy against him. The wicked Haman also happened to be wide awake that night and, despite the late hour, came to speak with the king of his plans to hang Mordecai. The king granted him an audience, but rather than listening to what Haman had to say, he began to ask him how best to honor someone to whom he felt indebted. Haman, assuming that he was the one being spoken about, answered accordingly, suggesting fantastic honors. When he realized that the king was, in fact, speaking of his enemy Mordecai, it was too late to recant his words. Adding insult to injury, the king happened to choose Haman to implement his own fantasies to Mordecai's benefit. The story continues along that line, with other "miraculous" or at least felicitous reversals of bad luck in favor of the diaspora Jews. Here, as well as in the Babylonian-Persian festival (or during Passover), therefore—but definitely on a historical rather than the cosmological level usual in Babylonia or Persia—Purim celebrates the passage from death to life. The old mythological demons of chaos in the Babylonian ritual have been replaced by historical anti-Semites with Haman at their head, on the model of the Babylonian goddess Tiamat, or, more fittingly, the demon Kingu.[65]

Purim, by attaching itself to the previous set of Jewish celebrations,[66] in many ways contrasts with them all. To recall, Shavuoth, "the Weeks" (Pentecost), is a very serious celebration of the reception of the Torah; Sukkoth, "the Booths," is a manner of ascetic return to the Sinai desert; Kippur, "the Atonement," is marked by a strict fast and an entreaty for forgiveness. Last but not least, Pesach (Passover) is based on remembrance of the time of slavery and, as we already know, is in an uncanny (but muted) conflict with Purim. All of the aforementioned festivals refer in one way or another to the land of Israel. So too does the later-added festival of Hanukkah. Not so Purim, which is a strong manifestation of *adaptive* and *creative* Judaism abroad.

This supplementary celebration in the Jewish calendar—lacking the Pentateuchal foundation of all the other feasts—is the most playful Jewish festival; it is animated by "the sense of the gay relativity of prevailing truths and authorities."[67] Haman is hanged; "cursed be Haman!" The evil is burned in effigy in the marketplace, and that makes the "victory" final.[68] Then a new era of freedom starts: it is a golden age.[69]

Purim encourages excess. The text itself speaks only of "feasting and gladness . . . gladness and feasting" (9:18–19, 22), but the repetition of the motif is traditionally understood as a superlative inviting participants to give free rein to their celebration. In sheer carnivalesque manner, Jews are to get inebriated.[70] Thus, the new law instituting Purim in the empire strikingly allowed for the lifting of all laws. And the fact that a woman, Queen Esther, inspired the movement constituted a resounding victory over all the Memucans of the kingdom, who initiated the misogynistic policy of Ahasuerus.[71]

Purim is carnival, and carnival is licentious. Purim mocks not only the sociopolitical authorities and their ideologies but also their "cold" consciousness and narrow standards of ethics and aesthetics. By way of such a dismissal of "law and order," however temporary, all elitism is also put into parentheses and "a common 'language,' native to all humans" is rediscovered.[72] On this score as well, on this score especially, perhaps, the book of Esther is universalistic and democratic.[73] Purim throws open Jewish "gladness and feasting" to include non-Jews who also experience—perhaps at the level of a vision—the defeat of evil (9:27). Because it invites a collective participation in that defeat, it ushers in a new world.

Purim Suspends the Ethical

"Untroubled by any moralism," said Thomas Mann.[74] I am tempted to apply to Esther the Kierkegaardian category of the "teleological suspension of the ethical."[75] From a normative ethical point of view, many aspects of the Esther story are suspect, at times shocking. Even before considering her resort to deceit[76] and murder, how could Esther-the-Magnificent hide her Jewish identity, eat nonkosher food, sleep with an uncircumcised bluebeard, and hesitate to intercede for the salvation of her people?[77] At some point, she even parties with her archenemy, Haman![78] How could she order the massacre of non-Jews in Susa and in the provinces and even insist on having a second day of vengeance? How could the "Elect People" kill seventy-five thousand people and clear their consciences by refraining from plundering the possessions of their victims?[79]

But the same and much more could be said about the insults and injuries of carnival in general. Who can in good conscience blame Kundera's carnivalesque hero for his sexual promiscuity when eroticism remained one of the rare expressions of liberty under an oppressive and dreary regime?[80] Who could blame the Jewish resistance fighters in the Warsaw ghetto for killing SS soldiers before being themselves crushed under a murderous machine? The utter destruction of seventy-five thousand enemies (a carnivalesque, extravagant number) parallels the spectacular drowning of Pharaoh's chariots in the Sea of Reeds in Exodus 14:28. In sixteenth-century literature, it also parallels the fate of the highbrowed sacristan in Rabelais's fourth book of *Gargantua*. Mikhail Bakhtin comments, "In this novel . . . [Rabelais] inflicts a severe punishment on his foe, the Gothic age."[81] Transposing this view to the age of the book of Esther is not difficult.

Furthermore, Esther's petition to the king for a second day of battle with the enemy must be put in context. The first edict (by the hand of Haman) is still in force. Accordingly, after being permitted to defend their lives during one day (according to the second edict), the Jews would be again prey to those who hated them. The only solution was to exterminate their enemies once and for all. True, the first decree had also designated a single day, the thirteenth of Adar, as the day of massacre, but the genocide contemplated could not have been accomplished in one day; the date set by lot is thus the first day of the operation and emphasizes the expected intensity of the slaughter; it does not set a chronological limit to it.

Significantly, the Jews kill hundreds of people in the capital, Susa. If Clines is right in seeing this number as the sign of an "immense hostility against the Jews within the Persian bureaucracy,"[82] this is hardly a revelation. From Esther 3:15 a clear distinction is made between the establishment and the populace of the empire. In Esther 8:17, again, the "peoples of the land" rejoice at the Jewish triumph.

A very important aspect of the slaughter of the seventy-five thousand is the popular Jewish participation in saving themselves; without that participation, the event would have remained a collective spectacle. Along the same lines, the reenactment of the event at Purim ensures that all generations of the people participate in both the renunciation of all evil and the reveling. The slaughter is both a horizontal and a vertical democratization process.

Furthermore, the folk cultural "grotesque" requires the death of the old, which is the very condition for the birth of a new fullness of life.[83] Carnival has much to do with death—an aspect particularly on display in the Día de los Muertos festivities in Mexico, the Mardi Gras Carnival in Rio de Janeiro, and Halloween celebrations in the United States, but also present in carnivals everywhere. People proclaim their collective immortality and "the ceaseless metamorphosis of death and renewal."[84] Death is part of life, the hollow side of the "embossed" laughing face. The book of Esther, of course, is an eminent exemplar of this.

As could be expected, the "resurrection" from a state of death leads to a celebration of life. Food plays a great role in carnival. It symbolizes communion with the material (and also the spiritual) world and a recreation in both senses of the word. This is true of both the Passover seder and the Purim banquet: they strongly symbolize renewal.[85] As we saw previously, the distribution of food during the festival is most important. Its obvious social bearing is part and parcel with dialogism, so much glorified by Bakhtin. But egalitarianism risked becoming a good excuse for vulgarity, as in the carnival setting par excellence, the market square, "a place of monosyllabic obscenities and hawkers' cries."[86] Purim avoids such a pitfall in a most remarkable way: it neutralizes the excesses of language as well as general aggressiveness by changing the focus to the care of one's neighbors.

More on Purim and Time

With Purim, calendar time is broken by the irruption of another sense of time. The circle is interrupted; the astrological predictions of all the Memucans of the empire (see 1:16) are defeated. Purim inaugurates a new time within time, a time not under the control of state law. Furthermore, the festival is surprisingly devoid of the customary liturgical and cultic elements, as these would not be conducive to reveling and laughter.

Thus, the temporality of Purim, like that of the Christian Eucharist, for instance, is "now and evermore."[87] The text of 9:31 makes this crystal clear: "These days of Purim should be observed at their appointed seasons." What could have remained at the level of the ephemeral and transient is made transhistorical, and the chronotope is broadened to the dimension of universality and fulfilled time.

The event becomes universal, and also perennial. The festival clearly represents remembrance of the past (the deliverance under Esther and Mordecai), but its fantasy reaches toward the future,[88] not just in terms of the repetition of the celebration year after year but in terms of hope and faith that, indeed, the salvation itself will be "perennial."[89] Thus, time is unified—past, present, future—and all the segmented events of the "*small time* (the present day, the recent past, and the foreseeable [desired] future)" occurring in the Jewish diaspora are brought together and integrated into the "great time—infinite and unfinalized dialogue in which no meaning dies."[90]

In order to spurn the powers that be, carnival demands a total exteriorization of human existence. The "Persia" of the tale is a dying world, already seized by rigor mortis, strikingly signified by the immutability of Persian law. The great King Ahasuerus is a ludicrous straw man, and Haman is a clown who does not laugh. A new world must be born. It is initiated by the carnivalesque celebration of Purim. The new world starts with laughter.

This point must be stressed, for it takes us to the antipode of cyclical time, a conception that prevailed so rigidly in the Mesopotamian region of the ancient Near East. It has often been noted by commentators that the casting of *pur* by Haman (3:7) purports to designate astrologically a special day in the annual calendar. As we know, the casting of the lot occurs "in the first [Babylonian] month" of the year (Nisan; see Exod. 12:2; Neh. 2:1), to discover what the gods had in store for the coming year (see Esther 9:24–26, 31).[91] This is an important indication that the tale is meant to be read against the background of the Mesopotamian Akitu festival. The god Marduk (of whose name, we recall, Mordecai is a variation) disposes of the fates during the coming year. Such a chronotope is particularly illuminating as regards the enthronement/dethronement motif we shall soon examine further.

When we take into account that the Jewish heroes' names have Babylonian origins and that the term *pur* is old Babylonian for "fate" (*puru*), it is not impossible, as we saw, that Esther may be a Judaized version of an older non-Jewish literary composition, originating in Babylon, that migrated to the West.[92] For the sake of *couleur locale,* the actual names of the heroes would have been preserved.[93] The phenomenon is exemplified in the book of Tobit, which Judaizes the ancient story of Aḥikar and makes him the pious nephew of Tobit (1:21–22; 2:10; 11:18; 14:10).

If such a derivation for the story of Esther is plausible, the Babylonian-Persian origin of the Purim festival and of the tale that leads to it is clarified. It has been argued throughout the present essay that the whole literary complex called Esther is to be read against the backdrop of the Akitu. The reference to the casting of lots is transparently Babylonian and so is the theme of the clash of good and evil, with good ultimately victorious. Similarly, the king's dethronement is a hoary ritual particularly well illustrated in Babylon but also present in most countries of the ancient Near East.[94] The king's demotion and "passion," on the model of the labors and travails of the god Marduk and his cohort, symbolize the *monde à l'envers* that will become so typical of carnival once they are reinterpreted by the populace (see *PDP,* 124–25).

At some point, however, the king, coinciding mythically with the eventual victory of the god Marduk, is reenthroned, and the new year can commence under favorable auspices. The whole festival adopts, therefore, a sort of a U-shaped movement—we have called it chiasmic previously—constructed of a deep dive followed by a dramatic rebound. In the book of Esther, this U-shape motion is evidently fundamental. There is a comic turn of the wheel of fortune by which Haman is first "enthroned," then "dethroned." Mordecai, at the other extreme, is first reduced to a stateless person, a noncitizen of sorts, before he is "enthroned" in place of Haman. Here, therefore, the pattern of the Akitu is apparent. It is even harped on, and the model is expanded to reveal its grotesque dimension. Exaggeration is an important characteristic of carnival. The polemic it carries indeed consists in overstressing aspects of what it caricatures. When the book of Esther seems to imitate the U-shaped chiasmus of the New Year festival, it is in reality proceeding to the deconstruction of a ritual meant to construct the established power of the regime. The book of Esther uses and caricatures the Babylonian movement of alternating demotion and promotion to show that, in the Akitu, these successive replacements and substitutions in reality undermine the stability of power. They never do so more forcefully than in Esther 6, where Haman himself describes to the king what he expects for himself in terms of honors and promotions—things eventually bestowed on his personal foe, Mordecai.

In both the Akitu and in the book of Esther, clothes and garments play an important role.[95] During the Akitu, the statues of the gods are undressed and dressed anew; on their model, the high priest and particularly the king change clothes. This obviously has nothing to do with pageantry. The dress is here the person. The cowl makes the monk. Similarly, changes of costume in Esther are highly symbolic. Mordecai in particular illustrates this: at first dressed as a courtier, he later dons sackcloth as a sign of his mourning mood (4:1); eventually, he is vested with royal attire. This latter development, which was dramatically "previewed" in Esther 6, echoes Esther's change of clothes in 5:1. All of these external transformations mark changes of fortune and are proper to carnivalesque travesty. Let us recall here the scene of Jesus mockingly clothed as a king by his foes and the sign affixed on the cross lampooning his claim to kingship. These things, forced upon him, may disparagingly allude to his earlier visits with common people and his participation in their parties.[96]

Changing clothes also signals freedom from gloomy ideological assertions of unchangeability, since any social change, of course, gives the lie to such claims.[97] But, important as they are for the carnivalesque spirit of the Esther tale, those changes are here liminal, in the sense that one way of dressing does not exclude its opposite. When Mordecai is dressed like a king, his ordinance regarding Purim is "for fasts and lamentations" (9:31), as befits a people in mourning. And when he dons the accoutrement of utter poverty and wails like a demented fool (4:1), he is still at the royal court—and the queen exhorts him to revert to proper attire.

Liminality belongs to dialogism. Its temporality is that of "midnight," the liminal point par excellence. Like the unstable moment when yesterday is no more but is not yet today, Mordecai never entirely maintains any one of his personae. He is never entirely this or that, for there is something of "this" in "that" and something of "that" in "this."[98] In this, that which is true of Mordecai is also true of Esther, and it is even true to a certain extent of the king when he is inspired by the queen. Only Haman is fettered to the monologism of his egomania. He cultivates his own solipsism and is deprived of a conscience with which he could somehow dialogue. In contrast to this, the change in Mordecai's fortune, signified by his change of dress, is not considered by him as immutable and definitive. If the king of Persia is able to write two contradictory edicts, he may well write a third one that again "dethrones" Mordecai and "enthrones" Haman or one of his ten sons once more. It is thus imperative for the survival of Mordecai and all the Jews that Haman and his progeny be expeditiously dealt with: they are all hanged (9:13–14). They play the part of the cosmic enemies of the gods of order in the Babylonian New Year celebration.

The central theme of the Akitu festival concerns the cosmic struggle of Marduk against the divinities of chaos, such as Tiamat, a frenzied goddess of monstrous proportions. To the extent that the Akitu forms the backdrop for the book of Esther, the congruence of the two tales is all the more striking in that the yearly victory of Marduk was later likely reinterpreted to include victory over the Elamite gods Mashti and Humman (variations of whose names were Vashti and Haman) by the combined forces of Marduk and Ishtar (variations of whose names were Mordecai and Esther).

The phenomenon of the annexation and deconstruction of pagan ritual is carnivalesque. It is particularly piquant in the historical context of the self-deification of Antiochus IV Epiphanes. To recall, Antiochus was addicted to Hellenism, leading him to renounce his own ancestral gods and to adopt the Greek pantheon, even coining his own effigy as Zeus-Baal-Shamem on the Seleucid currency. In Esther, the de-deification of the great gods of the Babylonian pantheon doubles back on that path. The personal unself-consciousness of Esther and Mordecai is antipodal to the ostentation of Antiochus or Haman. Their personal names may well have served as passports to Persian citizenship, but they also constituted carnivalesque masks, a nose thumbing at all potentates, whose grandiosity does not tolerate reduction to the human condition.

The setting-in-life of Esther invites further tallies. As the book of Esther was composed at the time of the Hellenization of the Middle East, we remember the *proskune* crisis that arose while the dazzling conqueror Alexander the Great was in Persia. To the profound displeasure of his Macedonian troops, Alexander adopted the Persian custom of having his subjects prostrate themselves before him as before a demigod. Antiochus IV, of course, shamelessly followed suit, even going much further in the same direction. Within this historical context, Mordecai's refusal to bow before Haman may be seen as iconoclastic. It is a carnivalesque gesture that derides all personal and collective self-aggrandizement. At that point, Mordecai is a perfect exemplar of the seriocomic Menippean player confronting someone to whom laughter is totally foreign. In this restricted context, we can understand Bakhtin's declaration that "laughter is a weapon like fists and sticks," to which he adds that, "unlike those latter two weapons . . . laughter must be absolutely fearless."[99]

The Calendar Issue

In concluding this chapter, I want again to stress the issue of the calendar, which occupies a surprisingly important place in the book of Esther. Not only are Ahasuerus's reign and special events chronologized (see 1:3, 10; 2:16; 3:7; 8:9; and so on), but the casting of the lot (*pur*) by Haman (3:7; 8:12; 9:1) on "the first month" (Nisan), singling out the date of the thirteenth of Adar (the last month of the year) for the genocide of the Jews, starts a deterministic course that seemingly nothing will be able to change. When the expiration date comes, however, the events as planned are changed (*nahaphokh*, 9:1),[100] and the Jewish reaction is spread over two days instead of one (9:1, 13, 15, 17, 18)—yet another way to break up the "inalterable" Persian destiny. Similarly, the festival that celebrates the serendipitous peripeteia is itself split, and it yokes together two days, the fourteenth and fifteenth of Adar.

This unusual insistence on the calendar or on chronology in general is arresting. It must be set on the same level as the issue of the law in the book. The story, as we saw, is about two laws colliding, the "immutable" law of the Persians and the "different law" of the Jews (see 3:8). Law and chronology do mix. Time is an ingredient in legislating. Declaring the law "immutable" freezes time and empties it of all substance. This notion perfectly fits the Mesopotamian conception of time as cyclical, as indefinitely repeating itself like a wheel spinning around its axis. Consequently, to have "a different law" is deemed intolerable, as it not only dictates another standard of behavior but corresponds to another conception of time, thus negating the immutability guaranteed by the gods. When Haman accuses the Jews of having a different law, he implies that they live according to a different time. From Haman's point of view, they are asynchronous. They may be scattered all over the empire, but they live in another world.

This is why the issue of time is crucial in the book of Esther. Haman possesses a rigid conception of calendar time. For him, all things are preordained and fall into place according to a predetermined schedule dictated by the stars. To this determinism, the Jews of Persia oppose an unfettered chronology marked by the unexpected and the extravagant. The mouse may at times roar like a lion, and the lion cower like a mouse. The calendar is defeated. It is no longer as immutable as the stars' configurations. It is an *agenda*, something not "given" but "made."

Nothing could have been more explosively subversive in a Mesopotamian context. Philosophy and religion in that part of the world were grounded for millennia on the false assumption of the fixity of time. By contrast, the Jews of Persia juggled with chronology: the events celebrated by Purim occurred on the thirteenth of Adar; no, on the fourteenth; well, on both days. Purim itself is to be observed on the fourteenth of Adar; no, on the fifteenth; well, on either day according to the chronotope of the celebrants!

While the law of the Persians is said to be immutable—we understand it to be like iron fetters—the law of the Jews is the law of freedom. "We Jews have received the commandment to be free," said Maimonides. Or, as Bakhtin said, "There is no alibi for being."[101] The Persian clock is a time bomb; the Jewish clock is Einsteinian: its chronology does not dictate events, it depends on events and their interpretation.

That is how the book of Esther parallels the book of Exodus. Both are liberation stories, but not just stories of one episodic and transient liberation from oppression. They are stories of the attainment of freedom: the restoration of people's humanity and the rejection, as degrading, of all tyranny—political, social, philosophical, ideological, and religious. As for the Jews, they celebrate Purim!

7

The Book of Esther Interprets and Is Interpreted

The Greek Versions of the Book of Esther

Before we consider the book of Esther as a reinterpretion of anterior biblical traditions—the main topic of this chapter—a few more words should be said about the reinterpretations of the Hebrew Esther in the Greek versions of the book. I have referred to those texts at various points throughout the preceding discussion, and the reader can easily find those references with the help of the index at the end of this volume. At this point, however, a few more words about one of the Greek versions, namely, the A-Text (sometimes termed Alpha-Text), are appropriate. As I said earlier, some scholars argue that the Hebrew Esther is not the original version.[1] Much closer to the "authentic" story, they argue, is the A-Text (hereafter, A-T), based on an earlier Hebrew model (*Vorlage*), and not, as other critics think, on a reworking of the LXX. In the A-T, they continue, after all contaminations with the LXX are discarded, two separate strands are clearly discernible: the Esther-source and the Mordecai-source. In this scholarly reconstruction, the refusal of Mordecai to bow before Haman is not explained, but, at any rate, the story is not about a threatened genocide but about a conflict between two courtiers.

Why Esther sees Haman as a threat also remains unexplained in this argument. Hence, Esther becomes the menacing one, and Haman becomes the victim-to-be. In fact, this theory does not know what to do with the Jewishness of the main characters.[2] The theory holds the motif in the Hebrew text of the inalterability of Persian law to be spurious, added only for the sake of elucidating the inauthentic Esther 8:3–10:3. Purim in this view is also a later addition.

I take exception to this reading on two grounds. First, I believe its reconstruction of the history of the composition of the book of Esther is flawed; second, I fault its understanding of the Greek A-T's literary genre. These two aspects of the problem are intertwined in the description above.

On the first point, it is clear that much if not all of the argument depends on the credibility of the claim that the last chapters of the Hebrew Esther are a later addition that originally had no place in the pre-Masoretic text. The proponents of the theory, therefore, try to disqualify chapters 9 and 10, judging that, "from 9.20 onwards, it is downhill all the way."[3]

Aesthetically speaking, it is true that, after reaching a climax with chapters 7 and 8, the rest of the story can appear anticlimactic. But the argument outlined above does not consider the possibility that these latter chapters might be just as important as the tale proper, only set on another level. If this is taken into consideration, the situation, in fact, is the following: in the Persian diaspora, Jews celebrated a more or less pagan festival at New Year. As was usual in such festivals, the pattern or rhythm of celebration was marked by the passage "from weeping to laughter." In order to assimilate this local folklore into the Jewish official calendar, a suitable *hieros logos* had to be created and fitted to a celebration renamed Purim (itself the philological outcome of the assimilation into Hebrew of a foreign term).[4] In the process, diverse elements of the original feast and its accompanying mythos were taken over and again translated from Babylonian-Persian mythology to Jewish storytelling in the form of a *Diasporanovelle.* Remnants of the old mold can be seen in the names Esther and Mordecai (Ishtar and Marduk) and in the throwing of the *pur,* among other things. The "weeping" aspect is now occasioned by the planned genocide of the Persian Jews by a demonic villain representing the loathed Amalek, and the "laughter" by a striking reversal of fortune. Consequently, as Esther 9:22 reads, "As the month [of Adar] turned for them from sorrow to gladness and from mourning into a holiday . . . so the Jews adopted as a custom [that is, as a consecrated custom] what they had begun to do [that is, what they were accustomed to do in the past, but now again did] as Mordecai had written to them." The deeper was the initial despair, the higher now the final rejoicing, although the two aspects must remain in dialectical tension.

Already at the level of the extant Masoretic text (hereafter, MT), there is an element of *ad extra* apologetics. It is clear, for example, in a text such as Esther 9:24–25, which credits the king with eradicating evil from Persia. It can also be discerned in the exoneration from anti-Semitism of King Ahasuerus, in particular, and of the Persian populace, in general, through an insistence on the guilt of an intermediary sociological layer, the bureaucrats in the capital, Susa, called in the A-T, Add. F, "those in power" (see MT Esther 3:15; 8:15–18). Pursuing this line of thought, the Greek versions present Haman as a foreigner, indeed, as a spy for Macedonia.

This element of apologetics, I contend, is indicative of the true generic nature of the A-T, in which it is much more pronounced than in other versions. As was the later document called the Letter of Aristeas, it is an apologue addressed to non-Jews.[5]

Reading the A-T stirs in readers familiar with the MT the sense that the A-T summarizes, emends, and sometimes augments the story as we have come to know it. Hence, a most important problem is to determine whether the points at which the A-T varies from the MT are due to the translator's use of a different Hebrew *Vorlage*,[6] or whether the translator-author writing in Greek deliberately altered his or her text for a purpose. I claim that this latter possibility is the right one.

As a matter of fact, an examination of the problematic elements shows that the A-T has eliminated all, or at least most, of the features that a non-Jewish audience could construe to be either offensive or uninteresting. Discarded as well were any details that might feed an anti-Semitic sentiment in readers. The additions similarly work toward the same end of pleasing potential gentile readers by contrasting the good Persian populace and their king with the alien, indeed, treacherous Haman. In this regard, what the A-T says of the events of the thirteenth and fourteenth of Adar is of particular importance. As the Persian law is *not* here described as inalterable, the king proceeds simply to annul Haman's decree (A-T 8:16). The Jews massacre their enemies in great numbers (8:20–21), and *they plunder* "whomever they wished" (8:46). It is not explicitly said whether this is in self-defense (Add. E = 8:29), but those who are slaughtered by royal permission are all *men* (so A-T 8:21, 47), in contrast with Haman's intention to destroy men, women, and children.

This turn of affairs demonstrates that "the Jews are not evildoers, but are governed by most righteous laws" (8:27), and that "the Almighty wrought for them salvation and rejoicing" (8:30). To this, the text of 8:31 adds, "And now they do well [to regard it] hereafter as salvation *for the Persians!*" It was therefore expected that, when "those in Susa saw [Mordecai], they rejoiced" (8:40). We remember that the MT at this point has Persians hurriedly proceeding to "Judaize" (MT 8:17), that is, presumably, to undergo circumcision. But such a development might give umbrage to the gentiles for whom the A-T translator was working. He or she wanted to stir in them feelings of empathy, not to shock them with a tactless ulterior motive of converting them to Judaism. Hence, the A-T author devised an amazing twist of the Hebrew model, whatever it may have been: those who circumcise themselves are—Jews! (A-T 8:41). The author adds that no one opposed them, and we are perhaps thereby invited to remember the persecution of the Jews by Antiochus in the 160s B.C.E., forbidding in particular the practice of circumcision. All the same, the deviation from the original intent of the story is evident.

A similar apologetic trait can be found in the accurate identification of the tale's king, named Xerxes in A-T 8:52. Now, a shift from *Ahasuerus* in the Masoretic text to *Xerxes* in the Greek version is much more logical than the reverse would be. Why would the MT obscure the king's name in an "original" text rather than historicizing him? This would already suffice to show that the A-T is a rereading of a former version (most probably the LXX). It is important to realize that the passage from story to history is an effective tool for reassuring gentile readers, who would feel more secure reading of historical events at some historical distance from them, even while sharing a comfortable familiarity with the place and the period—the setting-in-life—of the story.

More important yet is the insistence in the A-T, in parallel with the other versions of the story, on the "Jewish problem." For, in the A-T also, this is indeed a central issue, although de-emphasized by the theory under review. A simple summary of the A-T shows it clearly:

1. Haman attempts to slander the Jewish people and to annihilate them.
2. But he is himself a foe of the crown, while Mordecai, his chosen victim, is, on the contrary, the savior of the king.
3. Queen Esther is also Jewish, and when the king—a decent human being—discovers the truth about Haman, he has him hanged on the very gallows Haman had prepared for Mordecai; the king rescinds the decreed pogrom and allows the Jews to dispose of their enemies at will.
4. The gentiles learn with relief that their Jewish neighbors are exonerated, indeed, are recognized as trustworthy and the best of citizens. The gentiles conclude that the Jews' salvation is also their own (8:31).
5. Mordecai the Jew is put in charge of the empire (8:17), and the story ends with the mention of an annual festival (apparently not Purim, however) that will be observed in commemoration of the reversal of Jewish fortune.

Not only have important elements of the story as told in the MT now disappeared but, in the process, the A-T has significantly swerved in its trajectory. The story is no longer that told by the MT as a sequel to the Amalekite "solution of the Jewish problem," but rather a tale dealing with a rivalry among courtiers. True, the "Jewish problem" is not eliminated, but it is now envisaged from the standpoint of non-Jews. The A-T offers the answer "Esther and Mordecai" in response to their question, "Are Jews to be trusted as citizens or are they devious and subversive?" Mordecai's past demonstrates fidelity to the crown; he has even saved the king's life. Mordecai's ultimate promotion to the highest rank in the empire after the king is the just desert of an honest man who has proven, with the ancillary help of Queen Esther, that Haman's accusation was a calumny coming from a foreign agent who had infiltrated the Persian court. Haman belongs to a Macedonian fifth column. He has instinctively identified the Jews as his bitterest enemies precisely because of their just laws and their faithful citizenship.

The retelling in the A-T focuses on Mordecai, not on Esther. The king gives Haman's house, for instance, to Mordecai (8:15), not to Esther as in MT 8:1. The A-T speaks also of letters written to the whole expanse of the empire; but they emanate from the king and his Jewish second, not from Esther. In an apologetic narrative meant for a non-Jewish readership, the glorification of a woman does not occupy the same central place as it would in a subversive story told in the Jewish diaspora, where listeners would appreciate that Esther and Mordecai play much the same roles as did Deborah and Balak in the book of Judges.[7]

Finally, to pinpoint the work's genre and function, still another dimension of the A-T must be considered: namely, its use of *religious language*. It is far-fetched to claim that a proto-MT *deleted* such religious references, which were genuine in the hypothetical pre-MT.[8] Such a statement is highly surprising as, to my knowledge, no parallel to that phenomenon exists in the history of Jewish literature. The evolution is uniformly the reverse, as the other Greek versions or the Midrashim of the book of Esther attest.

The issue is not solved that way. The presence of religious references in the A-T (4:7; 5:9, 11; 6:23; 7:17, 22; 8:2; plus, of course, the Additions, which the A-T comprises in common with the LXX) is evidence of a later reworking; these are not the remnants of a pre-MT. Addressing non-Jews, the A-T author felt it improper to leave open the possibility that the turn of Jewish fortune occurred by sheer coincidence or chance.[9] Human piety and divine intervention add to the aura of mystery and to the intrinsic value of a people endowed with an appointed destiny. So that which the extant Hebrew text deftly left unsaid or understated for the internal use of the Jewish community was spelled out and explicated in an epigonic work influenced by the Greek mentality.[10] In the explicative process, nothing was left to the imagination; what was discreetly lying in the background—for example, the allusiveness of expressions such as "from another quarter" in MT 4:14—was forced into the foreground of religiosity and psychology. Furthermore, the carnivalesque all but disappeared. The "seriocomic" tale has been given a serious and grave mood. Laughter is out and, with it, the parodic and the subversive elements of the MT of Esther. We are now dealing with another kind of animal.

Esther 9 and 10 together cast their meaning back over all preceding peripeties. It is a grave mistake to eliminate that ending. By so truncating the book of Esther, the Greek reconstruction conveys another story, not the biblical one.

Intertextuality in the Book of Esther

The evident relationship of Esther and Exodus underscores the *intertextuality* of our book. And, as always in this type of relation, the texts, both the old and the new, affect each other. Esther changes the way one reads Exodus. Conversely, one cannot read Esther but against the backdrop of Exodus. Given this, the dialogue between the two works is decisive from a hermeneutical point of view. Esther as an interpretation of Exodus is also a transformation of it—but it is not its replacement. That is why both Passover and Purim are celebrated, side by side, although one of the celebrations is about *leaving* and the other about *staying*. As one could say, paraphrasing Ecclesiastes, there is a time for the one option and a time for the other.

Gerleman's comparison of the books of Esther and Exodus is thus very interesting—although Gerleman has missed the parodic nature of Esther and, therefore, speaks of it as a "replacement" when the term is inappropriate. Rather than seeing one book as replacing the other, one must think of a mutual back-and-forth reciprocity, for, in the parody and the text parodied, "languages and styles actively and mutually illuminate one another."[11]

Intertextuality is particularly important in the book of Esther. Itself the most secular document in the Bible, it happens to be in intertextual reference with one of the most central writings in the Scripture. The Song of Songs, for instance, a quasi-profane document, at least contains references to Palestinian topographical and personal names, such as Jerusalem, Tirzah, David, Solomon, and so on. In Esther, however, even those allusions have all but disappeared (with the exception of the casual mention of Jerusalem in Esther 2:6). Nothing can be more "Persian" than Susa, Ahasuerus, Mordecai, Esther, and Haman. In other words, were it not for Esther's intertextuality with Israel's Pentateuchal (and historiographical) traditions, the book would cease to have any justification for insertion into the category *biblical* or, more generally speaking, into the *Heilsgeschichte.*

This underscores how liminal the book is. If it were not so, one could understand Luther's negative judgment on Esther. But, when we acknowledge such a relationship, he was wrong. What confused Luther—followed by so many other Christian readers—is Esther's carnivalization of Exodus. It makes the kerygma of the great liberation from Egypt and its Passover celebration look awkward. By incorporating Esther, the Jewish calendar accommodates the coexistence of, on the one hand, a festival celebrating the hurried departure from thralldom in a western foreign land, punctuated with an austere meal taken standing, and, on the other hand, another festival celebrating the definitive Jewish settlement in an eastern foreign land, punctuated by a lavish banquet and popular revelry. The latter, we must recognize, appears to be a parody of the former, reversing as it does all of its terms into their opposites. At a minimum, it metaphorizes the movement of "leaving behind" into a claim of one's Jewishness, in contradistinction to assimilation, and it universalizes the perennial struggle against Amalek into a clash with evil persistent.

But the persistent evil has not become an abstraction in the process (as it would have been if transposed into an ancient romance). Evil is Haman, and the liberators are no idealized heroes. The place in which the action unfolds is concretely Susa, and the time during which events occur is that of the Persian Empire: the chronotope is clear. But this peculiar chronotope is itself liminal, as Susa may be interpreted as a condensation of all places in which a Jewish diaspora lives and the time of the planned pogrom, ostensibly the fifth century B.C.E. but much more fittingly the second century B.C.E., during the persecutions under Antiochus, can be any time before or since. Thus, Esther's chronotope is all-expansive but always identifiable as *Jewish.* Jewish are the "reflected and *created* chronotopes of the world represented in the work."[12]

In this respect, the striking scene of Haman "throwing himself on the couch where Esther was reclining" (7:8) is hermeneutically illuminating. What kind of event is that? Interpretation depends on the particular point of view of the actors and of the bystanders or readers. Haman intends by his gesture to beg for compassion. Had Esther been standing at this point, he would have thrown himself at her feet. But the decisive ingredient of the event is precisely that she is reclining. Hence, the king is entitled—especially after the revelation about Haman's wickedness—to interpret the gesture as an "assault on the queen in [his] presence, in [his] own house" (7:8). From a first interpretation as a search for pity, we have passed to its antipode, a rape that deserves to be punished by death. Furthermore, while Haman wanted Mordecai-the-Jew to "tremble" in his presence (5:9; compare Dan. 5:19; 6:27), he is now, in this kind of commedia dell'arte, "terrified" before a Jewess.

From among the three protagonists in the scene, one interpretation remains purposely unexpressed, namely that of Esther. This gap in the text is eloquent. Esther does not rectify the king's negative reaction, a move on her part that would rescue Haman. For her purpose from the beginning has been to destroy Haman, so that her people are not destroyed by him. "So they hanged Haman on the gallows that he had prepared for Mordecai" (7:10). The commedia dell'arte element is here again in full force. Haman is hanged on a spurious ground, as false as was his accusation of the Jews in 3:8. His indictment is for rape and lèse-majesté, while his crime is, in fact, an attempted genocide. In other words, even when presented with the blatant facts (7:4), the king is still unable to see and to arrive at the right interpretation. This is how he has appeared from the beginning: constantly missing the point. Exercising supreme power in the kingdom, his interpretation is the most decisive—but it is never correct.[13]

This is how the book of Esther cleverly uncovers the pernicious conjugation of hatred (Haman) and stupidity (Ahasuerus); of absolutism (Ahasuerus) and devastation (Haman); of political arrogance (Haman) and blind obstinacy (Ahasuerus). The antidote is supplied by Esther and Mordecai. It is compassion for one's own or for the weak in general, and this is wisdom (see 10:3). The chronotope of foolishness unto death is defeated by the chronotope of sanity unto life.

Thus, the book of Esther is a concatenation of reinterpretations proceeding by *displacements:*[14] of the *Heilsgeschichte* by a diasporic history; of the fight with Amalek by the struggle with a vicious anti-Semitism growing from a substrate of stupidity; of the Exodus from the Egyptian concentration camp by the threat of destruction defused by the wisdom of two Jewish courtiers; of Passover by Purim. The book of Esther is quintessentially a diasporic document. Its insertion into the Bible (through ulterior canonization, some three hundred years after its composition) is of the utmost importance. The book marks Judaism's bifurcation several centuries before the Common Era, and it marks the *legitimacy* of such a dyad—Jerusalem and Alexandria, Jerusalem and Susa, Jerusalem and Chicago—a dyad, not a duality. The Jews of Alexandria, of Susa, of Chicago, celebrate Passover; the Jews of Jerusalem celebrate Purim. There is here a potent mutual cross-fertilization.[15]

From this perspective, a unique and essential feature of Esther must be stressed. Carnival in the story reaches its acme precisely when all masks are dropped and the personae become themselves. See especially Esther 7: in removing Haman's deceitful mask, Esther by the same stroke unmasks herself and Mordecai—and removes the scales from the king's eyes (compare Acts 9:18). This process of revelation is especially true, of course, of the main characters, Esther, Mordecai, and Haman. This is an important phenomenon because, in general, carnival blurs all personal identity; in the crowd one becomes fully anonymous. But, with the dénouement of the Esther story and its paroxysm of the grotesque, we have paradoxically reached its limits. The parody goes so far and no farther because the carnivalesque in Esther is restrained by a pervasive sense of ethics that stymies the carnivalesque tendency toward depersonalization.

This inner conflict between putting on and removing masks explains to a certain extent the reader's mixed feelings as to the nature of the tale: comedy or tragedy? Irony or utter seriousness? Grotesque or sheer realism? Earlier, I used the Greek term *spoudageloion* (seriocomic) to encapsulate the inner tension in our story.

In the following section we shall see that the book of Esther's use of numbers contributes to the story's dialectic tension. The introduction of the stipulations of the royal edicts into the text, showing the author's keen interest in contemporary sociopolitical problems, contributes as well. For Esther deals with these grave issues, affecting immense populations of the Persian Empire, in a mode of derision. We thus find once again a mix of seriousness and comedy that furnishes the discourse with the "double-voiced word" that becomes parody.[16]

Let us take as an example the way the book of Esther speaks of the sociopolitical, or more accurately, of the socioeconomic realm. Clearly, the book's accent on consumerism in the empire is stark. According to 3:9, the annihilation of the Jewish community—this would, after all, represent a loss for the public treasury in terms of productivity and taxes—will be compensated by Haman, who will pay the fantastic sum of ten thousand silver talents (equal to a very large portion of the state's budget; see also 4:7). The king's response to Haman's proposition is highly ambiguous (3:11), inasmuch as one does not know at that point whether he will accept the money. The ambiguity, however, is removed in 7:4, where Esther says that her people have been sold—not into slavery, she adds, but to be annihilated. Thus, it retrospectively becomes clear that the king only pretended not to take Haman's money while actually uttering a refusal void of sense. One thinks of Abraham buying the cave of Machpelah from Ephron as a grave for Sarah (Gen. 23). Ephron seems to refuse payment for the land but quotes its price anyway, adding that it is a trivial matter between him and Abraham. The latter understands the clue and pays the four hundred shekels!

Furthermore, although the Jewish refusal to plunder the goods of their slain enemies must be analyzed in a much broader and more significant context, it certainly establishes a stark contrast with the empire's materialism and consumerism. It counteracts the promise of Haman to the anti-Semites that they will pillage the belongings of their Jewish victims. We must remember this economic aspect of anti-Semitism below when we deal with anti-Semitism as one of the book's themes.

The Dyadic in the Book of Esther

Regarding numbers in the tale, the author's predilection for twofold situations, on the model of the Joseph story in the book of Genesis, is worth noting:[17]

Two banquets offered by the king (1:3–8; 2:18)
Two banquets offered by the queen (1:9; 5:4–8)
Two queens (1:11; 2:17)
Two conspiracies against the king (2:21; 3:8–15)
Two king's viziers (3:1; 8:2)
Two mentions of the "*pur*" (3:7; 9:24–26)
Two royal decrees (3:13; 8:10–14)
Two fasts (4:3, 16)
Two oaths concerning "half the kingdom" (5:3, 6; compare 7:2)[18]
Two invitations to banquets organized by Esther (5:4, 8)
Two massacres (9:1–10, 11–15)
Two days of Purim (8:17; 9:17–22)

Last, but not least, the "hero" of the story is dual. Esther and Mordecai are the two faces of one reality: female and male, dynamic and static, audaciously ambivalent and lucidly Jewish.

The attempt by some scholars to split the present version of the Esther story into two "original sources," one centering on Mordecai, the other on Esther, that were later fused into one story by some manner of unoriginal epigones,[19] proceeds from a modern widespread misconception of the hero in general. Henri Cazelles, for example, suggests that the book of Esther resulted from the blending of two originally independent sources, which we shall here call *E* for Esther and *M* for Mordecai. *E* has a rather liturgical character and is at home in the Persian countryside. *M* is political; is located in the capital, Susa; and celebrates the Jews victory over Haman ben Hamdatha and his sons. Moreover, throughout the book a series of doublets occurs that correspond to the juxtaposition of *E* and *M*. In Esther 9, for example, there are two massacres, one on the thirteenth of Adar (source *M*) and the other on the fourteenth of Adar (source *E*); verse 18 collapses both into one. Similarly, there are two narratives of the death of the ten sons of Haman in chapter 9 (verses 10 and 13) and two decrees about Purim, one by Mordecai (verse 23) and the other by Esther (verses 29–32), harmonized in verse 31.[20] Thus, originally, the story had not two heroes, but one.

But, as Graham Pechey paraphrases Bakhtin, this is an "exciting though perverse fiction of the hero as self-authoring,"[21] while, in reality, the protagonists in the tale are mutually authoring: Esther needs Mordecai just as Mordecai needs Esther. In Esther 4:13–14, Mordecai is clearly "authoring" Esther, and, in the following verses, Esther is clearly "authoring" Mordecai (4:15–17). He may at times know Esther better than she knows herself. If so, there is clearly no Esther—as we know her from the novella—without Mordecai, and vice versa.[22]

We have seen the character of Esther evolve from a noncommittal royal princess to a full-fleshed heroine who saves her people from annihilation. Her initial reluctance to accept a vocation that only Mordecai's "surplus of vision" is capable of identifying for her is a striking motif in the story. Such hesitancy is far from unique in the Hebrew Bible, where on the contrary hero after hero resists his or her destiny. From Moses on (and even earlier, from patriarchal times), the prophets in particular are described as experiencing initial periods of denial (see, especially, Isa. 6; Jer. 1; and Jon. 1). The motif is too frequent not to reflect a certain Hebrew anthropological conception.[23] Bakhtin, *mirabile dictu,* had an acute understanding of the issue. Strikingly, he sees the hero (that is, the *I* authored by others as *I* author them) as a "whole of meaning" that the aesthetic activity of the individual only encompasses through her or his relation with the other and with the Other.[24] Mordecai, as the other of Esther, helps her to become a "whole of meaning," a fulfillment of herself that she had been on the verge of badly missing at some point of her being.

As a foil, Haman's solipsism prevents him from becoming "meaningful." His miserable death is fate's signature on a meaningless existence. True, as we saw, there had been an opening of sorts toward his wife and counselors in 6:12–13, but the alleged dialogue was in reality a monologue with alternate voices. Haman speaks only about himself, and his concern is strictly self-centered. Furthermore, the negative response he receives from others amounts significantly to a rejection (6:13). Haman has missed the opportunity to be "authored" and to "author." From the outset, his agenda and the purpose of his life were to destroy. Subtly, the story tells us that Haman empties himself of all substance until he brings on himself the death he had planned for others. Haman is self-destructive because his persona is so one-faced that his self-authoring amounts to a terrible flop.

Although in any conflictual situation it is tempting to demean the adversaries and to consider them nonpersons, Haman in Esther does not require such ill treatment by others, but by himself. In our parodic tale, his character slips ever downhill and appears soulless—that is, "nonauthored" and "nonauthoring." In a provocative Midrash to which I have already alluded, it is said that the meaning of Exodus 2:12 is the following: Moses, before killing the Egyptian taskmaster who beat a Hebrew worker, looked "here and there," that is, into the past and the future of the man, and he found *lo ʾish*, literally "no man" (2:12a).[25] Bakhtin's expression is strikingly close to the Midrashic; he speaks of "the man in man."[26] It can be said, therefore, that in the man Haman there was no "man." Esther, like Moses in Egypt, kills a "manless" man.

"It takes a village" to bring "the man in man" to fruition. It needs a *thou* to give substance to the *I*. The dyad characteristic is already present in the double names of the Jewish protagonists. As two queens, two viziers, two contradictory royal decrees, cannot coexist for long, those and all other pairs must also strive toward resolution, either through elimination of one of the elements or by merging, in some way, the two. In examples of mutual elimination, one official banquet eliminates the other; one queen substitutes for the other; one vizier is impaled to make room for his replacement; and one later edict invalidates a former one (although here the ambiguity of the substitution is such that the temporary coexistence of the two writs produces devastating "double signals"). Mergers or marriages of dyadic terms include the conjugation of the two Jewish fasts so that, through actions initiated separately by Esther and by Mordecai, Purim is instituted by both. As to the two days of festival, they are one entity accommodating two popular locations.

Juggling with Numbers in the Book of Esther

Dyads emphasize the Janus-like nature of reality. Other figures in Esther raise the same prospect of being at once precise and oblique, so to speak. What Bakhtin writes on the "desacralization" of numbers in Rabelais's work is applicable to Esther's use of numbers. In both cases, numbers either produce a "comic effect . . . obtained by a pretense of exactitude in situations where a precise count is impossible"[27] or include numbers that have no mystical meaning. I cite as examples in Esther "180 days" for the duration of the first royal banquet (1:4) in celebration of the rule of Ahasuerus over "127 provinces" (1:1; 8:9); "the thirteenth day of the twelfth month" (3:7) and "the thirteenth day of the first month" (3:12); "the second day" (7:2); and "the twenty-third day" (8:9). Among the exaggerated or grotesque elements of the story, one will notice the use of the adjective *all* in Memucan's speech to the king ("all the women," 1:17) and in the servants' proposal that "all the beautiful young virgins" of the kingdom be summoned into the royal harems (2:3). The adjective *all* reappears later in a text in which the grotesque reaches its apex, in 3:6 (whose language parallels that of 1:17, just mentioned). Haman deems it unworthy of himself to deal with Mordecai alone. Just as the king had inflated Vashti's insubordination into a state emergency regarding *all* the women of the empire (1:19–20), so Haman wants the death of *all* Jews in all 127 provinces (3:12–14). Furthermore, in parallel with the yearlong preparation of the virgins in chapter 2,[28] the whole population of the kingdom is given a full year to prepare for the massacre (3:14).

The numbers representing the "body-count" of the reversed massacre, discussed below, deserve our attention: "five hundred people" [in Susa] (9:6, 12); plus "three hundred persons in Susa" (9:15); and "seventy-five thousand" in the provinces (9:16). Even sacred numbers are used by the author in a less than reverend way: the third year of the king's reign is spoken of (1:3); he is drunk on the seventh day (1:10); the maidens apply cosmetics for twelve months (2:12);[29] we pass to the seventh year of the king's reign (2:16) and then to its twelfth year (3:7); Haman will pay ten thousand silver talents (3:9); the gallows is fifty cubits high (5:14; 7:9). In the "religious" biblical texts, all of these figures are found marked with a sacred indexing.

According to 9:7–10, Haman has ten sons, another instance of the use of a sacred figure. Their names are listed here in what is clearly a gamelike way.[30] As sons of Hamdatha (that is, Haman), six of them have names ending in *-tha* and six also have names starting with an *a* sound.[31] Only one, Dalfon, has a name different from the rest. The combination of *a-* and *-tha* (although ending with an *aleph* instead of a *hé*) gives *atthah*, that is, "you," the accusing address of Samuel to Saul in 1 Samuel 15, where this pronoun appears with unexpected redundancy three times (verses 13, 17a, 17b). The number of pronominal suffixes in *-kha* and *-tha* in the same chapter of Samuel is also striking. Furthermore, in his reply to Samuel, Saul uses the same second-person pronominal designation in return. Thus, the ending in *-kha* for Samuel is also found three times: in 1 Samuel 15:21, 24, and 30, including the striking use of *Eloheikha* (your God)! That the author of Esther had this text from Samuel in mind is evident from the mention in 9:10 that the Jews refrained from laying hands on the spoil, in conspicuous contrast to what happened under Saul's leadership in the book of Samuel.

Along the same line of thought, the numbers of the Jews' slain enemies given in 9:12, 15, and 16 (500 + 300 + 75,000) are also gamelike. All of them are multiples of five—$500 = [(5 \times 5) \times 2] \times 10$; $300 = [(5 \times 6) \times 1] \times 10$; $75{,}000 = [(5 \times 5) \times 3] \times 1{,}000$ ($= 10 \times 10 \times 10$)—a "Rabelaisian" enormity! Thus, it may well be that in specific cases the numbers in Esther regain their full symbolic value. An example of this is patent in the reference in 8:9 to "the third month," which marks the turn of fortune in favor of the Jews, and in the 9:1 reference to "the twelfth month" in a context that again stresses the peripeteia.

All of those figures, particularly the "body-counts" in chapter 9, underscore the violence in Esther, an element that has contributed to the historic negative reaction to the book among Christian readers. What we have considered here should qualify such a judgment. But it remains that carnival in general is not exempt from violence. Bakhtin seems to avoid this aspect, however, which nonetheless plays an important role in folk revelry. Earlier, I called attention to the undeniable atmosphere of carnival in the lynching of Jesus by the Romans and the mob, including of course the "crowning" of Christ, the sham interrogation to which he is submitted, his crucifixion alongside two hoodlums, the inscription on his cross deriding him as "King of the Jews," and so on. In addition, the Gospel scene is not itself exempt from serial numbers, but this time with a triadic base: the three crosses, the third hour, the three days in the tomb, and others.

In another geographic area, the inhabitants of Sardinia, according to Vladimir Propp, used to kill their old people while laughing loudly (hence the expression, "a sardonic laughter"). Emerson, who cites Propp here, adds that "laughter frequently accompanied death and magically transformed it into new birth" (a Bakhtinian point).[32] Such a link between death by (sanctified) murder and a collective rebirth strikes a familiar note among readers of the book of Esther, for, as we have seen, any pathos regarding death is totally absent from Esther. True, the work expresses a deeply felt urgency to divert the sword menacing the Jewish community in Persia, but when the massacre occurs in coarse fact, no feeling of sympathy is expressed concerning the victims. Death is here "an anatomical-physiological fact in an impersonal series"[33] even made grotesque by the sheer fanciful number of the anti-Semites slaughtered. That the slaughter has the joyous consequence of liberation for Esther and Mordecai's people is one more tie with the Rabelaisian comic. As in Rabelais, death is "a phenomenon of sociohistorical life."[34]

8

Otherness: The Women and the Jews

Sexuality in the Book of Esther

Although the Jews did not need the Greeks to write about sexuality (see Gen. 38–39 or 2 Sam. 11, for example), the setting-in-life of the book of Esther in the Hellenistic era—if such a late date is retained—would be conducive to a renewed literary interest in sexuality. The book of Esther, as noted in chapter 1, displays the supreme Bakhtinian quality of *novelness*, a generic identity that brings the book close to the Greek romance. As expected, the book focuses on female sexuality, especially that of Esther but also, fleetingly, that of Vashti. To recall, the story begins with a royal summons to Vashti to appear, perhaps naked but in any case as an erotic object, before the king's guests during an orgy. She is said to be beautiful, and she is expected to show her beauty to all (Esther 1:11: "to show the peoples and the officials her beauty" [NRSV]).[1] She refuses (1:12). Then, in a turn of events that belongs to the burlesque, Vashti's move becomes an affair of state leading to turmoil in the royal palace, a conference of the ministers, and consultation of astrologists and specialists in legal matters (1:12–15). The unanimous decision is that Vashti has wronged not only the king but every male in the kingdom (1:16). Her rebellion could be imitated by "all women," who might also refuse to make obeisance to their husbands (1:17), an unbearable situation for the men (especially those in power; see 1:18), and one that recalls the striking women under the leadership of Lysistrata in Aristophanes' comedy of that name (411 B.C.E.). Only one solution remains: the repudiation of Vashti (1:19) and her replacement by another woman "better" than she (1:19). This will serve as a lesson for all women in Persia, and they will again agree to be subservient to their husbands (1:20). The king agrees with this suggestion and declares as law that every man is master of his household (1:22).[2]

On the issue of sexuality in Esther, chapter 2 is particularly suggestive. For a whole year, the virgins gathered in the first harem think to the point of obsession about sex, but only in anticipation: the dream of their night with the king is carefully kept going by a band of eunuchs, whose very castration operates as a steady frustration to the females with whom they are constantly in contact for their "grooming." When at last the virgins are sexually used by the kingly stud, they join the group of concubines in a second harem, from which they may never again be called to "please the king."

As could be expected in an ancient first-line novelistic literature using what Bakhtin calls an "ennobled" language distant from "the crude heteroglossia of the real world and . . . cleansed of all possible associations with crude real life,"[3] the book of Esther does not lift the veil on life in the harem or in the king's bedroom. All of this is left to the reader's imagination.

The whole of Esther 2 is hilarious and contributes strongly to the generation of laughter from this point onward in the book—despite the tragic dimension of a story that, indeed, makes us contemplate the "unthinkable." To the extent that the *tremendum*[4] is planned but not realized, the story becomes a tragicomedy. Sexuality in the book is not foreign to the dual nature of that animal. Esther begins as a narcissistic pageant competitor (she certainly does nothing to discourage those in charge of her beautification),[5] and she goes through an endless "prep" for a honeymoon that could well be her last night with her bluebeard of a pseudohusband. To stress the point, the text says that Esther had to wait four years before being invited by the king (compare 1:3 and 2:16). She does not follow her predecessors to the concubine harem, however (see 2:19, where "a second time" refers to their being again together after Esther was first "used"). Under the guidance of her tutor, Mordecai, Esther's tactics are to exploit fully all feminine wiles and deception. She feels no qualms about sharing the bed and the table of a pagan and a tyrant. Up to this point, therefore, the Esther figure is reduced to the size of a consenting sex object.

But not for long. A major crisis erupts and—again under the leadership of Mordecai—Esther must undergo metamorphosis and emerge as a strong-willed head of state.[6]

The book of Esther achieved literary success[7] because of the presence in it of major themes of human existence, in particular the themes of love and death and rebirth. To these main ingredients are further added other eminent elements such as eroticism, riches and glory, envy, betrayal, crime, political shortsightedness and political astuteness, war and peace, defeat of the wicked and triumph of the righteous, and many more. The tale, in fact, is about the victory of life over death and of good over evil. It is a story of resurrection.[8]

All the ingredients would thus seem to be gathered for the creation of a symbolic or metaphoric narrative. But, on the contrary, we find instead a straightforward, concrete, sociohistorical, compact, and realistic story. So much so that any text analysis or "commentary" on Esther must by necessity remain at the level of a paraphrase. There is no hidden meaning and hardly any allusion, barring its intertextuality. This does not mean that the text is monoglossic; we saw above that the reverse is true, that the tone here is ironic and carnivalesque, rendering the text subversive, double-voiced, and dialogic.

All of the themes mentioned above are treated "lightly," despite the heavy atmosphere created by the threat of impending death hanging over a whole community. In short, pathos is here very much controlled, understated, tongue-in-cheek, as befits fine humor. For Esther is finally a comedy. It is a comedy playing with a tragic theme, like a cat with a mouse, or is it perhaps like a child with fire? Esther 4, for instance, is highly dramatic; it is "pathetic."[9] Had the book belonged to another genre, it is easy to imagine at this point the insertion of a dirge, similar to what we find in the book of Lamentations. The Greek text of Esther adds here a supplementary "Prayer of Mordecai" and a "Prayer of Esther" to this effect (Add. C).

But in the novelistic Hebrew text, the style is areligious and, therefore, more than ever, "such pathos is the discourse of a preacher who has lost his pulpit, a dreaded judge who no longer has any judicial or punitive powers, the prophet without a mission, the politician without political power, the believer without a church."[10]

Such a situation contributes strongly to the feeling that here "the discourse of pathos" comes only secondhand. The formidable danger represented by Haman is overcome, as Goliath is by young David, and the pathetic is lifted. David had a slingshot; Esther has her sexuality.[11] The reader is led to conclude that all the beauty is on the Jewish side and all the ugliness is with Haman and the conspirators.

Beauty here is not a static quality, however. It is a calling and an opportunity. Mordecai tells Esther that her accession to royalty is *Gabe und Aufgabe* (gift and task)[12]—a long way from the pageantry of chapter 2. Thus, sexuality suddenly takes on a meaning beyond eroticism and reproduction (the latter totally ignored in the tale, as is also childhood).[13] Sex becomes a sheer means of survival, which in the context of the story is also a means of salvation from annihilation. The same motif is present in the book of Judith, roughly contemporary with Esther. *Vagina vitae; vagina salutis.* While world literature offers a plethora of stories about feminine wiles and their devastating results, biblical literature displays a string of heroines whose sexuality is eminently positive, from the Pentateuchal matriarchs to Tamar, Ruth, the Shulammite of the Song of Songs, Esther, Judith, Susannah, and many others. This, by the way, does not necessarily indicate that the book of Esther was written by a woman,[14] although it remains a possibility (as in the case of the authorship of Ruth and Song of Songs).

Esther is no Barbie doll. It requires a strong will and determination not to accept selfishly the kingly offer of "up to half of the kingdom," to which Esther replies with the self-effacing request that the king and Haman appear at her coming banquet. True, we have not left the realm of fantasy. But, although Esther is in this way fattening Haman for the kill, as Levenson says,[15] her sheer obliviousness to her advantage contrasts starkly with Haman's insatiable appetite for royal favors. Her request also prepares the way for her denunciation of Haman's criminal project by deflecting any suspicion that she is waging a personal vendetta against a domestic rival.[16]

Esther even organizes a second banquet, and this delaying tactic is puzzling.

In addition to serving as a literary device of retardation, the image of the two banquets honoring king and vizier reflects Esther's dual psychological motives. First, she aims selectively to keep the king waiting; he must be the first to feel the delay. Esther here deploys enticement and suspense. Timothy Laniak astutely draws a parallel with Joseph in Genesis, who organizes a first banquet for his estranged brothers (Gen. 43:16–34) while keeping secret his identity. Only at a second banquet (45:3) does he identify himself to them.[17] This is neither the first time nor the last that we encounter a parallel with the Joseph story in Esther.

Accordingly, the sexual foreplay, so to speak, is overextended.[18] This is especially piquant if we follow Robert Alter's suggestion that Ahasuerus is impaired in the story by impotence, a "comic specter" symbolized by the king "holding out his golden scepter" (Esther 5:2), which, in fact, is the appendage of "a man with a shaky scepter." In that context, Ahasuerus, by misinterpreting as a rape Haman's gesture in beseeching the queen's mercy in chapter 7, attests to a fear that Haman is usurping not only his political power but also "the lovely woman he himself has possessed only intermittently, and perhaps precariously."[19]

Esther's second motive for retardation is that she is determined to have Haman present. Esther, evidently, does not want any kingly sentence in contumacy. The enemy must be trapped without any possible way out and—this time, in contrast to Saul's procrastination in 1 Samuel 15—without any delay between the indictment and the sentence. The effect of surprise, by depriving Haman of the opportunity for a premeditated alibi, is essential. The king will witness his vizier reduced to silence. The theatricality of the plot is enhanced by the villain's presence onstage. Logically speaking, he did not need to be there, but the carnivalesque performance demanded his presence. For drama, it certainly beats trampling the villain's effigy underfoot. Haman must be visibly confounded before spectators and readers. His death sentence must be seen to be executed on an immense gallows. It belongs to the show.[20]

With Esther's second banquet, all the ingredients are gathered for a potential sex orgy to commence. After all, Esther has invited two males—note the contrast with Vashti surrounded by women in the banquet she organized (Esther 1:9)—namely, her husband and someone who could easily think of himself as the king's substitute (see Esther 6). The ambiguities of state politics are shortchanged by the ambiguities of the grotesque. Thus, the Janus-like structure of the book is confirmed by internal events amphibologic in meaning. The defeat of Vashti is the triumph of Esther; the rags on Mordecai contrast with the royal vestments of the queen; the enormous ambitions of the wicked are fulfilled in the person of his enemy; the king's outrageous and senseless gluttony sees its meaninglessness reversed in the queenly banquets hiding a full agenda; the gallows of injustice becomes the instrument of the vindication of the just; the persecutors are persecuted; the defeated are victors; those who lose win; the arrogant reveling of those in power is replaced by the low-keyed but deeply felt festival of Jewish salvation; and the initial fast gives way to a shared abundance of food.

The theme of sexuality could retreat at this point in the narrative, but such is not the case. In the most dramatic scene of the story, Haman falls under suspicion of attempting to rape Esther (7:8), that is (in terms of political power, for the sexual and political realms are twins), of trying to snatch from the king not only his wife but also his kingship (compare 2 Sam. 3:7; 16:21–22; 1 Kings 2:22). In this new crisis, Haman loses his head, both figuratively and literally. As for Esther, her resolve becomes boldness (8:3–6). In conjunction with Mordecai, she is on her way to completely eclipsing her husband, who hangs Haman as a clear and present danger but unknowingly installs Esther in his stead over even more than the "half of the kingdom" he had promised her (7:2). Ahasuerus had by this point time and again demonstrated that he was a paper tiger (see 8:1, 7, 15; 9:4, 14, 20, 29; 10:3).[21]

From a scatterbrained pinup to a fifth-century B.C.E. Golda Meir, the evolution of Esther is amazing. The author has brushed up an image of a collective diasporic passage from carefree existence to panic, from panic to resoluteness, and from resoluteness to triumph. For Esther, this implied a profound transformation, a wrenching death-and-renewal personal process paralleling the death and rebirth of her people in the crucible of a threatened genocide.

As for King Ahasuerus / Xerxes, he is beset with anger, a theme often repeated in Esther to characterize the gentile protagonists. They are prone to anger (in regard to the king, see 1:12; 2:1; 7:7; 7:10 [a seesaw waxing and waning mood]; in regard to Haman "the Agagite,"[22] see 3:5; 5:9 [a steadily waxing mood]). By contrast, the Jews remain calm. Anger, of course, tends to become ridiculous.[23] It certainly indicates, in the ancient world at any rate, a lack of wisdom. When directed against others, it is meant to make them "tremble" (see 5:9). But events do not turn out as the angry Haman planned them. Just as Vashti was the victim of the king's ire and was replaced by Esther the Jewess, so Haman falls victim to the king's anger and is replaced by Mordecai the Jew.[24] Mordecai had saved the king's life; now Esther is beseeched to save Haman's life—the author might as well be Molière! And if there is any doubt about the genre, the scene following, in which the king reenters the banquet room, is "almost a farce."[25]

In Esther 7:7, as a matter of fact, the exit of the outraged king from the banquet room is theatrical and somewhat ludicrous. Looking for a motive to explain his stomping out is unnecessary. The room cannot contain his fury; he must breathe some fresh air. By starting with this tone, the text certainly encourages the reader to scoff at a king who acts like a cuckolded husband who has surprised his wife and an adulterous lover or, worse, a rapist in a compromising position. The comedy of the situation is compounded by royal indecisiveness. The king seems to be at a loss as to what he is supposed to do in the circumstances; someone among his subjects must whisper in his ear the obvious chastisement required for the traitor Haman

(7:9). Then, in one more ironic feature in the text, the king's discourse to Haman is simply inept; it is as much lacking in specifics as Haman's discourse to the king had been in chapter 3 when he was plotting the destruction of the Jews.[26] It is true, of course, that as king of the empire, Ahasuerus is on a firm ground in not giving an explanation of his decisions.

But such was not the case with Haman in Esther 3; he could hardly hide his ambition to reign in place of Ahasuerus, if only as an éminence grise, and thus he imitates the king himself in not bothering to reveal the identity of his intended victims. In the background of all this is the Akitu festival, discussed above, during which there was, indeed, a substitution of some commoner for the king,[27] although in the Akitu setting, it is true, the substitute was a caricature, a *minus habens*, whose "reign" was ephemeral, for he was summarily discarded as representing the nefarious deities slaughtered by Marduk.[28] It is tempting to speculate that, at a remoter time, the substitute was actually sacrificed in the image of those evil gods. The profound irony in Esther is that, unknown to him, Haman is a fool who fits the Akitu model. Bakhtin writes, "The buffoon and the fool, it's the metamorphosis of the king and the god in hell, in death (cf. the same trait of the metamorphosis of the king or the god into a slave, a murderer, a buffoon, in the Roman saturnalia and the Christian passion shows)."[29] All the more so, I would say, as the cosmic fight reenacted during the Akitu is, among other symbolisms, a "war of the sexes" (before Ishtar the goddess was associated with Marduk the god). The latter splits Tiamat in two—a clear allegory—and uses her two halves to fabricate the upper and the lower worlds. Mars has subdued Venus. In the popular carnivalesque orgy with which the festival culminates, the women are expected to accept the "services" of any male around. The complete reversal of situation in the book of Esther is striking.

One can also attribute to a deep anxiety the swift exit of the king after Esther's revelation at the banquet. As Pagán writes, "[the king] cannot condemn Haman for issuing a decree he himself had authorized and signed."[30] Coming back to the dining room, the king finds the pretext he was looking for: Haman is giving the impression that he is raping the queen.[31] This way, the king can affect to be incensed about his vizier's position, and he keeps a clear conscience in sending him to his death.[32] Haman is thus hanged for a crime he did not commit, even though he is guilty of another. The instrument of his torture is of his own making. The planned plunder of Jewish property ends with the grant of Haman's house to Esther and Mordecai (8:1–2)—not a trifle when one remembers the fantastic price Haman was able to pay the king in 3:9 (compare 5:11).

Even the eunuch Harbona's intervention—pointing out to the king that Haman's gallows would be a fitting chastisement—belongs to the commedia dell'arte. There, servants, male or female, often play the role of advisers and intermediaries.[33] Without them, their patrons are lost, out of wit, undecided. The patrons very much depend on their eloquent subordinates to orchestrate their lives.[34]

The story names the eunuch here, not leaving him anonymous, thus emphasizing his importance, albeit secondary.[35]

Then Haman's head is covered before he is hanged (7:8). Previously, he himself had covered his head, that is, his shame (6:12). The second act of covering is somewhat different in nature. One understands that Haman was once among those permitted to see "the face of the king" (see Esther 1:14). He is now blinded and stripped of this privilege.[36] Be that as it may, the second covering retrospectively ricochets back on the first: the cover was then and is now a shroud over Haman.[37] As the Jewish community had been branded with the sign of death, now Haman is marked with a bar sinister. "Who sows the wind . . ."[38] The false rapist is already dead for all practical purposes. Sex and death meet.[39]

Above, we have insisted on the Janus-faced notion of the carnivalesque pattern of death and rebirth. This ambivalent reality is indeed fundamental in carnivalesque literature—"the image of pregnant death," says Bakhtin.[40] Carnival combines the two. Ritually "put to death" here are, of course, institutions and people claiming authority and immortality. That is why the place for the enactment of carnival is, by predilection, the public square, the democratic place par excellence. Now, this peculiarity of carnival would be noticeably absent from Esther's background unless we are to understand the rather insistent motif of Mordecai sitting at the gate of the royal palace as an indication of exteriority from the seat of power. It is also said of Mordecai that he strolled the streets of Susa clamoring his laments. Clearly this represents a centrifugal movement that is not foreign to the essentially centrifugal thrust of carnival. Mordecai is off-center and wears the mask of death, an appropriate characterization for a chronotope that continues, remarkably, to occupy the royal court, with its habitual denial of death. That a large part of the action occurs at the royal court is attributable to the tale's nature as parody.[41] Carnival, as a matter of fact, has here penetrated the forbidden sphere, the "forbidden city." Nothing could be more sacrilegious. Even the most straitlaced figures, including king, vizier, courtiers, governors, and magistrates, are forced to play carnival roles. They all unwillingly and unknowingly become buffoons, and the Persian court becomes a lunatic asylum.

I have already referred to the conjunction of death and laughter in the Rio de Janeiro Carnival or in the American Halloween. Only in the satiric mode is it possible to make death a matter of derision, and no one is better suited than a woman, the fountain of life, to be the vehicle of such sarcasm.[42] One cannot overemphasize the importance of the revolutionary initiative of Esther's author in highlighting the role of a woman in the process of transforming history, almost single-handedly. Sexuality in the book is neither repressed nor glorified. It is a fact of life, indispensable as "the source of all flow and change."[43] In other words, Esther's sexuality in the tale is no narrative ornament for the erotic pleasure of the male reader. Even the pageantry in the first part of the book is not gratuitous, as it lays down the groundwork for what follows. Esther's sexuality is narratively comprehended in its striving toward bringing death-and-life, both in concomitance and in succession. She is birthing anew her people.[44]

Clearly, Esther belongs to a strain of carnival literature that promotes rather than scorns woman. Here, women have a powerful voice, and their sexuality is not what defines them—in contrast, we may add, to current carnival images of woman.[45] These latter are strikingly present in the parody of parody with which the tale begins. Women in the early chapters of Esther are little more than disposable wares. They are shown being treated by the Persian system just as they are by today's oppressive regimes. *Nihil novi sub sole.* I cannot but concur with Nicole Duran that "laughing off the court's turmoil over Vashti" is indeed muting the book's "gender politics."[46] Along that line, the sinister mention that the spousal candidates were shuffled from a first harem to a second when "used" (2:14) is a case in point.

It all started ominously with the king's Tonton Macoutes rounding up virgins from all over the country. These were incarcerated in royal harems and treated as inanimate pieces of property. So was, among them, the heroine of the tale. Whence did Esther come? The text says that she was "taken" or "snatched" from Mordecai's household (Esther 2:7) to "the king's house" (2:8) and from the guardianship of her stepfather to that of "Hegai, keeper of the women."[47] Although the text says nothing of Mordecai's reaction to this kidnapping, chances are that he was not too pleased about it. Esther's situation has been compared with the imprisonment of the patriarch Joseph, and it is while in these ominous places that both Esther and Joseph are singled out for favor (Esther 2:9, 15 and Gen. 39:4; Esther 2:17 and Gen. 39:21).[48]

The Esther story continues with other uncanny details, some of which may echo mythological motifs. In ancient Near Eastern folklore, to wit, the construction of a palace for the triumphant god occupies a place of choice. In Canaan, for instance, the motif is treated at length in the literature discovered at Ras-Shamra, Syria, anciently called Ugarit. This constitutes perhaps a backdrop to Esther's next story development. There is suspense but also folly in the king's distribution to Esther and Mordecai of the real estate formerly belonging to Haman without having addressed the issue of Jewish survival (8:1–2). The king is visibly embarrassed and, once more, does not know what to do next. He thus comes with a peace offering. Haman's property will hopefully assuage the feelings of Esther the queen.

The king's embarrassment comes from the nature of the foundation of Persian power as depicted here, namely, governance by means of immutable laws (1:19; 8:8). This very principle becomes an ominous trap into which the king himself falls without recourse.[49] Even he is manipulated by the very tool of his omnipotence.[50] It is a case of the biter being bit. The king, so to speak, dethrones himself. The royal seat made vacant, he delegates his former powers ("his ring") to someone more worthy of them, a woman, namely Esther (8:8). Was she not elected in the first place for being "better than" someone else (1:19)? In contrast to the first edict expressly sealed by the king (3:12), Esther is now the writer and disposes of the king's signet.[51] Not so long before, she was shaking with fear for her life and could have been reduced to a nobody (or to a corpse) by royal fiat. Now, in the *monde à l'envers*, she can mete out death to thousands.

There is, further, something theatrical in the dispatch of the second edict—this time issued by Mordecai, as the first one had been by Haman—to the 127 provinces by the fastest horses, while the events with which it is concerned are not to occur for nine months! In this and in its vocabulary, the second decree replicates the first (see 8:11 and 3:13).

The Feminine Subversive

To conclude this development on women's sexuality in Esther, it is worth our while to reflect on the intrinsic subversiveness of women's interventions in the story—a feature so constant in the Bible as to become a principle; one need only think of Sarah, Rachel, Rebecca, Tamar, Deborah, Jael, Ruth, Noadiah, Esther, and so many others. Where woman comes to the fore, a certain systemic social ideology is questioned and, more than once, deconstructed. The feminine author of the Song of Songs, for example, comes to mind.[52] Such "feminine unconventionality"[53] is a powerful counterbalance to the patriarchalism prevalent in some biblical literary genres. It is all the more striking as the concept of the *woman subversive* flies in the face of the archetypal hearth-bound housewife, pillar of immobility in comparison with her "nomadic" male partner. The very number of such heroines in biblical literature militates against seeing them as exceptional within their gender, however. Their pluralities as well as the consistently subversive nature of their interventions reveal a different and profound conception of femininity.

In my opinion, this core concept must deeply qualify the often denounced patriarchy of ancient Israel. Arguably, in most twenty-first-century societies the world over, the condition of woman lags, ideologically and practically, far behind the degree of "generosity" toward the female gender found in biblical literature. There, the feminine is not "unconventional" by exception but by vocation.

Esther is exceptional in comparison with the vast majority of her sisters in the world, but much less so in comparison with other biblical women. And this is true not just of Esther, but also of Vashti, in her resistance as described by a biblical author, or even of Zeresh, a Persian or Amalekite woman "naturally" endowed with the gift of prophecy. Zeresh is an amalgam of Balaam, prophet of the nations, and Rahab, the Canaanite who "knew" (see Joshua 2:9). Also like Rahab, when Haman and her ten sons are hanged, Zeresh is spared.

Esther's trio of women is one triadic woman. Three aspects of femininity are here united by a common sense of the transience and instability of absolutism. Confronted with Vashti (Esther 1:12) or with Esther (see especially 7:7), the hedonistic Ahasuerus seems no more than a Boy Scout in knee breeches. As for Haman, after Zeresh's "prophecy," he remains voiceless (6:13).

Power and grandiosity are a game played strictly among men. Ahasuerus's banquets are for men only. Summoning a woman to appear as a sex object before inebriated males would constitute the apex of the festivity, to the very extent that her femininity would be twisted, indeed annihilated, to conform to a destroying male will for power. Vashti's honor left her no choice but to refuse to participate.

The harem, of course, is the symbol par excellence of male dominion over women. This topographical and axiological burka amounts, even physically, to sheer eradication. The woman comes out only at night and "to please the king," before returning, perhaps forever, to the golden cage. There, the woman is well fed, well dressed, well groomed, but she sits in a living hell, in the humiliating company of other women "competitors" and of emasculated hybrids.

Esther goes to the king's private brothel, as Joseph went into the hole.[54] No woman can fall any lower. At first, Esther is said to play the game by its rules (2:15–18). The question is whether this is by consent or by coercion. If the former, young Esther is morally caught in the web of a slave mentality.[55] Pointing toward the latter possibility, however, is precisely Mordecai's command not to reveal her origins. For it is clear that the prohibition is antipodal to a closure. The dissimulation is in expectation of some event, even if the expectation would prove unfounded or paranoid.

Eventually, Esther emerges from the hole for good. From the start, she had used the harem and its contraptions to her advantage (2:15–18) instead of allowing herself to be used. Later, she is so much a free woman that she can organize her own banquets with selected guests, including the two most powerful men in Persia, indeed in the world. Again like Joseph in the book of Genesis, she has climbed the ladder from rags to riches and, more important, from coercion and self-denial to womanhood.

Parallels with the story of Joseph in Genesis have been drawn throughout this essay. They are striking. Of particular interest is that while in the cases of Joseph and Daniel (Dan 1:9) winning the favor of others is credited to God's intervention, in Esther's case no such divine action is reported: Esther's beauty and grace have "replaced" the divine performance. Once again Esther's theology is so subdued as to vanish altogether. The traditional religious vocabulary is used, but in parodic mode, as suits the carnivalesque.

In the religious texts of the Bible, where retributive justice is a principle, the just are rewarded.[56] At the outset of the Esther plot (chapter 3), however, the reward for saving the king's life goes not to Mordecai but to his archenemy Haman. Bypassing Mordecai and favoring Haman his enemy is not simply a slap in the Jew's face. It has enormous consequences in that Haman is now in a position to exercise the full extent of his vicious rage. An anti-Semite is substituted for the saving Jew in a literary derision of major proportions—but the historical examples of which are abundantly illustrated.[57] One is thus left to wonder where God's justice is in all this. Only through a combination of circumstances can the balance so unjustly tipped be restored.

Parallels with young Joseph's plight are again evident. Young Joseph, rather a brat, is perhaps not a model of justice, but at least he is innocent, and his blood is on his brothers, even though they substitute his enslavement for his murder.[58] It seems that God has abandoned the one whom he had destined for a bright future. As we saw above, Joseph goes to the pit, and Esther goes to the king's harem.

Furthermore, Esther is, again recalling Joseph, in exile in a foreign country. In fact, it has been shown by scholars that Esther is a metaphor for exiles. In Esther 2:6, "the root of the word for exile (*glh*) in four distinct constructions [is used], lest the full measure of the Jewish plight be overlooked."[59] As I have stressed all along, this identification with her people must be assessed in the context of the prototype roles played by the story's other characters: Haman for Amalek; Ahasuerus for the "nations"; Mordecai for Saul's royal line. Taking this into consideration will help in understanding the universality of an incident in Persia in the fifth century B.C.E.

The book of Esther is a celebration of the liberation of the Jews and of women. Their association is not accidental.

Anti-Semitism According to Esther

In biblical literature, customary attributions to God of felicitous or unfortunate courses of events may leave readers unmoved and skeptical, but in a tale such as Esther, narrowly focused on the Jewish drama, indifference is inconceivable, as was indeed again true during the modern Holocaust. The Persians of the story are either wicked or benevolent. In a time of crisis, neutrality in the face of the Jewish destiny is out of the question. Before the events related in the story, the Jews' distinctiveness may have passed unnoticed in Persia. Mordecai was a courtier before he became "Mordecai the Jew"; Esther was the king's wife before she was forced to reveal her "birth certificate." But the situation is entirely different once Haman and his followers force on their designated victims a half-true description of their identity and demean their Jewishness to a shameful "original stain." This kind of sham personality is a gentile projection. Jean-Paul Sartre is partly right: the gentile creates the Jewishness of the Jew. Haman exposes the singularity of Mordecai and the Jewishness of Esther; the Jewish presence becomes a "Jewish question" because the anti-Semites make it one.[60]

But the policy of hatred can provoke a backlash, as the book of Esther illustrates. "The city of Susa is in turmoil" (3:15) and "the opposite [of Haman's plot] happens" (9:1, 22). Persians start to "Judaize"; the king of Denmark wears the yellow star; Haman and Eichmann are hanged on the gallows of their own making; Mordecai is promoted to the post of prime minister of Persia. A mysterious force always saves a remnant of Israel (see, for example, Isa. 1:25–27; 11:10–16; 28:5–6; Jer. 23:3–4; 31:7–9; Joel 2:32). Help comes through an Esther or from some other quarter, but help always comes. The barber of Frederick II, challenged to prove the existence of God, soberly declared, "Sire, the Jews!"

The issue of the relationship between Jews and gentiles in the book of Esther provides yet another token of the nonreligious nature of the document. The treatment of the gentiles in the book is not without ambiguity. Some are depicted as capricious, whimsical, dangerously undecided, smug, greedy, arrogant, anti-Semitic, and bloodthirsty. Others, however, are seen to be distressed when their Jewish neighbors are threatened, and many at the peak of the crisis Judaize! (See 8:17; 9:27; compare Isa. 56:3–8; Zech. 8:19–23; and others.)

Such is the condition of the Jews in diaspora. Sometimes they are designated for extermination; sometimes they accede to the highest positions in governments of their hosts. The balance in Esther, however, finds the Jewish community celebrating the opportunity to stay in the empire and not to depart in a new Exodus. Jewish wisdom and shrewdness have made the difference between happiness and unhappiness, even between life and death. This is so true that intermarriage with a gentile Persian does not seem to cause a stir—in contrast to the rearrangements of the book in the Greek versions. Only in the Greek revisions of the Hebrew text does Esther become apologetic about sharing the bed and the table of the Persian king. In the original text,[61] this poses no problem—a far cry from the (attempted?) reforms of Ezra and Nehemiah in the fifth–fourth centuries B.C.E. The least one can say about Esther is that it is an unorthodox book.

In fact, the book of Esther is a subversive piece of literature. It belongs with other such productions in the Bible that react sharply against the Jerusalem establishment, especially after the reforms of Ezra and Nehemiah. Esther, like Daniel, lives far from Jerusalem, and her experiences demonstrate that the lot of diasporic Jews is part and parcel with the destiny of Israel.

Indeed, the intertextual parallels reviewed throughout this essay emphasize such belonging so broadly as to transgress even the limits of what has come to be considered the canon. Between Esther and Judith, for example, the rapprochement is far-reaching. In both stories, the central issue is Jewish survival in the midst of a lethal danger. The narrative sequence is the same in both documents: life threat, deliverance, vengeance, triumph, festivities. In the background of Judith's story, the author shows the immensity of the Assyrian army [*sic*], reflecting the overwhelming power of Nebuchadnezzar. In Esther's story, similarly, the unlimited wealth of Ahasuerus forms the background. Displays such as these are examples of a literary device used to impress the reader with the enormous odds the Jews must face in their efforts to survive. They are seemingly insurmountable. The dramatic effect of reversal is thus all the more impressive, and the ultimate victory of the weakest over the mightiest is seemingly miraculous. As Pierre Corneille said, "A victory without risk is a triumph without glory."[62] When, against all expectation, the Jews succeed in turning the odds to their advantage, they are said to inherit a great power for themselves, either through booty, as in the book of Judith, or by donning royal vestments and attributes, as in the book of Esther. This dramatic reversal of situation is characteristic of both stories.

In fact, Sidnie White Crawford goes so far as to "believe that one of the models for the author of Judith was the story of Esther."[63] There are carnivalesque features in the book of Judith. (See, for example, its blatant multiple incongruences: Nebuchadnezzar is king of the Assyrians; Holofernes is able to conquer the whole West but not the insignificant Bethulia; he moves his troops three hundred miles in three days (2:21); master of all, he is mastered by a woman; Achior the Ammonite displays a greater faith than do the Israelites; a hardened warrior, Achior faints when he sees Holofernes's severed head; and many others.) But these do not compare with the subtleties of Esther. Judith may be a reformer, but she does not need to live simultaneously in two worlds, as does Esther. The circumstances in the two books are totally different.

Once more, however, we note that these documents represent a stance that cannot be reconciled with the efforts of Ezra and Nehemiah to protect Jewish identity from contamination through contact with foreigners. As expressed in the literature of the Chronicler (to which the books of Ezra and Nehemiah belong), the restoration announced by the prophets would occur at Zion, excluding any other possible setting; it would occur among the returnees from exile and among no others; and it would occur within the revived cultic celebration in the Temple of Jerusalem and not through any other particular historical event.[64] From this perspective, it is clear that Esther constitutes an uphill apologia for the Jewish diaspora. Here, the Jews of Susa are bona fide members of the elect people. They are entitled to institute a festival of their own, a far-reaching decision running counter to Palestinian canonical rigidity. With Purim, the contrast between homeland and diaspora emerges in great relief.

An important issue in the Esther story is its display of the Jews' conflicting loyalties in diaspora. Mordecai refuses to prostrate before Haman—but this is not a gesture of rebellion against law and order, for he had already proved his loyalty toward the king (2:21–23). Esther disobeys the king (4:11)—but it is ultimately for the good of the state (7:4). She manipulates Ahasuerus—but only to open his eyes to the wickedness of his treacherous vizier. These examples show that an ethical (or religious or ethnic) Jewish allegiance supersedes all others, but ultimately the Jews with their double allegiance better serve the king than do his other subjects claiming a single, undivided allegiance.[65] Jews and Christians alike have made this argument from time immemorial. Its potency depends on the premise that God's will does not run contrary to the veritable interest of the res publica but, on the contrary, God knows best what is good "for the king." When the king realizes it, he elevates Joseph or Daniel or Esther-Mordecai to the highest position in the empire. Meanwhile, however, the danger coming from those "who do not know what they are doing" is great and even lethal, because the king is easily misled by court intrigues and power games. Then the Jew is falsely accused of disobedience, of particularism, of arrogant contempt, and of other such crimes. But making him a scapegoat is, in truth, meant to hide more effectively the turpitude of the real culprits.

The *Diasporanovelle,* be it the story of Joseph, Jonah, Daniel, Judith, or Esther, describes a tense situation for the Jews living in a foreign land. They must often bear two names and two faces, have two calendars and two agendas, don two sets of clothing, eat at two tables, hold two discourses, live at the edges of two worlds. Not so much in spite as because of it, they become prime ministers, princes, or queens. Their Jewishness raises them above the "monologic" mediocrity of soothsayers, above the morbid narcissism of cruel viziers. The option of serving God first (or, alternatively, the Jews' appointed destiny, as is the case in Esther) eventuates in an option *for* the state, for the world. Esther not only saves her people; she saves the Persian Empire from doom under the Hitler-like Haman the Amalekite. That is why we read in the book the surprising note that the inhabitants of Susa rejoice with the Jews at the "enthronement" of Mordecai (8:15) and that many even become Jews (8:17).

Just as the crowning of Esther was the de-crowning of Vashti, one could say that the "enthronement" of Mordecai was the dethronement of Ahasuerus. The book of Esther begins awkwardly, as all commentators have noted, with the enthronement of Ahasuerus (1:2). Although various explanations for this rough start have been offered, the motif of enthronement is clear and should be set in the context of the enthronement / dethronement pattern prevalent in the story. Eventually, Ahasuerus passes to Mordecai and Esther the royal powers symbolized by the signet ring with which he sealed the edict written by the two Jews (8:8; 9:29).

Before letting the king deservedly fade away from our interest, however, let us detain him by the sleeve, so to speak, for an extra brief moment. Ahasuerus is not seen in a positive light in the book of Esther. He remains on the throne at the end of the story, but this does not exonerate him of callous stupidity. The persistence of his reign was historically demanded and narratively expedient, the better to stress the magnificence of his vizier Mordecai. The king even enjoys increased revenues with Mordecai in charge, according to the text of 10:1. Laniak felicitously tallies this statement with Genesis 39:5 and 41:7–49 (both in the Joseph story) and sees here "an example of the blessing promised those who properly honor the Jews."[66]

True, but the picture drawn of the king, even in these final reflections in the book, remains ambiguous. All things considered, Ahasuerus is eventually reduced to a shadow; for all practical purposes he is now even more the impotent puppet he had been all along.[67] He will be such forever. The tiger was a paper tiger and his anti-Semitism a vain attempt to make himself important, recalling the same striving in the little square-cut mustache of the little corporal.[68] In our tale, Ahasuerus continues officially as king, indeed as the statue of kingship, but he is deprived of all authority, legitimacy, and life. Esther accedes from king's bedfellow to real queenship in Persia,[69] and Mordecai becomes the vizier of the kingdom. All is well in the carnivalesque world.

Bakhtin for one insists that what the carnivalesque literature puts in motion is less a given individual or a social character than an idea or truth itself. In Esther, it is clear that the fate of the diasporic Jews is at stake, a social reality here idealized in its anonymity and self-inclusiveness. Haman wants to blot out "Jewishness," and his irritation with Mordecai is because he is "*the* Jew"; Haman clearly understands that Mordecai's defiance is a "Jewish thing." Hence, Mordecai is, strikingly, called "the Jew" seven times in the story (2:5; 5:13; 6:10; 8:7; 9:29, 31; 10:3). In the context of anti-Semitism, this emphasis is clearly defiant, a thumbing of the nose directed at the Jew-haters. In reply to the caricature of the "Semite" in propagandistic depictions, the carnivalesque comes with a countercaricature exaggerating the very features loathed by the "enemy of the Jews."

Characteristically, Haman had "denounced" the Jewish laws (3:8). As in so many other manifestations of historical anti-Semitism, the irritant could be said to be "nothing personal"; it is found, not so much in the persons of the Jews as in their "Jewishness." Put bluntly, killing Jews means eradicating an idea. Hitler said,

> I am freeing the mind from what is generally called conscience and morality. Judaism has brought two defects in men: in the body through circumcision and in the soul because of conscience, a sheer Jewish invention.[70]

That is why, incidentally, anti-Semitism is self-defeating, for even if no Jews remained in the world—God forbid—the idea would live on.

In Esther, this ideologizing of a social body, through both anti-Semitism and Jewish pride, is the key to the underlying idea that Jewishness is an "ultimate question," not just a sociopolitical phenomenon. Mordecai's intervention in Esther 4:14 sheds light on this: "For if you keep silent at such a time as this, relief and deliverance will rise for the Jews from another quarter."

I have spoken above of the absence here of immunity for the Jewish heroes: verse 4:14 clearly alludes to their vulnerability. One can seriously doubt, however, that the king would have allowed the anti-Semites to slaughter the queen, once her ethnic origins were known, or one of his courtiers, in the person of Mordecai, who by his functions at the court is under the king's protection and by his kinship with her is also under the queen's. If this is correct, then it has not been sufficiently noticed by the book's commentators that Haman's manipulation of the king into annihilating the Jewish people would wipe out anyone Jewish *except* the one "offender," Mordecai!

In fact, Mordecai must be dealt with individually, which is why Haman erects a gallows for this specific purpose (5:14) and comes to the king with a special petition to that effect in 6:4, well after the king has already ordered the massacre of "all the Jews" (3:13). Haman's plot against the people of the Jews is thus made all the more grotesque. Truly, what is at stake is much less the crime of lèse-majesté committed by one of them than the crime of Jewishness embodied by all of them. Esther understands this right away after Mordecai's report in 4:13, and she betrays it when, for a while, she envisages not intervening. Haman also betrays as much when his wife and friends show him they have not been blinded by his camouflage and highlight the Jewishness of Mordecai (6:13). Mordecai's refusal to bow to Haman is the pretext Haman seizes, and, as all pretexts, it "claims full responsibility" for the impending disaster while concealing another agenda.

Now, on the model of ancient and recent examples, the Persian Jews could have turned their wrath against their own and blamed Mordecai for an alleged lack of diplomacy and spirit of accommodation.[71] It did not happen, either because of popular wisdom at the time or because evidence provided by contemporary events prevented anyone from looking elsewhere for the real culprit.

To recall, the book of Esther was composed during the late Second Commonwealth, when Jews were victims of violent persecutions at the hands of Hellenizers in Palestine and Alexandria, in particular. Since those events, anti-Semitism has erupted time and again. On this score also Esther is astonishingly relevant. Ahasuerus / Xerxes seems not to understand that lesson at first. Making the Jews outlaws excluded them from the empire and, certainly, from royal protection. Even before their physical extermination, they would be without rights of any kind and could be abused and plundered with impunity. Ironically, those accused by Haman of being unruly were in fact submitted to unjust, ungrounded, and outrageous conditions, allegedly to protect ludicrous laws requiring such behavior as bowing before a megalomaniac courtier or risking one's head if daring to appear before the king when not officially summoned. By contrast, the Jews also saved the king's life, while others pretended to be law-abiding but either plotted against him or dreamed of substituting their own power for his (chapter 6). Implicit, of course, is the idea that the laws the Jews observe, and that Haman describes with an astounding superficiality as "different from every other people's" (3:8), might be better than those in force at the Persian court.[72]

The book, albeit without express mention of the Torah, recounts the clash between two laws and, beyond that, between two worldviews. One could also define the problem as a contest between two inviolabilities. The dénouement of the story demonstrates that what is inviolable is, in fact, the Jewish people,[73] not an abstraction such as the "Persian law" (6:13; compare 4:14). When ideology prevails over humanity, the machine indiscriminately crushes friends and foes. It belongs again to satire to show that the first victim of legal inflexibility in the story is neither a Jew nor an outlaw, as intended. Summoned by her godlike husband to appear at the royal banquet at Susa, Queen Vashti refuses and is summarily put aside. Her refusal—which should be seen in the probable context that the presence of women at Persian drinking affairs was limited to concubines[74]—raises a grave legal problem. As the king is personified law, he has himself a very narrow margin of choice. He must set an example, which he confirms by decree, ironically degrading Vashti to the status of concubine, the role she tried to avoid in the first place. The fateful cycle of tragedy locks into place, revolving on itself, allegedly for the sake of law and order.

Within the ironclad determinism of cause and effect—or of Persian law—one must always consider the possibility of (or should we say the faith in?) deliverance coming "from some other place" (4:14). The storyteller wisely left the existential questions as questions, leaving the facts to speak for themselves. However one answers the "Jewish question," the Jews endure: for when they seem to disappear by attrition or by massacre, "help comes from [still] another quarter." Whatever name is given to this fact—luck, chance, or maybe God—through an uncanny peripeteia,[75] a turn of fortune, time and again Israel emerges from the grave.[76] Any statement more precise would almost inevitably become systematized. The book of Esther is, in many ways, postmodern.

At the end of this study of the book of Esther, we may say retrospectively that a number of questions raised by the story have here received inchoative solutions. These remain in an embryonic stage because they are necessarily tentative and, more important, because "any response gives rise to a new question" ad infinitum.[77] An author's greatest gratification comes when her or his responses give rise to the right types of questions. It is my conviction that Bakhtin's questions, responses, and prompts to new questions are uniquely and challengingly heuristic. "Dialectically"—a concept that Bakhtin, however, does not hold dear!—he says that our reading will be ever infinite, but also:

> Nothing is absolutely dead: every meaning will someday have its homecoming festival.[78]

Appendix: Outline of the Book of Esther

I. *The accession of Esther to the queenship:* 1:1–2:23
   a. Ahasuerus organizes great and protracted banquets in the kingdom: 1:1–9
   b. Queen Vashti disobeys the king and is rejected as queen: 1:10–22
   c. Plans for providing the king with a new harem and a new queen: 2:1–4
   d. Esther is brought to Susa, the capital: 2:5–14
   e. Esther is selected as the new queen: 2:15–18
   f. Mordecai saves the king by denouncing two conspirators: 2:19–23

II. *Haman's plan to destroy the Jews; Esther saves her people:* 3:1–8:2
   a. Haman's accession to post of vizier; he is incensed by Mordecai's refusal to bow down before him: 3:1–6
   b. Haman plots to annihilate all the Jews; a first royal edict gives him carte blanche: 3:7–15
   c. Mordecai presses Esther to intervene; she agrees but is fearful: 4:1–17
   d. Esther comes uninvited to the throne room, risking her life; the first banquet of Esther: 5:1–8
   e. Haman erects an immense gallows on which to hang Mordecai: 5:9–14
   f. Haman is compelled to honor Mordecai: 6:1–14
   g. Second banquet of Esther; she denounces Haman; Haman is hanged on his own gallows: 7:1–10
   h. Mordecai is appointed the new vizier: 8:1–2

III. *Second royal decree, this time in favor of the Jews:* 8:3–10:3
   a. New edict: the Jews receive permission to defend themselves (the first edict being still in force): 8:3–17
   b. The Jews inflict a total rout on their enemies but refrain from plundering; the ten sons of Haman are killed: 9:1–15
   c. Preparations for the institution of Purim: 9:16–19
   d. Institution of Purim under the authority of Mordecai and Esther: 9:20–32
   e. Mordecai's final triumph: 10:1–3

Notes

Chapter 1

1. Michael Holquist, Introduction to *M. M. Bakhtin: Speech Genres and Other Essays,* ed. C. Emerson and M. Holquist; trans. V. W. McGee (Austin: University of Texas Press, 1986), xxii, note 2; *Speech Genres* hereafter cited as *SG.*

2. Mikhail Bakhtin, *Rabelais and His World,* trans. Hélène Iswolsky (Bloomington: Indiana University Press, 1984), 116–17; hereafter cited as *RAHW.*

3. See Michael André Bernstein, "When the Carnival Turns Bitter: Preliminary Reflections upon the Abject Hero," in *Bakhtin: Essays and Dialogues on His Work,* ed. Gary Saul Morson (Chicago: University of Chicago Press, 1986). Bakhtin himself in later works insists on the presence and the power of frames (such as conventions, the situatedness of the subject, and so on); compare his "Notes Made in 1970–71," *SG,* 132–58.

4. Gary Saul Morson and Caryl Emerson, *Mikhail Bakhtin: Creation of a Prosaics* (Stanford, Calif.: Stanford University Press, 1990), 228, 229. "Carnival itself addresses catastrophe and terror in a highly benevolent and unrealistic way. Bakhtin ignores the danger of carnivalistic violence and antinomian energy. In short, it is not carnival but the 'carnival symbolic' that inspires him, not real individual bodies in interaction, but the potential for extending, transcending, and rendering immortal the collective body" (ibid., 470). In other words, besides being a literary phenomenon, it is also a style, as is the satiric in oral and written literature.

5. Bakhtin writes that carnival "is opposed to that one-sided and gloomy official seriousness which is dogmatic and hostile to evolution and change, which seeks to absolutize a given condition of existence or a given social order. From precisely that sort of seriousness did the carnival sense of the world liberate men" (*Problems of Dostoevsky's Poetics,* ed. and trans. Caryl Emerson [Minneapolis: University of Minneapolis Press, 1984], 159; hereafter cited as *PDP*).

6. To quote Morson and Emerson again, "By detaching Bakhtin's concepts from his specific application of them, we might better appreciate the appeal of the carnival view of the world" (Morson and Emerson, *Mikhail Bakhtin: Creation of a Prosaics,* 452).

7. T. H. Gaster and H. Ringgren have shown that there were New Year rituals on the Babylonian model in Persia (see Theodor H. Gaster, *Purim and Hanukkah in Custom and Tradition* [New York: Henry Shuman, 1950]; and K. V. H. Ringgren,

"Esther and Purim," *Svensk exegetisk årsbok* 20 [1955]: 5–24). That the parallel with this in Esther is not overdrawn is demonstrated by the Babylonian origin of the names Esther and Mordecai (see Heinrich Zimmern, "Zur Frage nach dem Ursprung des Purimfestes," *Zeitschrift für die Alttestamentliche Wissenschaft* 11 [1891]: 157–69; and P. Jensen in "Elamitische Eigennamen," *Wiener Zeitschrift für die Kunde des Morgenlandes* 6 [1892]: 47–50, 209–26). Furthermore, one remembers that King Xerxes quelled a rebellion in Babylon and carried off the statue of Marduk (in 486 B.C.E.).

8. *SG*, 34–35.

9. Sergei Averintsev, in "Bakhtin, Laughter, and Christian Culture" (*Bakhtin and Religion*, ed. S. M. Felch and P. J. Contino [Evanston, Ill.: Northwestern University Press, 2001]), would concur. He makes a judicious distinction between the respective temporalities of laughter ("an impulse, as impetuous as an outburst . . . a transition") and of humor ("the sovereign use of freedom"); see 80–81.

10. The terms are those of Morson and Emerson; see *Mikhail Bakhtin: Creation of a Prosaics*, 440.

11. *The Contemplations* (1856), bk. 6, 23.

12. Bakhtin writes, "A genre is always the same and yet not the same, always old and new simultaneously" (*PDP*, 106).

13. Bakhtin mentions Pindar (fifth century B.C.E.). Let us note that a book with which Esther presents striking parallels, namely Judith, is a typically Hellenistic novel, an analogy also stressed by Ulrich von Wilamowitz-Moellendorf in *Die griechische und lateinische Literatur und Sprache* (Leipzig: Teubener, 1912), 189.

14. A *chronotope* is an alloy of time and space. The royal castle is a perfect example; it is not only a locus but also represents a number of cultural markers (historical, economic, political, social, religious, and so on). See Bakhtin, "Novy Mir," *SG*.

15. Richard Klein ("Prolegomena to Derrida," *Diacritics* 2, no. 4 [1972], 31–32) writes, "It is [an] illusion to think that we can merely step outside of the house of metaphysics and dance freely in the sunshine. . . . The only possible strategy is the much more patient and laborious one . . . by which the foundations of the structure may be carefully but decisively deconstructed, displaced, disorganized—giving rise, *not* to a new space *outside* of the old structure, but to new angles, new possibilities and organization within it. The process requires that one use the elements of structure against the structure" (quoted by Barbara Babcock in "Arrange Me into Disorder: Fragments and Reflections on Ritual Clowning," *Rite, Drama, Festival, Spectacle: Rehearsals Toward a Theory of Cultural Performance*, ed. John J. MacAloon [Philadelphia: Ishi, 1984], 122).

16. It is genuinely Bakhtinian to see his oeuvre as marked by unfinalizability and as essentially providing a style of inquiry.

17. W. Lee Humphreys, "The Story of Esther and Mordecai: An Early Jewish Novella," *Saga, Legend, Tale, Novella, Fable*, JSOT Suppl. 35, ed. George W. Coats (Sheffield, Eng.: Sheffield Academic Press, 1985), 100.

18. Adele Berlin, in *The JPS Bible Commentary: Esther* (Philadelphia: Jewish Publication Society, 2001), 21, says "the excess of wine in chapter 1 is matched by the excess of women in chapter 2."

19. According to Sanhedrin 74b, Esther remained inert like a clod in the embrace of her Persian husband! In the Greek Add. C = Esther 14:15, Esther "abhors the bed of the uncircumcised or of any gentile." She also refused to eat nonkosher food (14:17–18).

20. It is true that between the straightforward discourse and its parody (the "parodically refracted word"), the border is "flexible." See Bakhtin, *The Dialogic Imagination*, ed. Michael Holquist, trans. Caryl Emerson and Michael Holquist (Austin: University of Texas Press, 1981), 73; hereafter cited as *DI*.

21. Of interest is the rabbinic reaction to any negative opinion regarding Song of Songs or the book of Esther—the most areligious writings in the Bible—equating them axiologically with the Torah itself! (For Esther, see j. Megillah 70d. Maimonides [1135–1204] considered Esther second only to the Torah in importance, as reported by R. B. Dillard and T. Longman, *An Introduction to the Old Testament* [Grand Rapids, Mich.: Zondervan, 1994], 189.) On Song of Songs, see my *Romance, She Wrote: A Hermeneutical Essay on Song of Songs* (Harrisburg: Trinity Press International, 1998).

22. As Bakhtin says, "Parodic-travestying literature introduces the permanent corrective of laughter, of a critique on the one-sided seriousness of the lofty direct word, the corrective reality that is always richer, more fundamental and more importantly *too contradictory and heteroglot* to be fit into a high and straightforward genre" (*DI*, 55). And he recalls a parallel phenomenon in Rome, where so-called *agelastes* were in charge of "weeding" the literature of any comic elements considered to be profanatory (*DI*, 58–59).

23. Isaac Kalimi ("The Book of Esther and the Dead Sea Scrolls' Community," *Theologische Zeitschrift* 60, no. 2 [2004]: 101–6) mentions the presence of "many fragments of [Esther] in the Cairo Genizah, more than any other biblical composition, aside from the Torah" (102) and opines that the book was not in the covenanters' library because the fast ordered by Esther contravened the seder meal of Passover (105). I shall emphasize this point below.

24. Jeffrey Rubenstein ("Purim, Liminality, and Communitas," *AJS Review* 17, no. 2 [1992], 175) quotes j. Megillah 1:5 to the effect that Purim was rejected as a festival for "Moses told us that no prophet should add anything to the Law from now on and henceforth."

25. This possible first version was Midrashic in nature and did refer, as 10:2 attests, to the annals of the kings of Persia and Media.

26. Morson and Emerson, *Mikhail Bakhtin: Creation of a Prosaics*, 277.

27. Bakhtin called for "a special history of speech genres . . . that reflects more directly, clearly, and flexibly all the changes taking place in social life" (*SG*, 65).

28. As to its significance, it can perhaps be compared with the Greek diaspora after Alexander's Asian and African conquests.

29. Bakhtin points to the romance's subcategory of "novel of ordeal," which has left traces in a "considerable majority of all the novels [ever] produced" (*SG*, 11). See Adele Berlin, "Greek Storytelling About Persia," in *Esther*, xxviii–xxxii.

30. *DI*, 100.

31. The figure belongs to the grotesque. The Persians reckoned rather between twenty and thirty-one satrapies (see Herodotus 3.89). Concerning the king's flippancy, one thinks of Rabelais's story of the ridiculous King Picrochole who, "sans plus outre s'interroger qui ni comment," proclaims a state of war against the falsely accused King Grangousier! (François Rabelais, *Gargantua* [1534], *Oeuvres de Rabelais, avec introduction et notes critiques*, ed. Abel Lefranc, vol. 2 [Paris: Champion, 1912]; ed. and trans. Samuel Putnam, *The Portable Rabelais* [New York: Penguin Books, 1978], ch. 26).

32. Joseph in Egypt never has the benefit of a theophany, in contrast to his father, Jacob, in the Land.

33. See Morson and Emerson, *Mikhail Bakhtin: Creation of a Prosaics*, 292.

34. One of the main themes of Bakhtin's *Speech Genres* is that one commits a major error by reading a text with the presumption of its naive realism.

35. But violence does not prevent the *Iliad*, for instance, from being sublime!

36. M. Luther, *Table Talk* (Philadelphia: Fortress Press, 1967), xxiv.

37. *RAHW*, 30.

38. Kenneth Craig, *Reading Esther: A Case for the Literary Carnivalesque*, Literary Currents in Biblical Interpretation (Louisville, Ky.: Westminster / John Knox Press, 1995).

39. B. Green, *Mikhail Bakhtin and Biblical Scholarship: An Introduction* (Atlanta, Ga.: Society of Biblical Literature, 2000), 146.

40. See D. C. Muecke: "The phenomenon [of irony] existed before it was named and consequently before there could have been a concept of it." (*Irony*, The Critical Idiom Series. [London: Methuen, 1970], 14). Bakhtin speaks of millenniums of popular laughter (see "Discourse in the Novel," *DI*, 259–422).

41. The issues of precise dating, textual criticism, and history of interpretation, for example, are almost entirely ignored.

42. Sergei Averintsev says that "Bakhtin treats Rabelais not as an individual author of a given period but as a universal philosophical-anthropological paradigm" ("Bakhtin, Laughter, and Christian Culture," 82). Even a negative critique by Vladimir M. Boriskin acknowledges that the carnival celebrated by Mikhail Bakhtin is an attitude, a threshold valued for the aspect of "change and renewal in it, its striving toward the future" (V. M. Boriskin, *Ateizm i tvorchestvo* [Saransk: Mordovskoe knizhnoe izdatel'stvo, 1986], 105, quoted by C. Emerson, *The First Hundred Years of Mikhail Bakhtin* [Princeton, N.J.: Princeton University Press, 1997], 103).

43. Gary Saul Morson and Caryl Emerson, eds., *Rethinking Bakhtin: Extensions and Challenges* (Evanston, Ill.: Northwestern University Press, 1989), use this expression in a different sense (see 81).

44. See 1:3–5; 1:9; 2:18; 3:15. Drinking parties: 1:7–8, 10; 3:15; 5:6; 7:2. Also in 1:3, 9; 2:18; and 3:15, the banquet is ironically called *mišteh* (this occurs twenty times in the book), that is, a "drinking bout"! Contrast this with the Jewish fast in 4:3, 16.

45. In the seventeenth century, Rabelais's characters were also annexed by court masquerades!

46. The royal banquet lasts half a year (1:1–3), and there would be no reason to stop after 180 days—were it not for Vashti, whose refusal to present herself interrupts the feast (1:12).

47. R. Alter, *The Art of Biblical Narrative* (New York: Basic Books, 1981), 33–34.

48. Alter adds that it is "a kind of fairy tale—the lovely damsel guided by a wise godfather, is made queen and saves her people—richly embellished with satiric invention; its comic art departs from historical verisimilitude in ways that pre-exilic Hebrew narrative seldom does" (ibid., 34).

49. *RAHW,* 94. Many a critic has cringed before such a statement that may, indeed, appear as one of the most paradoxical in Bakhtin's works. Long before Bakhtin was known in the West, Harvey Cox wrote in *The Feast of Fools: A Theological Essay on Festivity and Fantasy* (Cambridge, Mass.: Harvard University Press, 1969): "a stated occasion for political persiflage can be exploited by the powerful to trivialize criticism." Cox adds, "The divine right of kings, papal infallibility, and the modern totalitarian state all flowered after the Feast of Fools disappeared" (5).

50. Sandra B. Berg (*The Book of Esther: Motifs, Themes, and Structure,* SBLDS 44 [Missoula, Mont.: Scholars Press, 1979]) calls attention to the correspondence between the king's two banquets in chapter 1 (one for the provinces and another for the residents of Susa) and Purim on the fourteenth of Adar for the Jews of the provinces and on the fifteenth of Adar for the Jews of Susa. "The author of Esther could, for all we know, have been a woman!" says W. W. Hallo ("The First Purim," *Biblical Archaeologist* 46 [1983]: 25).

51. In the first chapter of his *Pantagruel,* Rabelais says that his hero was born during a terrible drought that lasted "thirty-six months, three weeks, four days and thirty hours or more"! (In reality, the 1552 drought lasted six months.) See *RAHW,* 439. Bakhtin writes, "Exaggeration, hyperbolism, excessiveness, are generally considered fundamental attributes of the grotesque style" (*RAHW,* 303).

52. An attitude derided by wisdom literature; see Prov. 11:28; 28:11; and so on.

53. See Molière, *Le Bourgeois gentilhomme;* La Fontaine, "La Grenouille qui veut se faire aussi grosse que le Boeuf" ("elle s'enfla si bien qu'elle en creva").

54. It may be said of the Jewish festival what Bakhtin wrote of Mardi Gras: "The feast was a temporary suspension of the entire official system with all its prohibitions and hierarchic barriers" (*RAHW,* 89).

55. See Mikhail Ryklin, "Bodies of Terror: Theses Toward a Logic of Violence," *New Literary History* 24 (1993): 51–74.

56. Bakhtin writes, "A passive understanding of linguistic meaning is no understanding at all. . . . Even . . . an understanding of the speaker's intention insofar as that understanding remains purely passive, purely receptive, contributes nothing new to the word under consideration, only mirroring it . . . in no way enrich[ing] the word" (*DI,* 281).

57. Erich Auerbach, *Mimesis* (Princeton, N.J.: Princeton University Press, 1953), 549. Montesquieu, in the eighteenth century, said, "Je n'ai pas plus faict mon livre que mon livre m'a faict" (*The Spirt of the Laws,* trans. by Thomas Nugent and J. V. Prichard, public domain ed. of 1914, London: G. Bell & Sons, bk. 2, sect. 18, 666).

58. Bakhtin, *SG,* 7, cited by Morson and Emerson, *Mikhail Bakhtin: Creation of a Prosaics,* 55.

59. *SG,* 103–31.

60. In "Response to a Question from the *Novyi Mir*" (in *SG,* 1–9), 5, Bakhtin also writes that a great artist produces works with "immense treasures of potential meaning that could not be fully revealed or recognized in his [own] epoch. . . . The author is captive of his epoch, of his own present. Subsequent times liberate him from his captivity and literary scholarship is called upon to assist in this liberation."

61. See the section titled "Purim's Place in the Book of Esther" in chapter 6 of this volume.

62. Bakhtin notes, "Laughter and the kingdom of ends (means are always serious)" (*SG,* 135). As Michael Fox notes, "Peripety is essentially ironic. . . . When [the planner] is an object of antipathy, it means comic irony" ("The Structure of the Book of Esther," *Isac Leo Seeligmann Volume,* vol. 3, ed. A. Rofé and Y. Zakovitch. [Jerusalem: Rubenstein, 1983], 296). Other authors have also emphasized the humorous in Esther. So Bruce W. Jones, "Two Misconceptions About the Book of Esther," *Catholic Biblical Quarterly* 39 (1977): 171–81; and Samuel Sandmel, *The Hebrew Scriptures: An Introduction to Their Literature and Religious Ideas* (New York: Oxford University Press, 1978), 497–98, and following. Robert Alter perceives Esther to be "a comic fantasy utilizing pseudo-historical materials" (*Art of Biblical Narrative,* 34). Edward L. Greenstein goes even further and sees in Esther "a cartoon, and thus precisely the sort of show one would expect to see on Purim" ("A Jewish Reading of Esther,"*Judaic Perspectives on Ancient Israel,* ed. Jacob Neusner [Philadelphia: Fortress, 1987], 231). Adele Berlin, in her commentary on Esther in the JPS Bible advocates a comic reading of the tale.

63. Pace D. J. A. Clines and others.

64. Bakhtin's "collective ancestral body of all the people" (*RAHW,* 19).

65. See my *Feminine Unconventional: Four Subversive Figures in Israel's Tradition,* Overtures to Biblical Theology (Minneapolis, Minn.: Fortress Press, 1990), 57–58.

66. E. K. Bennett, *A History of the German Novelle from Goethe to Thomas Mann*

(Cambridge: Cambridge University Press, 1934), 18–19. (As we shall see below, Bennett's choice of the term *epic* is somewhat infelicitous.)

67. See Moshe Gan, "The Book of Esther in the Light of the Story of Joseph in Egypt," *Tarbiz* 31 (1961–62): 144–49; Arndt Meinhold, "Die Gattung der Josephgeschichte und des Estherbuches: Diasporanovelle," Pts. 1 and 2, *Zeitschrift für die Alttestestamentliche Wissenschaft* 87 (1975): 306–24, and 88 (1976):72–93; Joyce G. Baldwin, *Esther: An Introduction and Commentary,* Tyndale Old Testament Commentary (Leicester: Inter-Varsity Press, 1984), 28; and many others.

68. André Neher, *The Exile of the Word: From the Silence of the Bible to the Silence of Auschwitz,* trans. David Maisel (Philadelphia: The Jewish Publication Society of America, 1981), 24–27.

69. As Pavel Medvedev (of the Bakhtinian school) writes, "Every genre has its methods and means of seeing and conceptualizing reality, which are accessible to it alone" (*The Formal Method in Literary Scholarship: A Critical Introduction to Sociological Poetics,* trans. A. Wehrle [Baltimore: Johns Hopkins University Press, 1978], 133).

70. Strikingly, faith and love are here conspicuous by their absence.

71. Is it possible to straddle the gap between the embryonic (or absent) theology of Esther and the explicit theology of the Pentateuchal sagas? According to a monologic conception of truth, there is no such bridge—and Martin Luther's ire is understandable. But Bakhtin claims that truth is dialogic and follows the paradigm of the *conversation.* Truth is an *event* (*PDP,* 93). The "bridge" is not a synthesis but an "in between" field in which both the voice of one and the voice of the other are heard.

72. The events narrated by the novella need not be strictly contemporary with the composer. *Present* here means an absence of distancing: "there is no epic distance, and contemporary reality provides the point of view" (*DI,* 23).

73. The denunciation of the Jewish laws does not lack irony when we realize that it comes from people who, while affecting to be law-abiding, either plot against the life of the king or dream of substituting their power for his. (See Esther 6:8. One's cloak is part of one's being; compare 2 Kings 2:13–15.) According to the Greek Esther Addition A, Haman intended to kill Mordecai because of his denunciation of the two eunuchs in Esther 2:21–23.

74. Bakhtin, "Epic and Novel," *DI,* 25–26.

75. Ibid., 34.

76. Ibid. Bakhtin's characterization of the epic or, more generally, of the "noble [literary] genres"—to which Esther does *not* belong—is illuminating: "[The] idealization of the past in high genres has something of an official air. All external expressions of the dominant force and truth (the expression of everything conclusive) were formulated in the valorized-hierarchical category of the past, in a distanced and distant image (everything from gesture and clothing to literary style, for all are symbols of authority)" (*DI,* 20).

77. Mentioned by Bakhtin, *DI*, 13 (alluding to "Über epische und dramatische Dichtung," cosigned by Goethe and Schiller).

78. On cyclicity, Bakhtin says that it is "a negative feature, one that limits the force and ideological productivity of this time. . . . For this reason even growth does not achieve an authentic 'becoming' " (*DI*, 209–10). Bakhtin speaks at length of the difficult emergence of historical time from cyclic time in the eighteenth-century Enlightenment (see *SG*, 26, for example). There is, however, some kind of inner contradiction in Bakhtin's rejection of cyclicity since, arguably, carnival's temporality is cyclical. But, as Caryl Emerson writes in her introduction to *Bakhtin in Contexts: Across the Disciplines*, Amy Mandelker, ed. (Evanston, Ill.: Northwestern University Press, 1995), "carnival rhythm and folkloric time, although cyclical, are *not* static" (16).

79. The absence of all reference to Zion is thus clarified.

80. After the beautiful title of David Banon's book, *La Lecture infinie: Les voies de l'interprétation midrachique* (Paris: Seuil, 1987). As Bakhtin says, "characteristic for [the novel] is an eternal re-thinking and re-evaluating" (*DI*, 31).

81. Erich Auerbach, "Drama of European Literature," 29. He adds that the connection between the two events "is not regarded as primarily chronological or causal development but as a oneness within the divine plan, of which all occurrences are parts and reflections" (Epilogue to *Mimesis*, 555).

82. The typological reading of the "timeless covenant" is nothing novel. A large part of the Hebrew Bible is built that way.

83. This brought Carey A. Moore to state that the characters of the plot are "superficially drawn" (*Esther: A New Translation with Introduction and Notes*, Anchor Bible 7B [Garden City, N.Y.: Doubleday, 1971], liii).

84. Both terms are Bakhtin's; see "The *Bildungsroman*" (in *SG* [10–59], 21). Note the reversal of the stereotypical roles of male and female here.

85. See my development of this point in chapter 4, in the section titled "Dualities."

86. In contrast to Esther and Mordecai and their humble withdrawal behind their people, Bakhtin speaks of subcategories of the *Bildungsroman* in which one finds "the image of the *ready-made* hero. . . . Events change his destiny, change his position in life and society, but he himself remains unchanged and adequate to himself" (*SG*, 20). Note the contrast with Joseph in Genesis.

87. From this perspective, it is somewhat paradoxical that Purim is called "The Day of Mordecai" in 2 Maccabees 15:36.

88. Bakhtin, *DI*, 36.

89. Ibid.

90. We remember Hegel's phrase that in every action "something further may be implicated than lies in the intention and unconscious of the agent" (*The Philosophy of History* [1837], trans. J. Sibree [1899] [New York: Dover, 1956], 28).

91. "It is atypical of biblical literature to provide the names of the servants, especially when they have no direct acting or speaking roles" (Linda Day, *Esther,* Abingdon Old Testament Commentaries [Nashville: Abingdon Press, 2005], 34; contrast with Ezra 7:14). This contributes to "a humorous impression."

92. About this ludicrous episode, David J. A. Clines uses terms such as "amusing," "histrionic," "pure farce," "more than faintly satirical," and notes that "the story of Vashti's independence will spread like wildfire throughout the empire, with no need of assistance from the famed Persian communications system" (*Ezra, Nehemiah, Esther,* The New Century Bible Commentary [Grand Rapids: Eerdmans, 1984], 280).

93. In Esther 9:26, the Greek has *phrourai,* a lesson that is supported by Josephus, *Ant.* 9.295, *The Works of Josephus,* trans. William Whiston [Peabody, Mass.: Hendrickson, 1987].

94. See the section "A Carnivalesque Closure to an Ancient Historical Flop" in chapter 5. On the Sabbath that precedes Purim on the calendar, the commandment to annihilate Amalek is read in all the synagogues (see Sanhedrin 20b).

95. Auerbach, *Mimesis,* 17.

96. The familiarity of the author with ancient Persia is manifest. There are a number of Persian terms and of personal names in the book. D. J. A. Clines counts eight terms and thirty-five proper names of Persian origin! (*Ezra,* 261).

97. Bakhtin, in *Speech Genres,* 41–42, speaks of "the fullness and clarity of the visibility of time in space, the inseparability of the time of an event from the specific place of its occurrence (*Lokalität und Geschichte*) . . . the necessity that penetrates time and links time with space and different times with one another [etc.]." Bakhtin also writes, "The ability to *see time,* to *read time,* in the spatial whole of the world and, on the other hand, to perceive the filling of space not as an immobile background, a given that is completed once and for all, but as an emerging whole, an event—this is the ability to read in everything *signs that show time in its course,* beginning with nature and ending with human customs and ideas (all the way to abstract concepts). . . . The work of the seeing eye joins here with the most complex thought processes" (*SG,* 25).

98. R. Bracht Branham, "Inventing the Novel," in Amy Mandelker, ed., *Bakhtin in Contexts,* 87.

99. Auerbach, *Mimesis,* 11.

100. Ibid., 12.

101. Ibid., 13.

102. Ibid., 17.

103. See *PDP,* chapter 1.

104. Similar to the public pantomimes of a Mussolini, a Hitler, or, nowadays, a Kim Jong Il.

105. The stress on the plurality of languages in the empire is striking, all the more so as official documents would, in reality, use the so-called Empire Aramaic as

a lingua franca. We are on the way to the discovery that language defines the human being and is the basis of social reality.

106. *DI*, 60.

107. Harold Bloom notes the following, "At *Republic* 398A, Plato insists no one can compose both tragedy and comedy, but at the close of the *Symposium*, Socrates says that the same dramatist ought to be good at both comedy and tragedy. Athens had no such playwright, but Shakespearean women and men are both comic and tragic" (*Where Shall Wisdom Be Found?* [New York, Riverhead Books, 2004], 39). Bloom adds that also "*Don Quixote* is tragedy as well as comedy" (ibid., 80).

108. "The book of Esther represents a definitive shift of literary style" (Jacob Licht, *Storytelling in the Bible* [Jerusalem: Magnes, 1986]), 109.

109. See. F. Hvidberg and F. Loekkegaard, *Weeping and Laughter in the Old Testament* (Leyden: Brill, 1962). This combination has nothing to do with the Nietzschean Dionysiac, where "pain awakens pleasure while rejoicing brings cries of agony from the breast. From highest joy there comes a cry of horror or a yearning lament at some irredeemable loss" (Friedrich Nietzsche, *The Birth of Tragedy and the Case of Wagner* [1872], trans. Walter Kaufmann [New York: Vintage, 1967], sec. 2). The biblical alloy of weeping and laughter is ethical in nature. Underpinning it is the "as if" principle: "[We are treated] as sorrowful, yet always rejoicing; as poor, yet making many rich; as having nothing, and yet possessing everything" (2 Cor. 6:10). Otherwise, the rejoicing of the happy one is an affront to the weeping of the wretched, and vice versa.

110. Some seventy-five feet high!

111. As David Clines writes (but what he says is only valid for the Persian monoglossia in the book of Esther), "In Esther, reality tends towards inscripturation, and attains its true quality only when it is written down" (*The Esther Scroll: The Story of the Story*, JSOT Suppl. 30 [Sheffield, Eng.: Sheffield University Press, 1984], 22).

112. Clines pointedly criticizes the alleged Jewish duplication of the Persian rigidity in 9:25–28. He writes, "No Persian bureaucrat could have phrased it more impeccably" (ibid., 25). This is formally right, but the critique falls flat because we are in the realm of parody, which Clines missed.

113. Clines remarks that this "inscripturation" means only that the story has "inbuilt its own hermeneutical rules, specifying how it is to be read and thus what it really means" (ibid.). Things are not that simple, as Clines demonstrates, having missed the very key to what the story "means."

114. Again a feature much favored by Bakhtin.

115. A further development on this point is found in the section "Esther and Mordecai's Masterstroke" in chapter 4.

116. The Bakhtinian unfinalizability. Bakhtin writes, "[Represented] reality as we have it in the novel is only one of many possible realities; it is not inevitable, not arbitrary, it bears within itself other possibilities" (*DI*, 37). The profound finale of

Sophocles' *Oedipus the King* comes to mind: "We must call no one happy who is of mortal race, until he hath crossed life's border, free of pain." Hans-Georg Gadamer strikes a very similar note in *Truth and Method* (New York: Continuum, 1975): "We are always within the situation, and to throw light on it is a task that is never entirely completed. . . . To exist historically means that knowledge of oneself can never be complete" (269).

117. More on this point later; see especially chapter 8.

118. Note that a three-day-long fast observed day and night is unparalleled. It belongs to the grotesque, especially as the fast would then extend to the time of Passover and thus would run against the law of Exodus 12. In anthropology, mourning rites mark liminality, that is, the passage from one basic human state to another. Food deprivation, like the stripping of proper clothes and the abandonment of grooming, marks the shift from "visible to invisible social existence," as Arnold van Gennep would say. In this connection, Purim is to be seen as a counter-ritual marking the passage from invisibility back to visibility, attuned as it is with the emergence of cyclical rebirth.

119. See Jon Levenson, *Esther: A Commentary,* Old Testament Library (Louisville, Ky.: Westminster/John Knox Press, 1997), 116.

120. Hans Bardtke, *Das Buch Esther,* Kommentar zum Alten Testament 17.5 (Gütersloh: Mohn, 1963), 374.

121. This text, incidentally, is quoted by St. Paul in Galatians 3:13 and applied to the crucifixion of Jesus.

122. *DI,* 75.

123. Bakhtin speaks of carnival as "shaped according to a certain pattern of play" (*RAHW,* 7).

124. *DI,* 76.

125. In Esther, the parodic never degenerates into the vulgar.

126. Levenson, *Esther,* 99.

127. As D. C. Muecke writes, "A satirist who wishes to condemn a particular vice or folly can do it very effectively by putting a self-contradictory argument into the mouth of a would-be wise or virtuous character" (Muecke, *Irony,* 59).

128. Levenson, *Esther,* 94–95.

129. As Barbara Babcock writes, "As both Socrates and the Zen masters demonstrate, there must be a frustration and confounding of the intellect for thinking to occur. And in . . . Zen . . . clowning, humor is 'fully developed'" ("Arrange Me into Disorder," 123).

130. See André LaCocque, "A Psychological Approach to the Book of Jonah," chap. 6 in *Psychology and the Bible: A New Way to Read the Scriptures,* vol. 2, ed. J. H. Ellens and W. G. Rollins (Westport, Conn., and London: Praeger, 2004).

131. *DI,* 116 (see, for example, Esther 4:14).

132. *DI,* 116.

133. The celebration of this non-Pentateuchal feast did not easily impose itself in the land of Israel (and elsewhere?). The adamant terminology used in the legalization of Purim in Esther 9:27–32 shows that obstacles had to be overcome: "established and imposed upon themselves . . . without failing to do . . . from year to year . . . from generation to generation, from family to family, from state to state, from city to city . . . without fail . . . its commemoration will be without end . . . [Esther] wrote with full authority to confirm . . . [Mordecai] confirmed . . . as prescribed . . . and as they had decreed . . . the decree of Esther confirmed . . . it was written in the book."

134. Bakhtin, "The Chronotope," in *DI* [84–258], 91.

135. According to Michael Fox (*Character and Ideology in the Book of Esther,* 2nd ed. [Grand Rapids, Mich.: Eerdmans, 2001], 22), no state could be governed with unchangeable laws. Perhaps. But Zaleucus of Thurium, says Michel de Montaigne, ordered that anyone who would bring forward a proposal to institute a new law or to cancel an old one should come to the people with a rope around his neck—and be strangled with it if his proposal was not accepted by all! (See *Essays* [1575], trans. John M. Cohen, New York: Penguin, reprint 1993, bk. 1, ch. 23, "Of the custom and of not changing a received law.")

136. In the Middle Ages, the money business into which the Jews had been coerced was in a similar way held to be contemptible and was seen as a sign of an atavistic Jewish greed.

137. This was the title of a 1996 made-for-television movie.

138. *DI,* 68.

Chapter 2

1. In 1950, Theodor H. Gaster suggested that the prototype of Purim was the Persian New Year festival, and he saw in Esther "simply a Jewish adaptation of a popular Persian novella" (*Purim and Hanukkah in Custom and Tradition,* 35; see also K. V. Helmer Ringgren, "Das Buch Esther," in *Das Hohe Lied, Klagelieder, Das Buch Esther,* Das Alte Testament Deutsch 16, ed. K. V. H. Ringgren and A. Weiser, 113–44 (Göttingen: Vandenhoeck and Ruprecht, 1958). I realize that invoking the Babylonian festival of the Akitu in this context is a double-edged sword, for one can legitimately conclude from this that carnival is as much the affair of kings, high clergy, and nobility as it is of the populace. (More on the Akitu follows in this chapter and in the sections in chapter 6 "Did Purim Replace 'Mosaic' Passover in the Eastern Diaspora?" and "More on Purim and Time.") This fact might indeed relativize Bakhtin's statements in this respect. But, as I said from the outset of this essay, what interests us here is the heuristic application by Bakhtin of the "carnivalesque." As Simon Dentith writes (*Bakhtinian Thought: An Introductory Reader* [London and New York: Rout-

ledge, 1995]), Bakhtin's "orientation is not to the past but to the future" (78). Furthermore, modern criticism of the Bakhtinian "idealization" of carnival, invoking as it does practical experiences of repressive carnivalesque violence in different parts and different times of European history, is somewhat missing the point. Bakhtin himself acknowledged that the spirit of carnival declined during and after the Renaissance. The grotesque in literature, for example, became a "subjective" grotesque fixated on the individual. Moreover, as Bakhtin insists, the grotesque is characterized by *degradation* (*RAHW,* 19). It could be expected that such a powerful weapon for dehumanizing the adversary would fall into the hands of ruthless people, as happened during the religious massacres in sixteenth-century France, for instance.

2. Jacob Klein, "Akitu," *Anchor Bible Dictionary,* vol. 1 (New York: Doubleday, 1998), 139a.

3. I shall return to this point in chapter 3, in the section titled "A Nonreligious Document in the Bible," with emphasis on the protracted torture of the designated victims, who will know a full year in advance of their appointed death and its precise date.

4. It is striking that in both "worlds," that of the Persians and that of the Jews, the events and festivals condensed in the story are preliminary to major festivals already established, that is, the Akitu or New Year festival in Susa and Passover in the Jewish communities. In both worlds, as well, the great festivals represent order and structure—what Victor Turner termed, in "Liminality and the Performantive Genres," *societas*—for Passover celebrates "the formation of the nation and the acceptance of the law," as Jeffrey Rubenstein noted in "Purim, Liminality, and Communitas," *AJS Review* 17, no. 2 (1992): 267. Thus, the calendrical orgy in the Jewish blood of the thirteenth of Adar, and "Purim, thirty days before Passover, [represent] antistructure, a state prior to the establishment of society and its legal system . . . a time of communitas, of the absence of structure and law" (Rubenstein, 267). In this respect, we can refer to what René Girard calls the "sacrificial crisis." Ethnological studies have found numerous examples of it. During the ceremony meant to ritually repeat the explosion of violence and its eventual canalization into unanimous violence against a designated scapegoat, the latter is massacred *by all* (we remember the fate of the buffoon king or *pharmakos* of the Akitu). Peace and tranquillity are restored, and the New Year can commence. (See René Girard, *La Violence et le sacré* [Paris: Grasset, 1972], passim.)

5. In their book on Bakhtin (*Mikhail Bakhtin* [Cambridge, Mass.: Harvard University Press, 1984]), Katerina Clark and Michael Holquist judiciously stress the unusual nature of the eras in which Rabelais in the 1530s and Bakhtin in the 1930s lived. The carnivalesque is a fitting if courageous response to the darkness of the world. Behind the extravagances in the book of Esther, one should not miss the tears of a suffering community. Extravagance is called by Bakhtin the scandalous or the eccentric. Reflecting on this notion, David McCracken terms "the scandalous,

an artistic category between the tragic and the comic" ("Character in the Boundary: Bakhtin's Interdividuality in Biblical Narratives," *Semeia* 63 [1993]: 29–42), 38).

During the period of the "cold war," I had the opportunity to travel to Bucharest, where I was deeply impressed to see that no one in the streets laughed or even smiled. Adding to the impression of the grotesque, the Romanian army was in a state of war readiness against the threat of an invasion by the U.S. Marines!

6. Bakhtin says that "feasts were linked to moments of crisis. . . . Moments of death and survival, of change and renewal" (*RAHW*, 9).

7. In the background of the story is not in all likelihood a Mesopotamian pogrom, but a second-century B.C.E. Palestinian or perhaps Alexandrian one.

8. There is here, as generally in the literary genre to which the book belongs, an absence of memory. Bakhtin wrote, there is "nothing for memory and tradition to do" (*DI*, 23). Only the initiation of Purim will retrieve the virtue of remembrance.

9. See chapter 3 of this volume.

10. Adele Berlin, *Esther*, xlii, thinks that "a burlesque [of Persia] would be less effective after the Persian Empire ceased to exist." But interest in the defunct Persian Empire continued long after its demise; see Plutarch, Diodorus Siculus, Quintus Curtius, and others, all writing after the turn of an era.

11. Montesquieu, *The Spirit of the Laws*, XI, 6. Strikingly, Sophocles' fateful Oedipus accepts full responsibility for his acts. Bakhtin follows suit; he says that, concomitantly with the explanation of man by way of laws, one must also understand human freedom. Long before Bakhtin, Rabbi Akiba (second century C.E.) said that everything is determined in advance, but the human is free (*Pirqei Aboth* 3, 19).

12. Elias Bickerman, *Four Strange Books of the Bible: Jonah, Daniel, Koheleth, Esther* (New York: Schocken, 1967).

13. This is what the cuneiform texts call *datu ša šarri*, "the royal command." As Joseph Blenkinsopp says, "all legal enactments of any kind . . . are . . . theoretically 'law of the king.'" He refers to Ezra 7:26; see "Was the Pentateuch the Civic and Religious Constitution of the Jewish Ethnos in the Persian Period?" in *Persia and Torah: The Theory of Imperial Authorization of the Pentateuch*, ed. James W. Watts (Atlanta, Ga.: Society of Biblical Literature, 2001), 44. The unchangeability of such law emphasizes the "arbitrary power exercised by Persian rulers" (45).

14. A refinement of this idea in some modern empires involves equating any dissidence against the regime with mental illness.

15. The Jews' "surprise" is relative, however, for the Jews were the "beneficiaries" of the Persian principle when the Torah became state law in Judea under Ezra-Nehemiah. Then, the inner contradictions of the written texts were maintained side by side (the so-called sources *D* and *P*) because the laws were immutable, according to the Persian patrons. See Frank Crüsemann, "Le Pentateuque, Une Tora: Prolegomènes à l'interprétation de sa forme finale," in *Le Pentateuque en question*, ed.

Albert de Pury (Geneva: Labor et Fides, 1989), 339–60; and also from Crüsemann, *The Torah: Theology and Social History of Old Testament Law* (Minneapolis, Minn.: Fortress Press, 1996), 349–50. Jean Louis Ska also stresses the Pentateuch as an "irrevocable document" once it had been written down (see "Persian Imperial Authorization, Some Question Marks," in Watts, *Persia and Torah,* 170 and note 30). The irrevocability of Persian law is seemingly confirmed by Diodorus Siculus (see, for example, Book XVII: 30). The text reports the case of a man put to death under Darius III (336–330 B.C.E.) even though he had been shown to be perfectly innocent. "[Darius III] immediately repented and blamed himself for having committed such a great error, but it was impossible to have undone what had been done by royal authority."

16. Esther 3:10; 8:1; 9:10, 24; compare 7:6; 9:22.

17. Haman's accusation against the Jews was a common one in the Hellenistic world. Josephus reports it in several of his writings; see *Ant.* 4.5.8 (137) or *Apion.* 2. 7 (79). Tacitus and other Roman historians later sharpened their criticism and accused the Jews of being misanthropes (see Tac. *Hist.* 5.5, among other texts).

18. Haman's terms for Jewish annihilation correspond to the biblical "ban" (*ḥerem*) (see 1 Sam. 15:3; 22:19; and so on). The Jews responded with a counterban against the persecutors. If we understand Esther 8:11–12 as referring to a Jewish massacre of the women and children of the anti-Semites, an illuminating text is to be found in 1 Kings 20:40–43.

19. David Daube, "The Last Chapter of Esther," *Jewish Quarterly Review* 37 (1946–47): 140. (The author defends the authenticity of Esther 10. The loss incurred by the king in cancelling the massacre, that is, Haman's ten thousand talents, is now compensated for by a legitimate tax, probably proposed by Mordecai.)

20. In the LXX, the book of Judith follows that of Esther. The irony of this pairing says it all: one presents the face of Ishtar within the realm of the goddess; the other is the Jewess in a context of resistance. See Sidnie White Crawford, "Esther and Judith: Contrasts in Character," in *Esther in Modern Research,* JSOT Suppl. 380, ed. Sidnie White Crawford and Leonard J. Greenspoon (New York: T. & T. International, 2003), 61–76. See also my *Feminine Unconventional,* 71 esp.

21. In opposition to this, as we know, Bakhtin, with Rabelais, praised the carnivalesque laughter of derision. This laughter is indestructible and ever renascent, as even death becomes a precondition of reproduction.

22. *RAHW,* 9.

23. Ibid., 52.

24. It is generally taken for granted that Haman's concocted persecution of the Jews was limited to the eastern Jewry in diaspora, but we should remember that Yehud (that is, Judea) was part of the Persian Empire (as was also Egypt).

25. Julian Pitt-Rivers, "Honour and Social Status," in *Honour and Shame: The Values of Mediterranean Society,* ed. J. G. Peristiany (Chicago: University of Chicago Press, 1965), 22, also cited by Timothy Laniak, *Shame and Honor in the Book of Esther,*

Society of Biblical Literature Dissertation Series 165 (Atlanta, Ga.: Scholars Press, 1998), 40.

26. Under the fascist regimes, Jewish veterans of World War I in Germany or Italy were not saved by their medals or by their war-inflicted infirmities.

27. Bakhtin, *PDP,* 122, in French in the text.

28. See Clines's works, for instance.

29. *RAHW,* 94.

30. Hans-Georg Gadamer, *Truth and Method,* 16.

31. In fact, Mordecai is the only contact between Esther and the other Jews. Without him, she is cut off from the community.

32. Note that the expression "Mordecai the Jew" appears seven times in the book, including three times in the often disputed "appendix" to the story: 9:29, 31; 10:3. Bruce William Jones sees in this total one more argument in favor of the "authenticity" of chapters 9 and 10 of Esther (see "The So-Called Appendix to the Book of Esther," *Semitics* 6 [1978]: 36–43).

33. Mordecai's greatest triumph is to be forever associated with the king: both their names are registered in the Persian annals (Esther 10:2).

34. The Persian king or kingship is mentioned 190 times in 167 verses (see Carey A. Moore, *Daniel, Esther, and Jeremiah: The Additions,* Anchor Bible 44 [Garden City, N.Y.: Doubleday, 1977], 157).

35. Carol Meyers calls attention to Esther 3, in which the king transfers his royal power, symbolized by his signet ring, to Haman. Hence, when Haman dies, his death "will mean that the subject people will have overcome the 'ruler,' who is not the actual ruler" ("Esther," in *The Oxford Bible Commentary,* ed. John Barton and John Muddiman [Oxford: Oxford University Press, 2001], 327b).

Chapter 3

1. See my *Romance, She Wrote* (esp. 179–80).

2. In fact, the ironic depends on the lack of irony in others. See Muecke, *Irony,* 1970.

3. Pace Clines in his *Esther Scroll.*

4. *DI,* 245, note 31.

5. See Morson and Emerson, *Mikhail Bakhtin: Creation of a Prosaics,* 221.

6. These notions of assimilation and reaccentuation are Bakhtinian. See *SG,* 89.

7. Compare with Exodus chapters 25–28; 35–38; and so on.

8. As my student Ruth Billington said (paper of June 1991, about Esther 1:22), "the ridiculousness of drunken men who activate the entire Persian Empire communication system to save face."

9. When this ironic note is downplayed, the festival may be called the Day of Mordecai; see 2 Maccabees 15:36.

10. Clines, *Ezra,* 316.

11. See Esther 9:17 and the notion of "relief, rest, peace"; see also 9:30; 10:3.

12. Bakhtin, *SG,* 132.

13. Morson and Emerson, *Mikhail Bakhtin: Creation of a Prosaics,* 345.

14. Berlin (*Esther,* xxv) states, "To keep the characters flat . . . befits the comic genre." In a way, the reported events are themselves stereotyped as they are, as it were, unfolding "on their own, without human or divine agency," a feature underlined by the frequent "use of the passive voice and passive constructions" (ibid., xxvi). And, of course, Persia is stereotypically described in a *conventional* manner (ibid., xxx). Incidentally, Berlin agrees that the author did not necessarily live in the region.

15. See chapter 4, especially the section "Outsideness."

16. See *DI,* 384.

17. *PDP,* 106–7.

18. The comic side can include, as it does in Esther, a reduced degree of laughter that Bakhtin—paraphrasing Gogol—calls "laughter unseen by the world" (*PDP,* 178, note 4).

19. *SG,* 133.

20. *RAHW,* 34.

21. For Bakhtin, the theatrical unity of time, space, and action is monoglossic. But he speaks of Dostoevsky's tendency to conform to the theatrical principle of unity of time and of "catastrophic swiftness of action" (see *PDP,* 29).

22. These things are also present in Rabelais, with his use of familiar names of places, objects, and people.

23. *RAHW,* 447.

24. J. Levenson (*Esther*) refers to biblical texts such as Isaiah 14:1 and 56:3, 6, in which the term points to non-Jews joining the community.

25. The Scroll of Esther may be recited in any language, according to rabbinic opinion. Furthermore, in the celebration of Purim, "one is permitted to . . . dress as Haman. In the wearing of gentile clothing one becomes a gentile, if only for a little while" (Monford Harris, "Purim: The Celebration of Dis-Order," *Judaism* 26 [1977]: 164).

26. Roberto Da Matta stresses the openness of carnival groups; in Rio de Janeiro, onlookers are free to join the *desfile* at any time ("Carnival in Multiple Planes," in MacAloon, *Rite, Drama,* 228–35).

27. Johanna W. H. van Wijk-Bos, *Ruth and Esther: Women in Alien Lands* (Nashville, Tenn.: Abingdon, 2001), 67.

28. Some years ago, visiting with some prelates at the Vatican, I was flabbergasted by an isolation that blinded many of them to the outside world.

29. Proverbs 31:4–5 seems created as an illustration of this: "It is not for kings

to drink wine, or for rulers to desire strong drink; or else they will drink and forget what has been decreed and will pervert the rights of all the afflicted" (NRSV).

30. Compare to the situation in Germany between World War I and World War II.

31. Significantly, in the LXX, Add. C (= Vulg. 14:1–9), Esther defends herself from the charge of enjoying the bed and the table of non-Jews.

32. Were it not that the Babylonian name Mordecai confirms the Babylonian origin of the name Esther, one could also think of the striking resemblance of the root *ʾstr* in Hebrew with the redundant stem *ʾstr* (to hide) in Deuteronomy 31:17–18: God says "I shall hide my face from them . . . many evils and enmities will visit them . . . and hiding will I hide my face." There may be allusions to this Deuteronomic text and to the "hiding" of God or of Esther's identity in the book of Esther, but the context is entirely different in the two pericopes.

33. The names Mordecai and Esther correspond to the nicknames that Rabelais gives to his characters, for example, Gargamelle, Grangousier, Gargantua, and so on. Let us note at this point that, as the name Mordecai derives from the name Marduk, the Babylonian god, it should be no surprise to find, with Arthur Ungnad, the name Marduka in a tablet of the Amherst collection. And let us be much less "certain" than is Ungnad that this Marduka is to be identified with Esther's Mordecai! (See "Keilinschriftliche Beiträge zum Buch Ezra und Esther," Pt. 1, *Zeitschrift für die Alttestamentliche Wissenschaft* 58, no. 1 [1940]: 240–44.)

34. A piece of crucial information—the association of the Jewish name Esther with the name Hadassah (Myrtle)—is missing in the Greek versions. It is a significant absence, shedding a further light on the intended gentile readers of the Greek texts of the book of Esther. The Greek versions are discussed further later in chapter 7.

35. *RAHW,* 415–16 (emphasis Bakhtin's). It is rather piquant that in the traditional Jewish celebration of Purim one is invited to become so inebriated as to be unable to distinguish between "cursed be Haman" and "blessed be Mordecai" (so Rava [fourth century C.E.] in Megillah 7b).

36. The term *dialogism* neatly defines the central philosophical tenet of Bakhtin's thinking, but he did not use it in his writings.

Chapter 4

1. See Mieke Bal, "Lots of Writing," in *Ruth and Esther,* ed. Athalya Brenner (Sheffield, Eng.: Sheffield University Press, 1999), 233: "Vashti is eliminated only to be restored as Esther, who takes her place and avenges her by reformulating disobedience as achieving power. . . . Esther's insistence on appearing before the king and using the tools of display to do so . . . is the positive version of Vashti's nega-

tive act. . . . Finally, to drive this continuity between Esther and Vashti home, it is Esther who then makes the king appear at her banquet." Along the same line of thought, Linda Day (*Three Faces of a Queen: Characterization in the Books of Esther* [Sheffield, Eng.: Sheffield Academic Press, 1995], 213) writes, "Because of Vashti's example, Esther knows what to expect if she makes the wrong move in her own decision to make request for her people."

2. As Bal writes (237), "the generalization of Vashti as 'all women' . . . [is a] mirror [that] also reflects more insidious generalizations from a single individual to an entire people, more subtle expressions of hatred for the Other, whoever he or she might be." One is reminded of the "Christian" generalization of Jesus' rejection by some Jewish authorities of the time to apply to all Jews then and ever since.

3. Note the reversal of the Persian legislation initiated by Esther "entering the royal courtyard" (4:11) "against the law" (4:16).

4. Not everyone would agree with this and would rather see in Vashti's refusal to do obeisance to her husband the protest of a queen against being treated as a dancing girl. The sequel of the story, however, with its interpretation of Vashti's disobedience as a female rebellion against male authority, goes rather in the direction I indicate in the present essay.

5. W. Lee Humphreys writes, "To this point [4:11] she has been the object of most verbs" ("The Story of Esther and Mordecai: An Early Jewish Novella," in Coats, *Saga, Legend,* 106).

6. R. Alter, *Art of Biblical Narrative,* 126.

7. Bakhtin, *Esthétique de la création verbale* (Paris: Gallimard, 1984), 28 (also published as "Author and Hero in Aesthetic Activity," in *Art and Answerability: Early Philosophical Essays by M. M. Bakhtin,* ed. Michael Holquist and Vadim Liapunov [Austin: University of Texas Press, 1990]; *Art and Answerability* hereafter cited as *AA*).

8. Bakhtin, *AA,* 15–22.

9. This is not without recalling the young Moses or the mature Joseph at the court of Egypt. The parallel with Moses is drawn by Gillis Gerleman (*Esther,* Biblischer Kommentar, Altes Testament 21 [Neukirchen-Vluyn: Neukirchener, 1973] 11–23), followed by Clines, *Ezra,* 289, and Charles E. Hambrick-Stowe ("Ruth the New Abraham, Esther the New Moses," *Christian Century* 100 [1983]: 1130–34): Esther is also a lawgiver and, as Moses instituted Passover in the Torah, Esther sanctioned the celebration of Purim. Initially, both Moses and Esther are "secret Jews" and must choose their own people against their adopted one. Carey Moore, however, takes exception to this tally ("Esther Revisited Again: A Further Examination of Certain Esther Studies of the Past Ten Years," *Hebrew Annual Review* 7 [1983]: 175). I am not convinced by Moore's arguments here; on the contrary, I think that there is an intentional irony in the fact that, in the story of Moses, the people's clamor goes up to God's ears (Exod. 2:23), while in Esther's story the people's shouts reach Esther (4:13–17). On affinities with the Joseph story, see Ludwig A. Rosenthal, "Die

Josephgeschichte, mit den Büchern Ester und Daniel verglichen," in *Zeitschrift für die Alttestamentliche Wissenschaft* 15 (1895): 278–84.

10. Levenson, *Esther,* 52.

11. "It is significant that . . . Esther does not feel anything for herself but only for the Jewish people" (Day, *Three Faces,* 177).

12. Although the historical Xerxes inaugurated the practice of monogamy in the dynasty, he kept a harem with hundreds of concubines and was known for his numerous adulterous love affairs.

13. The king is inaccessible and invisible (4:11), in flagrant and ironic contrast with what had been said of royalty in chapter 1, where everything pertaining to the king is a show (including the queen).

14. It is unnecessary to see this A addition as an independent tradition. The Alpha-Text correctly interprets the king's blindness.

15. Note that Mordecai in chapter 4 (see verse 2) is now outside the official perimeter, on the city square (4:6), the place in which carnival has its setting, even though it starts in the present case with rites of mourning (4:1), as it does also during the Akitu festival in Babylon.

16. Bakhtin, *Esthétique de la création verbale,* 55 ("Author and Hero"): "notre individualité n'aurait pas d'existence si l'autre ne la créait."

17. On this, see van Wijk-Bos, *Ruth and Esther,* 110.

18. *Contra* van Wijk-Bos (*Ruth and Esther,* 108), for instance. Let us note, again in contradistinction to the same author, that Esther 9:13 is not necessarily a duplication of 9:7–10; texts such as Joshua 10:26, 1 Samuel 31:10–13, and 2 Samuel 4:12 (see also Herodotus 3.125; 6.30) have shown that dead bodies can be hanged as a sign of loathing. Similarly, in 9:20, Mordecai, as prime minister, sends letters to the Jews inviting them to put the fourteenth and fifteenth of Adar on their feast calendars, and in 9:29–30 a second set of letters confirms the first, under the authority of Queen Esther in lieu of the kingly seal that legally validates a writ. My contention is not that a secondhand writer is out of the question. But, when alleged duplications and inner contradictions are so easily "discovered" by modern readers, chances are these flaws would have been just as evident to any supposed later redactor. The latter, if she or he ever existed, would arguably have done a better job, unless precisely the duplications were by design.

Within the context of Esther's "indifference" to the law, let us note here that the Targum Sheni to Esther 9:4 sees in the exposure of the bodies of Haman's dead sons, left out overnight, a neglect of the commandment in Deuteronomy 21:22–23. The hanging of Haman's ten sons, of course, is the counterpart to the seventy-five-foot-high gallows erected by Haman to hang Mordecai, thus exposing his corpse to public shame. Incidentally, Adele Berlin calls attention to this height as unparalleled in the Bible. "Even Solomon's temple is only thirty cubits high" (*Esther,* 55).

19. Bakhtin, *Estetika slovesnogo tvorchestva,* ed. S. G. Bocharov (Moscow:

Iskusstvo, 1979), 373. This article, translated as "Toward a Methodology for the Human Sciences," appears in *Speech Genres*; see 170.

20. Berg, *The Book of Esther,* passim.

21. Baldwin, *Esther,* 28.

22. Susan Niditch, *Underdogs and Tricksters: A Prelude to Biblical Folklore* (San Francisco: Harper and Row, 1987).

23. Ibid., 106.

24. See Susan Niditch, "Legends of Wise Heroes and Heroines," in *The Hebrew Bible and Its Modern Interpreters,* ed. Douglas E. Knight and Gene M. Tucker (Philadelphia: Fortress Press; Chico, Calif.: Scholars Press, 1985), 445–63.

25. Ibid., 450.

26. Bakhtin, *Toward a Philosophy of the Act,* trans. Vadim Liapunov (Austin: University of Texas Press, 1993), 2.

27. *PDP,* Appendix 2, 289.

28. On the "dyadic person," Bruce J. Malina says that it is "a person always in relation with and connected to at least one other social unit, usually a group" ("Dealing with Biblical [Mediterranean] Characters: A Guide for U. S. Consumers," *Biblical Theology Bulletin* 19:127–41; the quote is from 127–28, cited by David McCracken, "Character in the Boundary," 39, note 5).

29. See *AA,* 15–22.

30. The buffoon who substitutes for the king in the Akitu finds his homologue in numerous societies. These are tragicomic characters of substitution "who are regularly sacrificed at the end of their brief triumph" (R. Girard, *La Violence et le sacré,* 379).

31. See *AA,* 108–9. The following comment from Bakhtin about the importance of meeting cannot be more to the point when applied to the encounter between Mordecai and Haman: this chronotope "is marked by a higher degree of intensity in emotions and values" (*AA,* 243). In the book of Esther, these deep (but unexpressed) feelings are contempt and defiance on the one hand and rage and murderous intent on the other.

32. See C. A. Moore, *Esther* (1971), liii.

33. See Morson and Emerson, *Mikhail Bakhtin: Creation of a Prosaics,* 345.

34. Auerbach, *Mimesis,* 15.

35. *RAHW,* 39–40.

36. See S. White Crawford (Crawford and Greenspoon, *Esther in Modern Research,* 64): "Ahasuerus has aspects of the buffoon in his character." See also Adele Berlin, *Esther,* xx.

37. *DI,* 92, 94: "Should something happen a minute earlier or a minute later, that is, should there be no chance simultaneity or chance disjunctions in time, there would be no plot at all, and nothing to write a novel about. . . . One day, one hour, even one minute earlier or later have everywhere a decisive and fatal significance."

38. As in the Sophocles' tragedy *Oedipus the King,* the audience is always one

step ahead of Oedipus in knowledge of the truth. Here and in the book of Esther, this discrepancy between the two consciousnesses creates a successful dramatic irony.

39. Even this last recourse was denied to the Jews of the Middle Ages and of the Third Reich by the imposition on them of a special clothing.

40. If there is still some possible ambiguity in chapter 7 as to the identity of Esther's kin, it is cancelled out in chapter 8 (verse 5), when Esther names the designated victims of Haman as "the Jews," even if she still feels it necessary to add "my people . . . my kindred" (8:6).

41. See my development on this point in the section "A Carnivalesque Closure to an Ancient Historical Flop" in chapter 5.

42. To recall, the Greek version of the LXX begins with Mordecai having a premonitory dream.

43. *DI,* 159.

44. James Sanders, "The Canonical Process," in *Guide des Nouvelles Lectures,* ed. André LaCocque (Paris: Bayard, 2005).

45. Harry Sieber, *The Picaresque* (London: Methuen, 1977), 73. See Nicole Duran ("Who Wants to Marry a Persian King?" in *Pregnant Passion: Gender, Sex, and Violence in the Bible,* Semeia Studies, ed. Cheryl Kirk-Duggan [Atlanta, Ga.: Society of Biblical Literature, 2003], 79). She wonders whether Esther's initial ignorance of her people's plight might not be due to a self-imposed blindness (see 4:4).

46. Vashti exemplifies the type of person trapped in the carnivalesque?

47. For "it is often very difficult to establish precisely where reverence ends and ridicule begins" (*DI,* 77).

48. The collective fast in 4:16 is more ambiguous than is acknowledged by Levenson (see his *Esther,* 19) or by his disciple Timothy Laniak (see *Shame and Honor,* 91, note 77, for example). Levenson says that it is "a totally impotent and senseless gesture if there is no higher power that it can influence." But modern experience shows that Jews worldwide go through circumcision and celebrate Passover, for instance, without much religious conviction. It is safer to see the fast as a process of moralization that enables a morally devastated community to overcome a psychological and religious impasse provoked by grief and despair. At any rate, the book of Esther does not elaborate on the "potency" or "sense" of the gesture, and commentators are not warranted to speculate about its alleged allusiveness.

49. See also J. A. Loader, "Esther as a Novel with Different Levels of Meaning," *Zeitschrift für die Alttestamentliche Wissenschaft* 90 (1978): 417–21. In an excellent article, "The Religion in the Book of Esther" (*Judaism* 39, no. 2 [1990]), Michael Fox takes seriously the absence or even the elimination of any reference to God in Esther and says, "The frustration of these [the readers'] expectations must be purposive." There is a veil over God because "the author would have us hold to confidence even when lacking certainty. . . . He is teaching a theology of possibility" (146, 147).

50. No one among the commentators came, to my knowledge, closer to this conclusion than did Adele Berlin (*Esther*) or Edward L. Greenstein. The latter writes, "on Purim . . . anything goes. Consequently, it has been customary for Purim celebrants to flaunt and parody Jewish practice and teaching. In Esther, both Esther and the Jews similarly transgress or ignore Jewish law" ("A Jewish Reading," 231). Jeffrey Rubenstein ("Purim, Liminality, and Communitas," 266) says, "These abrogations of the law are themselves sanctioned by law, a type of nomian antinomianism." Pace Clines, for whom, "it would be going too far to speak of a deliberate 'concealment' of God or of a 'hidden' causality (cf. Berg, *Esther*, p. 178f.)." Clines also takes exception to J. A. Loader, "Esther as a Novel," 417–21; see Clines, *Ezra*, 269.

51. Especially, regarding the book of Esther, their Jewish traditional world.

52. *AA*, 211 (I have revised the translation).

53. *DI*, 296.

54. *PDP*, 185.

55. Van Wijk-Bos writes, "His wife and friends are almost indecently quick to point to his beginning downfall" (*Ruth and Esther*, 104).

56. Day, *Esther*, 107.

Chapter 5

1. Paraphrase by Emerson, *First Hundred Years* (203), of Liudmila Gogotishvili's article, "Varianty i invarianty M. M. Bakhtina," in *Voprosy Filosofii* 1 (1992): 135.

2. *DI*, 342.

3. Matt. 26:52 (NRSV).

4. I have elsewhere used the category of the Menippean literature; see André and Pierre LaCocque, *Jonah: A Psycho-Religious Approach to the Prophet* (Columbia: University of South Carolina Press, 1990). As Bakhtin says, "The menippea loves to play with abrupt transitions and shifts, ups and downs, rises and falls, unexpected comings together of distant and disunited things, mésalliances of all sorts" (*PDP*, 118). See also Auerbach, *Mimesis*, 72 ("The Arrest of Peter Valvomeres" [about St. Augustine]).

5. See W. McKane, "A Note on Esther IX and 1 Samuel XV," *Journal of Theological Studies* 12 (1961): 260–91.

6. Berg (*The Book of Esther*) is right in stressing that Mordecai is not said to descend from David, in spite (or because) of the renewed interest in David during the Second Temple period. The book of Esther is not interested in a restoration of the Davidic independence of Palestine. On this score, once again, we note the distancing of Esther from Israelite tradition.

7. Laniak, *Shame and Honor*, 78. But, such abstention is strikingly one-sided. Haman, as we saw, does mobilize the numinous in his favor in Esther 3:7.

8. This, however, is just a term of comparison, for the absence of references to David (or to his dynasty) is blatant here (see note 6, above).

9. For Amalek as the absolute evil, see Psikta Rabbati 12.47; Psikta Rav Kahana 27; Mekhilta Tractate "Amalek" (see II, 171–86).

10. *DI,* 130.

11. "The essence of a man is realized not by his condition, but by his activity" (*DI,* 140). The term *energeia* comes originally from Aristotle. See also the dictum of William von Humboldt, writing in the nineteenth century, that language is not *ergon* (completed work) but *energeia* (creative process). William von Humboldt, *On Language: On the Diversity of Human Language Construction and Its Influence on the Mental Development of the Human Species* [1836], Cambridge Texts in the History of Philosophy, ed. Michael Losonsky, trans. Peter Heath (New York: Cambridge University Press, 1999).

12. See Harold Fisch, *Poetry with a Purpose: Biblical Poetics and Interpretation* (Bloomington: Indiana University Press, 1988), and also Bakhtin, *PDP.*

13. *PDP,* 84.

14. Bakhtin says, "As long as a person is alive, he lives by the fact that he is not finalized, that he has not yet uttered his ultimate word" (*PDP,* 59). Because Haman is not literally a robot and because no human being can totally avoid the process of communication, he is described as dialoguing with his wife and friends in an intimate scene parenthetical to his "biography": it is the exception that confirms the rule (Esther 6:12–13). Haman's speech to his wife and friends about his superior status is a beautiful case of what Bakhtin calls a "double-voiced" discourse, that is, an utterance in which two or more voices can be heard at once, the voice of the character and the voice of the author. This happens, in particular, as here, when the character's words are parodied or ironicized.

15. Moore, *Esther,* liii.

16. As Meir Sternberg notes, "the Greeks and Trojans have the same gods, arms, manners, codes of honor." But the Bible contains no such thing as an idealized Israelite, "the Woman," "the Righteous," and so on (M. Sternberg, *The Poetics of Biblical Narrative* [Bloomington: Indiana University Press, 1985], 253). Furthermore, David McCracken's remark (about the Gospels) is valid here as well. He writes, "in conveying these 'worlds'—the normal world, the carnival of violence [termed in this essay on Esther *parody of parody*], and the kingdom of God—the gospels focus not on who individual characters *are,* as essential beings, or on their roles as actants, but on their relational activity" ("Character in the Boundary," 39).

17. As is true in general in Esther, the reader also knows little about the person Haman; but from the little we know, one thing is sure: Haman would not pass the test as described in Proverbs 6:16–19 (NRSV): "There are six things that YHWH hates, seven that are in abomination to him: haughty eyes, a lying tongue, and hands that shed innocent blood, a heart that devises wicked plans, feet that

hurry to run to evil, a lying witness who testifies falsely, and one who sows discord in a family."

18. See Proverbs 26:27 (NRSV): "Whoever digs a pit will fall into it, and a stone will come back on the one who starts it rolling."

19. To such a plot can be applied the following Bakhtinian judgment on Dostoevsky's work: "Catastrophe is not finalization. It is the culmination, in collision and struggle, of points of view" ("Toward a Reworking of the Dostoevsky Book," appendix 2 in *PDP,* 298).

20. See Revelations 3:16.

21. The Greek version more modestly claims fifteen thousand people killed (9:16).

22. See above, in chapter 4, the discussion of *first line* and *second line* in novelistic history. To see Esther as belonging to a second-line novelistic category is simply implausible. The reverse, however, is not inconceivable. Dostoevsky *could* have written a first-line type of novel. That he did not is what makes him a genius deserving the praise that Bakhtin showers on him.

23. See *DI,* 400.

24. That the Jews in Esther refrain from taking any booty from their enemies provides yet another means of distinguishing Purim from Passover; see Exodus 12:35–36.

25. Megillah 7a mentions this extraordinary fact as a proof that Esther was inspired by the Holy Spirit.

26. Bakhtin credits Dostoevsky with the *creation* of the polyphonic novel. It is well-deserved praise for one of the greatest novelists of all time. I would, however, suggest that the author of Job came at the very least close to such a literary creation. This, by the way, seems to have been intuited by Bakhtin himself (see appendix 1 to *PDP,* especially 280).

27. See Philippians 3:7.

28. André LaCocque, *Ruth, A Continental Commentary,* trans. K. C. Hanson (Minneapolis, Minn.: Fortress Press, 2004), 6.

29. This, by the way, applies also to the author of Ruth. If the author can be said to identify with Naomi, it is evident that she is at least as much in need of Ruth as Ruth is in need of her.

30. See chapter 4, "A Trio of Women."

31. Compare Jean Racine, *Esther,* act 2, scene 7:

ESTHER: "Mes filles, soutenez votre reine éperdue
Je me meurs . . . (Elle tombe évanouie).

32. So Esther 9:30, in the Miqra'oth Gedoloth, without indication by Rashi on which rabbinic source he relies.

33. Without identifying Mordecai as the author of the book, Shelomo D. Goitein sees in the avoidance by the author of any mention of God the sign of a modest and humble man who wanted to distance his work from earlier sacred writings ("Omanuth hassippur ba-mikra," in *Torath shimushei ha-lashon ha-ivrith beyameinu*, vol. 1, 82–101, Beer-Sheba: Ha Makhon Haskalah Gabohah Banegeb, 1967).

34. Some critics understand Esther 9:20 to mean that Mordecai wrote only what is found in verses 24–25, and here again Mordecai describes the events as occurring without him.

35. I shall say more about an ambiguous aspect of Mordecai's personality in what follows. (See chapter 6 of this volume, the section titled "Purim's Place in the Book of Esther.")

36. This is especially conspicuous in Esther 6:6. See chapter 1 in this volume, the section titled "Is There an Evolution of the Characters in Esther?" On this, see also Jack Sasson, "Esther," in *The Literary Guide to the Bible*, ed. Robert Alter and Frank Kermode (Cambridge, Mass.: Harvard University Press, 1987), 336.

37. *DI*, 257.

38. *DI*, 105.

39. *DI*, 95.

40. Contrast with the book of Deuteronomy, for instance, in which the protagonists are YHWH and Moses, while the people have practically no voice.

41. Bakhtin, *Mikhail Bakhtine, Esthétique et théorie du roman*, 239–60.

42. Note that, in both cases, the people's response is a collective fast (see Zech. 7:5; 8:19).

43. As Harold Bloom writes, "the [present] ideologies of Resentment have largely displaced theology" (*Where Shall Wisdom*, 44). See also note 45.

44. Shemaryahu Talmon, " 'Wisdom' in the Book of Esther," *Vetus Testamentum* 13 (1963): 441.

45. M. A. Bernstein writes, "Indeed, to be abject is never to have experienced the monster's single-mindedness. Instead, there is a cringing defiance deprived of any trust in one's own power and vitiated by a self-contempt at least equivalent to one's loathing for others. His whole being is, in essence, a helpless dialogue between the urge to curse and attack without restraint and the anxiety immediately aroused by even the slightest danger" ("The Poetics of *Ressentiment*," in *Rethinking Bakhtin*, 222).

46. As to Vashti, I refer the reader to my discussion in the preceding chapter. One will also find an extensive reflection on Orpah in my recent commentary on the book of Ruth (*Ruth*).

47. See René Girard's *Le Bouc émissaire* (Paris: Grasset, 1982), 34.

48. Auerbach, *Mimesis*, 404.

49. These unprotected people were called *hooligans* by the Stalinist regime.

50. The same is true of Hitler's "final solution."

51. Earlier, as Van Wijk-Bos points out, Ahasuerus did "forbid Vashti to come where she did not want to be in the first place, the king's presence" (*Ruth and Esther*, 75). It belongs to farcical comedy to have the king use his sham authority strictly to forbid the insubordinate party to do what the latter has already decided she would not do anyway. This element of humor is darkened, however, by the substitution of a coercive command for a free declaration of independence.

52. Berg has stressed the comic paradox of Haman's "elevation" by the king until he is "elevated" physically on the huge gallows of his own making (7:9, 10).

53. See Exodus 4:21; 7:3; 10:17; and 11:10; and Romans 9:18; among others.

54. See Daniel 7:8, 11.

55. Gerleman, *Esther*, 23.

56. McKane, "A Note on Esther IX and 1 Samuel XV." Clines (*Esther Scroll*, 30) sees in the Jewish restraint a sign of "the weakness of the plot's conception." The same critic is, however, right to observe a "downplay of the 'victory' idea" in that the text characterizes the festival as days of "rest."

57. So Rav Valerio, *Yad Hammelek*, on Esther 9:15 (a sixteenth-century commentary, quoted by Meir Zlotowitz, *The Megillah* [New York: Mesorah, 1979], 123).

58. Clines, *Esther Scroll*, 18.

59. It is not the place here to fully discuss the question, already mentioned above, of "authenticity" as regards Esther 9–10. In an essay such as the present one, the *textus receptus* is the literary authority. Even if Paton, Eissfeldt, Clines, and others were right in seeing these chapters as an addition to an "original" story, the chapters would still require interpretation. Furthermore, one can find convincing arguments in favor of these chapters' "authenticity" in the beautiful and concise development by Adele Berlin on chapter 10 as a "coda" in perfect parallel with the beginning of the story in chapter 1 (*Esther*, 94–95); in addition, see the work of Bruce William Jones ("So-Called Appendix") and Sandra Berg (*The Book of Esther*).

60. See LaCocque, "The Different Versions of Esther," *Biblical Interpretation* 7, no. 3 (1999): 301–22.

61. See note 52 above. In the Gospel of John, and from an antipodal perspective, Christ is "elevated" on the cross before being elevated to the right hand of God. In Esther, Haman ends up by being hoisted to the pike. (The book of Esther rather uses the verb "to hang.")

62. The LXX is not entirely wrong, however. The Hebrew text tells us that, when Haman was promoted to the premiership in the kingdom, courtiers did prostrate and bow down before him. The combination of the two verbs is "otherwise reserved for the homage to God." (See Levenson, *Esther*, 67.)

63. See Moore, *Esther*, 36–37. Levenson calls this reading a possible theory but one without corroboration (*Esther*, 67).

64. Unless one understands the words "children and women" in Esther 8:11–12, with Robert Gordis, to be in apposition to "waging hostility against them"

[their children and women]. See Gordis, "Studies in the Esther Narrative," *Journal of Biblical Literature* 95, no. 1 (1976): 43–58. Actually, the text of Esther 9:6 seems to indicate that the Jews only killed men.

65. I do insist on this point in my book on Genesis 2–3, *The Trial of Innocence* (2006).

66. Morson and Emerson, *Mikhail Bakhtin: Creation of a Prosaics*, 138.

67. This way, older works "have proved capable of uncovering in each new era and against ever new dialogizing backgrounds ever new aspects of meaning; their semantic content literally continues to grow, to further create out of itself" (*DI*, 421).

68. "Great novelistic images continue to grow and develop even after the moment of their creation" (*DI*, 422). Bakhtin also says, "The text lives only by coming into contact with another text (with context). Only at the point of this contact between texts does a light flash, illuminating both the posterior and anterior, joining a given text to a dialogue" (*SG*, "Toward a Methodology for the Human Sciences," 162).

Chapter 6

1. Note that the NRSV translation is weak here. The theme of "reversal of fortune" is common in the Bible (see Ps. 30:11; Lam. 5:15; Isa. 61:3; Jer. 31:13; and so on). It is, however, generally attributed to a divine intervention.

2. See Levenson (*Esther*, 8): he draws a V-shape picture, showing Esther 6 as the crucial turning point at which the descent ends and the ascent begins. This is all the more interesting in that Esther 6 is pure carnival. René Girard summarizes carnival as an "effacement général des différences" (*La Violence et le sacré*, 179). This is often associated, he says, with violence. The festivities celebrate the foundational unanimity of the crowd and transfer the meaning of the past to the opposite of its initial malignancy. The mourning ingredient in Purim illustrates Girard's statement that the festivals in general suppose the continuity of the "sacrificial crisis" and its resolution (ibid., 181).

3. If only by sorrow for the slain enemy, see Megillah 10b; Sanhedrin 39b (about the Egyptians drowning in the Sea of Reeds). Cox added, "At such times we affirm life and gaiety despite the facts of failure and death. . . . [Besides,] the ability to celebrate with real abandon is most often found among people who are no strangers to pain and oppression" (Cox, *Feast of Fools*, 23–25).

4. As also Rainer Maria Rilke thought, "He who has not felt that reality is terrifying has no awareness of what it means to be real" (Maurice Blanchot's paraphrase in *Faux Pas* [Paris: Gallimard, 1993], 49).

5. Paraphrasing the Danish philosopher's little work, *Does a Man Have the Right to Let Himself Be Killed for Truth?* Maurice Blanchot says about the persecuted man

that he is a true witness, "because the persecutors, by striking him, establish in him a complete relationship of interiority between idea and existence" (Blanchot, *Faux Pas,* 21).

6. Death, Bakhtin said, "is the necessary link in the process of the people's growth and renewal. It is the 'other side' of birth" (*RAHW,* 407). Although Bakhtin rejects in principle the Hegelian dialectic, we recognize in this Bakhtinian maxim a Hegelian synthesis. Misery is everywhere but always surpassed to the extent that the fault is overcome by reconciliation, and so on. See also René Girard, *La Violence et le sacré,* 379, for example.

7. Bakhtin said, "Nothing is absolutely dead; every meaning will have its homecoming festival" ("Methodology," in *SG,* 170).

8. See the section "Purim's Place in the Book of Esther," later in this chapter.

9. Sometimes, it is true, reality surpasses fiction, and a tyrant is found disheveled in a rat hole.

10. Bakhtin speaks of private reveling as being "no longer the 'banquet of all the world,' in which all take part [see here Esther 9:27: "and all who joined the Jews"], but an intimate feast with hungry beggars at the door." He adds, "It is a picture of ghettoing, not an expression of social justice" (*RAHW,* 302).

11. Shelomo D. Goitein goes so far as to suggest that the recurring banquets in the book of Esther are the diaspora equivalent of the Palestinian "land flowing with milk and honey." See Goitein, *Iyunim ba-Mikra* (Tel-Aviv: Yibeneh, 1958), 59.

12. Those females are unwilling prostitutes and the uncanny precursors of numerous modern sisters, particularly the thousands of Korean women herded into brothels by the Japanese army in World War II.

13. As a period of four years elapses between Vashti's revocation and the selection of Esther (compare 1:3 and 2:16), "there may be a hint of comedy in the length of the [king's] period of anger," says Levenson (*Esther,* 54). Levenson adds, "Even the king's sex life requires commissioners. The personal has become the political, and both have become laughable" (ibid.).

14. Theodor H. Gaster, *Myth, Legend, and Custom in the Old Testament,* vol. 2 (New York: Harper and Row, 1969), 655.

15. Bakhtin mentions, among the secondary rituals of carnival, the "exchanges of gifts" (*PDP,* 125). The *manoth* (portions) in Esther 9:19 (see also 2:9) are a general exchange of presents; the analogy with Nehemiah 8:10–12 is real. But Ezra's and Nehemiah's commands to eat rich food and drink sweet beverages, to revel and send food to the poor, happen in a noncarnivalesque context.

16. One remembers the passage in Ecclesiastes 10:16 (NRSV): "Alas for you, O land, . . . when your princes feast in the morning!"

17. Levenson, *Esther,* 92.

18. J. Lewy, "Old Assyrian puru'um and purum," *Revue Hittite et Asianique* 36 (1939): 117–24. See. A. Ungnad, "Eponymen," *RLA* 2 (1938): 420, 448.

19. So Theodor H. Gaster, *Purim and Hanukkah,* 4; Carey A. Moore, *Esther,* xlix; J. C. H. Lebram, "Purimfest und Estherbuch," *Vetus Testamentum* 22 (1972): 208–22; and Bernhard W. Anderson, *The Book of Esther,* IB 3 (Nashville: Abingdon, 1954), 824. For Arndt Meinhold ("Die Gattung der Josephgeschichte," 87), Purim was a preexistent foreign festival, already celebrated by Jews in the diaspora. To shore it up as a Jewish celebration, the authority of both Mordecai and Esther was necessary (see 9:20–21; 9:29–32).

20. The three-day fast Esther ordered the community to undertake in chapter 4, surprisingly, contravenes the seder meal of Passover; this may be an important reason why Purim and its accompanying legend, the book of Esther, are conspicuously absent in Qumran (see Isaac Kalimi, "The Book of Esther and the Dead Sea Scrolls' Community"). Indeed, Esther displays an astounding indifference, to say the least, toward Pentateuchal ordinances. As I said earlier, the subversive character of the scroll is its main ingredient; it cannot be overstated.

21. Several books in the Bible begin or end with a celebration: Exodus, Nehemiah, Job, the noncanonical Judith, and Esther.

22. The displacement of Purim from the thirteenth of Adar to the fourteenth and fifteenth is probably due to a conflict on the thirteenth of Adar with festivities celebrating Judah Maccabee's victory over General Nikanor (1 Macc. 7:48–49; 2 Macc. 15:36). It explains retrospectively Esther's request for a second day of resistance in 9:13 (see notes in *Traduction Oecuménique de la Bible,* ad loc.).

23. And, also like the Sabbath day, as described by *P,* loaded with words about work (nine within three verses; see Genesis 2:1–3), so painful memories are not absent during Purim.

24. Barbara G. Myerhoff says, "Ritual states enduring and underlying patterns, thus connecting past, present, and future, abrogating history and time" ("A Death in Due Time: Construction of Self and Culture in Ritual Drama," in MacAloon, *Rite, Drama,* 152). Roberto Da Matta ("Carnival in Multiple Planes," 224) agrees, "In Carnival, in its typical space, the instant overcomes time."

25. Victor Turner says about "some propositions" that they are "liminal, in the sense that they are suspensions of daily reality, occupying privileged spaces where people are allowed to think about how they think, about the terms in which they conduct their thinking, or to feel about how they feel in daily life" ("Liminality and the Performative Genres," in MacAloon, *Rite, Drama,* 22). He adds, "Any society that hopes to be imperishable must carve out for itself a piece of space and a period of time in which it can look honestly at itself" (ibid., 40).

26. Cox, *Feast of Fools,* 82.

27. See Michael Fishbane, *Text and Texture: Close Readings of Selected Biblical Texts* (New York: Schocken Books, 1979), xii, 98.

28. Samuel Pagán, "Esther," in *The International Bible Commentary,* ed. William Farmer, Sean McEvenue, Armando Levoratti, and David L. Dungan (Collegeville, Minn.: Liturgical Press, 1998), 707–21.

29. Liminal but not subaltern, for the same phrase is used of Daniel when he was vizier of Babylonia (Dan. 2:48–49).

30. Later on, Purim will parody this "through reversals of status. Many communities in medieval times appointed a Purim king. Typically a young boy, the king received a type of mock authority for the course of the holiday" (Rubenstein, "Purim, Liminality, and Communitas," 253). The substitution of the god Marduk or his representative, the king, for the paternal figure is evident. The succession of weeping and laughter during the ceremony recalls the ancient pattern going back to totemism (see Freud, *Totem and Taboo*).

31. Laniak, *Shame and Honor,* 101.

32. We may here echo Cox's saying, "In heaven, hope . . . held only in the most daring act of effrontery . . . is no longer necessary and laughter reigns" (*Feast of Fools,* 156).

33. See the discussion in chapter 2 of this volume.

34. So says Charles Lock. He adds, "If folk culture is hegemonic there can be no carnival, no rebellion from *below,* no celebration of the lower bodily stratum, because there is no axis to provide degrees of comparison" ("Carnival and Incarnation: Bakhtin and Orthodox Theology," *Journal of Literature and Theology* 5, no. 1 [1991]: 75). Even in the arguably wildest of all carnival manifestations, in Rio de Janeiro, there is "a center, a subject, or a destiny for which [it] take[s] place," says Roberto Da Matta ("Carnival in Multiple Planes," 225).

35. "Paradoxically, [the ritual] uses repetition to deny the empty repetitiveness of the unremarked, unattended human and social experience," says Barbara Myerhoff ("A Death in Due Time," 173). She quotes (175) Adam Mendilow: "These [moments] are pinpoints of great intensity, concentrations of universal awareness, antithetical to the diffuseness of life" (*Time and the Novel* [London and New York: P. Nevill, 1952], 137).

36. Cox, *Feast of Fools,* 7.

37. An expert in ritual theory, Barbara Myerhoff writes, "ritual . . . is unique in its capacity to convince us of the unbelievable and make traditional that which is unexpected and new" ("A Death in Due Time," 151).

38. Contra Clines, *Esther Scroll,* 42.

39. In contrast, the fifth-century B.C.E. Jewish colony of Elephantine (South Egypt) requested the backing of the Jerusalem authorities (see the "Yedoniah Communal Archive" [letters], *ANET* 491–92).

40. See John M. Wiebe, "Esther 4:14: 'Will Relief and Deliverance Arise for the Jews from Another Place?' " *Catholic Biblical Quarterly* 53, no. 3 (1991): 413.

41. So Michael Fox, *Character and Ideology,* 63; also his "Religion in the Book of Esther," 139, note 19.

42. Karen H. Jobes, *Esther,* has called attention to the lexical parallel of Esther 4:14–16 with Joel 2:12–15, a text that is unambiguously religious (see Jobes, *Esther,* New International Version [Grand Rapids, Mich.: Zondervan, 1999], 135–

37). Contrary to Jobes, however, Esther does not necessarily depend on Joel here; the vocabulary in both places may be traditional in a context of mourning and fasting. If there is, nevertheless, dependence, one must still explain why the borrowing text has stripped the Joel text of its religiosity.

43. See Numbers 22–24. See also the discussion in chapter 4 of this volume.

44. A similar expression ("peoples of the lands") is found in Ezra 9:2, 11, and in Nehemiah 10:29, 31, designating gentiles.

45. As Adele Berlin judiciously says, "religious conversion [of the "Judaizing" Persians] seems far-fetched in a book in which any mention of religious practice is studiously avoided" (*Esther,* 80).

46. Gerleman, *Esther,* 132.

47. This is no trifle. Elias Bickerman (in chapter 6, "The Law of the Jews," of his work *The Jews in the Greek Age*) says the situation that obtained "in Jerusalem meant the triumph of orthodoxy and, further, the establishment of the Temple and its priesthood as preeminent in the Holy City. The second phase . . . was the promulgation in 458 of the Torah as the authoritative code for the Jews" (*The Jews in the Greek Age* [Cambridge, Mass.: Harvard University Press, 1988], 30).

48. See, for example, Laniak, *Shame and Honor,* 134, note 22.

49. As David Clines says, the message here is "a reassurance to diaspora Jewry that collaboration with the authorities is no sin against Jewish identity. For it is possible for Mordecai *the Jew* to stand next in rank to the king, *and* at the same time to be popular with his coreligionists (10:3). The story has given the lie to Haman's initial charge that 'it is not for the king's profit to tolerate' the Jews (3:8)" (*Ezra, Nehemiah, Esther,* 262).

50. Gerleman, *Esther,* especially 11, 14.

51. See Bickerman, *Four Strange Books of the Bible,* 198.

52. See Arndt Meinhold, "Die Gattung der Josephgeschichte," part 2.

53. Note, in Esther 1:13, the close association of "times" and "laws."

54. Characteristically, when Judaism became a diaspora religion, Rabbi Joshua ben Karchah, writing in the second century C.E., said there were weightier reasons to celebrate Purim than there were to celebrate Passover (Megillat Taanit, 12).

55. Morphologically speaking, the controlled breaking of a taboo is foundational to human society. In "The Horror of Incest" (chapter 1 in *Totem and Taboo*), Freud reports that, among those whom he calls "the savages," even the taboo of incest at times is cancelled and all rules admittedly broke down during sacred orgies. "A festival is a permitted, or rather an obligatory, excess, a solemn breach of a prohibition . . . the festive seeking is produced by the liberty to do what is as a rule prohibited" (*Totem and Taboo,* 140).

56. *SG,* 126.

57. "Author and Hero," *AA,* 127–28.

58. *AA,* 56.

59. *SG,* 126.

60. *SG,* 127. Even with the sublime Torah, we are still dealing with human accommodations of Truth. Speaking of the law regarding divorce in Israel (see Deut. 24:1–4), Jesus told his followers, "Moses wrote this prescription because of your hardness of heart" (Mark 10:5). The Law is a "pedagogue," said St. Paul. It shows the way to the Master, but it is not the Master (see Gal. 3:24).

61. Cited by Abraham Joshua Heschel in *The Wisdom of Heschel,* translated by Ruth Marcus Goodhill (New York: Farrar, Straus and Giroux, 1970), 255.

62. See Proverbs 11:10 (NRSV): "When it goes well with the righteous, the city rejoices; and when the wicked perishes there is jubilation."

63. As Bakhtin writes, "The author [of the novel or novella] may also make use of someone else's discourse for his own purposes, by inserting a new semantic intention into a discourse which already has, and which retains, an intention of its own" (*PDP,* 193).

64. Bakhtin, ibid. In Thomas Greene's words, "Every creative imitation mingles filial rejection with respect, just as every parody pays its own oblique homage" (*The Light in Troy: Imitation and Discovery in Renaissance Poetry* [New Haven, Conn.: Yale University Press, 1982], 46; cited by Linda Hutcheon, "Modern Parody and Bakhtin," in Morson and Emerson, *Rethinking Bakhtin,* 92). Hutcheon astutely states that parody is "not always at the expense of the parodied text." Parody, she says, involves "a productive-creative approach to tradition" (ibid., 87–89). Parody, says Morson, in his turn, presupposes "the existence (or reader's assumption of existence) of a set of conventions governing the interpretation of those works" [that is, the "target" work and its parody]. He adds, "parodies are often directed at narrative genres in which the action unfolds in a time radically different from everyday time or discontinuous with the time of reading (e.g., epic, romance, and pastoral)" (Morson, *Rethinking Bakhtin,* 74).

65. As Abraham D. Cohen writes, "Purim which, to the nemesis of the Jew and to an alien system of thought, affirmed the operation of chance and fate in the universe, becomes, for the Jew, the anti-chance symbol, the symbol of that which God so readily controls to *His* ends" ("'Hu Ha-Goral': The Religious Significance of Esther," *Judaism* 23 [1974]: 94).

66. Although, consequent with its secularism, the book of Esther does not use the term *ḥag,* as in the Pentateuch, but the word *mishteh* to designate the multiple banquets in the story.

67. *RAHW,* 11.

68. For, irony is "an all-embracing crystal-clear and serene glance, which is the very glance of art itself, that is to say: a glance of the utmost freedom and calm and of an objectivity untroubled by any moralism," said Thomas Mann ("The Art of the Novel," in *The Creative Vision: Modern European Writers on Their Art,* ed. H. M. Block and H. Salinger [New York: Grove, 1960], 88).

69. According to some Jewish traditions, in the days of the Messiah all the festivals but the days of Purim will become obsolete (see Harris, "Purim," 170).

70. This manifestation of carnival has not been emphasized by Bakhtin.

71. See also on this Nicole Duran, "Who Wants to Marry a Persian King?" 83. She speaks accurately of female power as "deconstruction of the male edifice."

72. Caryl Emerson, *First Hundred Years,* 163.

73. See ibid., 164: "This body [celebrated in carnival] is inviting and available to all without discrimination."

74. See note 68 above.

75. About carnival, Roberto Da Matta speaks of suspension, inversion, and dislocation. See his "Carnival in Multiple Planes."

76. One example of which is found in 7:8: Esther does not protest when the king erroneously thinks that Haman is attempting to rape her!

77. As Sidnie Crawford writes, "in fact, since Ahasuerus and his court, including Haman, have no idea that [Esther] is a Jew, she must be quite assimilated" ("Esther and Judith," 68).

78. See Esther, chapters 6–7; the text pushes the irony to the point of slapstick when it describes a gesture of Haman's that the king mistakes for an attempt to rape the queen.

79. In the "corresponding" book of Judith, the whole Assyrian army is killed on the battlefield.

80. Milan Kundera, *The Unbearable Lightness of Being* (New York: Harper and Row, 1984).

81. *RAHW,* 268.

82. Clines, *Ezra,* 322.

83. The death in the Sinai desert of a whole generation is the condition for entrance into the Promised Land (see. Num. 32:13; Deut. 2:14).

84. *RAHW,* 255–56. See Carl G. Jung: "Ultimately, every individual life is at the same time the eternal life of the species" (*Collected Works of C. G. Jung,* vol. 11 [Princeton, N.J.: Princeton University Press, 1969], par. 146).

85. Within the tension that exists between the respective meals of Passover and of Purim, the carnivalesque is maintained in the tradition surrounding Purim. As one of the names of Passover is *leil shimurim,* "the night of watching," the parodic haggadah for Purim is called *haggadath leil shikurim* (the night of the drunkards); see Jeffrey Rubenstein, "Purim, Liminality, and Communitas," 259.

86. *RAHW,* 167.

87. But not automatically, that is, cyclically, as the celebration of Purim is the outcome of a decision, even an oath, on the part of the Jews (Esther 9:27–32).

88. See chapter 2, note 1.

89. Cox says, "The religious man is one who grasps his own life within a larger historical and cosmic setting. He sees himself as part of a greater whole, a longer story in which he plays a part" (Cox, *Feast of Fools,* 14).

90. Bakhtin, "Toward a Methodology," *DI*, 169–70. All this belongs to a time conception that Bakhtin calls "the unified time of collective human life" (*DI*, 214), when its distinction from private life and the focus on the individual had not yet occurred (say, through the Hellenization of the known world in the fourth century B.C.E.). Until then, human life was lived in a "folkloric time" (see, for example, *DI*, 218), such as it was in the classic epos, where "*Individuums* are representatives of the social whole, events of their lives coincide with the events of the life of the social whole, and the significance of such events (on the individual as well as on the social plane) is identical" (ibid.). Purim is reenactment of the social drama, in which Victor Turner sees "the major form of plural reflexivity in human social action" ("Liminality," 25). Again in parallel with the remarkable lack of individual inner life and of "what a character is thinking, what he is experiencing, his internal dialogue" in Rabelais (*DI*, 239), we find the same obvious absence in the Hebrew Esther.

91. See Abraham D. Cohen, "Hu Ha-Goral." For Cohen, however, the *pur* is a symbol of chance-fate. But, as Michael Fox responds, "fate is the *opposite* of chance—it is its negation," and Fox concurs with the idea that the casting of *pur* is "a means of divination, and it presumed Divine control of events" ("The Religion in the Book of Esther," 141).

92. It lies within the range of possibilities that the story of Esther and Mordecai existed before its present connection with Purim in Esther 9. There is no certainty about it, but the same suspicion is valid as regards Daniel 1–6, which may date to the fourth century B.C.E., thus preceding by two centuries the rest of the book (see my *Daniel in His Time* [Columbia: University of South Carolina Press, 1988], 62–69).

93. See Irwin Rhode, *Der griechische Roman und seine Vorläufer*, 4th ed. (Hildescheim: Georg Olms, 1960). Already in 1891, Heinrich Zimmern ("Zur Frage nach dem Ursprung des Purimfestes," *Zeitschrift für die Alttestamentliche Wissenschaft* 11 [1891]: 157–69) identified Haman, Zeresh, and Vashti as three Elamite gods: Humman, his consort Geresh, and Mashti, the latter goddess dethroned by the Babylonian Ishtar (Esther). In Susa, Ishtar appeared among other things as *ʾstr šarrat* (Ishtar the Queen), and Humman was replaced by Marduk.

94. S. Averintsev rightly says "that is as old as the world itself" ("Bakhtin, Laughter, and Christian Culture," 86). J. G. Frazer (*Taboo and the Perils of the Soul: The Golden Bough, a Study in Magic and Religion, Part 1* [Oxford: Oxford University Press, 1994], 7–8) speaks of the primitive kingships and says that the king "lives hedged in by a ceremonious etiquette, a network of prohibitions and observances, of which the intention is not to contribute to his dignity, much less to his comfort. . . . He is dismissed ignominiously, and may be thankful if he escapes with his life. Worshipped as a god one day, he is killed as a criminal the next."

95. A feature of the carnivalesque is the uncanny donning of royal attires. The swapping of sorts of clothes, first by Haman, then by Mordecai, belongs to satire. As Bakhtin writes, "The object is broken apart, laid bare (its hierarchical orna-

mentation is removed): the naked object is ridiculous; its 'empty' clothing, stripped and separated from its person, is also ridiculous. What takes place is a comical operation of dismemberment" (*DI*, 24). Adele Berlin, in another context altogether, mentions Plutarch's *Artaxerxes* 5, where a certain Teribazus decks himself with the king's coat and with women's jewels (*Esther*, 60). The king laughs and says, "I permit you to wear the trinkets of a woman, and *the robe of a madman*" (my emphasis).

96. Cox speaks of "the harlequinesque Christ" (*Feast of Fools*, 141).

97. The "powers" understandably feel shaken when their inalterability is questioned. The often violent or demeaning treatment of blacks by white supremacists finds here one of its roots.

98. "A person has no sovereign internal territory, he is wholly and always on the boundary," says Bakhtin (*PDP*, appendix 2, 287).

99. *RAHW*, 98.

100. Note this element of chance—as in Ruth 2:3—that both recalls and forecasts the advent of the Greek romance, where chance constantly has the initiative, the heroes being in fact "acted" by *tukhè*. When about one century after the composition of the Masoretic text the LXX version of Esther creates a preface to the tale with a premonitory dream of Mordecai, we approach still more closely to the blossoming of that Greek literary genre, where such predictions appear in profusion.

101. Bakhtin, "Toward a Philosophy of the Act," in the Russian text, 112, 119 (cited by Morson and Emerson, *Mikhail Bakhtin: Creation of a Prosaics*, 31, 38).

Chapter 7

1. See Clines, *Esther Scroll: The Story of the Story*, 71–114.

2. Ibid., 151.

3. Ibid., 50.

4. Examples of such assimilation to "orthodoxy" abound, of course, both in biblical times and in Christian history.

5. If my thesis is right, incidentally, it will cast a shadow of doubt on Clines's rejection of alleged "non-authentic" developments that crept into the A-T. Note that, close to one century later, the same apologetic reworking is true in Josephus, whose *Jewish Antiquities*, for example (and all of his writings) aimed to demonstrate the congruity of "Judaism" and the Roman worldview. Not surprisingly, Ahasuerus is here a positive figure. In the A-T similarly, the abuse planned by the king and Haman is drastically reduced. The Jews here are to be sold as slaves and their children plundered (7:4). Esther finds this intolerable here, although she hypothetically evokes the same treatment in the MT without raising a complaint! The A-T also depicts the king as much more emotional, merciful, and upset by injustice.

As to Haman, he is a deceptive friend to the king, a traitor. For a more detailed discussion of the Esther A-Text, see my "Different Versions of Esther."

6. So Clines.

7. See Judges 4–5.

8. Clines, *Esther Scroll,* 152–53.

9. Clines writes (ibid., 153), "To the unbeliever . . . to the pagan, 'chance' is a name for chance, without any design or tendency or reliability."

10. In the secular world, a nonreligious document is simply profane. In the Jewish world, the same document becomes cryptically referential to religious traditions with, at times, a polemical purpose. The "Greek mentality" condemned Socrates for atheism.

11. Bakhtin, *DI,* 76.

12. Bakhtin, "The Chronotope," *DI,* 253.

13. As J. G. McConville astutely notes, "The only offenses which King Xerxes recognizes . . . are offenses against himself" ("Esther" in *Ezra, Nehemiah, and Esther,* Daily Study Bible Series [Edinburgh: St Andrew's Press; Philadelphia: Westminster Press, 1985], 184). He adds, "It is possible for peoples to survive under such kings. But there is no salvation in *trusting* them" (185).

14. See André LaCocque, "Esther: Enjeux théologiques des déplacements," *Lumière et Vie* 260 (October–December 2003): 33–48.

15. As Clement of Alexandria, speaking of the Christians in the world, said, "Every foreign country is a fatherland to them, and every fatherland is a foreign country" (*Exhortation to the Greeks,* 2). Timothy Laniak writes, "Esther is a reminder of the ancient order of priorities: Israel is a people first, and then a place. God is available to them first, and then as a designated somewhere (cf. 1 Kings 8:27)" ("*Esther's* Volkcentrism and the Reframing of Post-Exilic Judaism,"in Crawford and Greenspoon, *Esther in Modern Research,* 82).

16. Morson and Emerson write, "As a double-voiced word, parody, like stylization, allows us to sense the discourse of the other. Unlike stylization, parody subjects the other's words to harsh treatment. Specifically, it 'introduces into that discourse a semantic intention that is directly opposed to the original one' (*PDP,* 193). Parodistic discourse consequently becomes 'an arena of battle between two voices' (ibid.)" (Morson and Emerson, *Mikhail Bakhtin: Creation of a Prosaics,* 152).

17. Joseph has two dreams (Gen. 37:5, 9); two brothers intercede in his favor (37:21, 26); Joseph is twice described as imprisoned (39:20; 40:3); and so on. The parallels between the two stories are numerous. They become a verbatim similarity in Esther 3:4 and Genesis 39:10 (the enticement of Joseph by Potiphar's wife). The same situation obtains in Esther 4:16 and Genesis 43:14 (Jacob says that if he is to be bereaved, he will be). In Esther 7:4, Esther says about her and her people, "we have been sold," as is stated in Genesis 37:28 and 45:4. Many other examples could be offered.

18. In fact, there are three such mentions in the text, but while in 5:3 and 5:6, the verb is in the masculine form, in 7:2 it is in the feminine (to distinguish the latter from the other occurrences).

19. See Hermann Gunkel, *Esther* (Tübingen: J. C. B. Mohr, 1916); Henri Cazelles, "Note sur la composition du rouleau d'Esther," in *Lex Tua Veritas: Festschrift für Hubert Junker,* ed. H. Gross and F. Mussner, 17–29 (Trier: Paulinus, 1961); Hans Bardtke, "Neuere Arbeiten zum Estherbuch: Eine kritische Würdigung," *Ex Oriente Lux* 19 (1965/66): 519–49; J. C. H. Lebram, "Purimfest und Estherbuch"; compare Clines, *Esther Scroll,* 119–30.

20. Henri Cazelles, "Note sur la composition"; K. V. Helmer Ringgren, in "Das Buch Esther," also sees two motifs: "Esther" and "Mordecai-Haman" (7, 134).

21. Graham Pechey, "Philosophy and Theology in 'Aesthetic Activity,' " in Felch and Contino, *Bakhtin and Religion,* 48.

22. As Bakhtin writes, "A man never coincides with himself," and this, he adds, is due to the "unfinalizability of the person" (*PDP,* 59).

23. See André and Pierre LaCocque, *Jonah.*

24. See Bakhtin, "Author and Hero," *Art and Answerability,* 138.

25. Exodus Rabbah, ad loc.

26. *PDP,* 59.

27. *RAHW,* 464.

28. Interestingly enough, there exists a ritual in the Tunisian Djerba called in Arabic *chajba,* claustration, to which young maidens are subjected before marriage, in preparation for husbands they do not know in advance. They go through an elaborate treatment to make their skin as white as possible, to increase their weight, and so on.

29. Note that, in the ancient world, cosmetics and perfumes are indiscriminately used before lovemaking or war (see Ugarit, *Baʿal* I, ii, 1–42). Indeed, as regards Esther, she is preparing for competition with the other "candidates," and, more indirectly, for a fight with the wicked Haman.

30. There is "Humour in Names," as reads the subtitle of Yehuda T. Radday's article. He writes, the "no fewer than thirty nonentities who crowd the Persian Royal Court give the impression of a dumb chorus in an opera bouffe . . . the author describes a Byzantine-like court" (71, 72). It is also with a good deal of humor that the book of Esther lists Haman's sons' names. See "Humour in Names," in *On Humour and the Comic in the Hebrew Bible,* ed. Yehuda T. Radday and Athalya Brenner, 59–98 (Sheffield, Eng.: Almond Press, 1990).

31. I understand the last name listed, literally Vaizatha, to be a contraction of the conjunction *we-* followed by the name Aizatha.

32. Vladimir Propp, "Ritual Laughter in Folklore: A Propos of the Tale of the Princess Who Would Not Laugh, Nesmejana," in *Theory and History of Folklore,* ed. Anatoly Liberman, 124–46 (Manchester: University of Minnesota Press, 1984), 134; Emerson, *First Hundred Years,* 176.

33. *DI*, 195.
34. *DI*, 202.

Chapter 8

1. The biblical accent on the aesthetic is a remarkable element, showing the influence of Hellenism on late Hebrew literature: Joseph in Genesis is handsome (Gen. 39:6); Daniel and his companions are as well (Dan. 1:4); and so is Esther (Esther 2:7). Joseph, Daniel, and Mordecai are each described at some point as wearing magnificent kingly vestments (see Gen. 41:42; Dan. 5:29; and so on). Many other examples could be listed.

2. W. Lee Humphreys writes, "[It is] a harem story satirically showing how the willfulness of one pretty woman compelled the king and the highest officials of the realm to marshal all the instruments of government to assure male supremacy in the home" (Humphreys, "Esther, Book of," in *Interpreter's Dictionary of the Bible*, Suppl. vol. [Nashville, Tenn.: Abingdon, 1976], 280). Jon D. Levenson adds, "The council of ministers that is called to deliberate the king's inability to make his wife come to his party is a masterpiece of satire . . . the irony is exquisite [in the evocation of all the women's possible uprising]" (Levenson, *Esther*, 51).

3. *DI*, 385.

4. See Arthur A. Cohen, *The Tremendum: A Theological Interpretation of the Holocaust* (New York: Crossroad, 1981).

5. In contrast, see Daniel 1:4, 8, 12.

6. Bakhtin writes, "Metamorphosis serves as the basis for a method of portraying the whole of an individual's life in its more important moments of *crisis*: for showing *how an individual becomes other than what he was*. We are offered various sharply differing images of one and the same individual, images that are united in him as various epochs and stages in the course of his life. There is no evolution in the strict sense of the word; what we get, rather, is crisis and rebirth" (*DI*, 115). On Esther's development, see also William W. Hallo, "First Purim," 24.

7. Barring the Torah, among Jews the scroll of Esther is the most frequently copied book of the Bible.

8. See chapter 6, "Did Purim Replace 'Mosaic' Passover in the Eastern Diaspora?"

9. This chapter of Esther is the closest the author comes to what Bakhtin calls "the discourse of pathos."

10. *DI*, 394–95.

11. Susan Niditch writes, "Clearly, the folktale writer has no qualms about women using sexuality to obtain benefits for themselves or others. . . . Tricksters toy with the establishment. . . . They embody chaos, marginality, and indefinability" (*Underdogs and Tricksters: A Prelude to Biblical Folklore*, 141).

12. The Russian language contains similarly derived words in the terms *zadan* (the posited) and *zadanie* (the task); both appear in Bakhtin's vocabulary.

13. In this Late Hebrew document, sexuality is strikingly separate from reproduction—an aberration in earlier times. Sex as fecundation is now sex as (egotistic) pleasure, before becoming in our days, through a dramatic reversal of symbolism, sex as deadly. Incidentally, note that Esther is without parents and without progeny; Mordecai is without wife! "This is not a Jewish situation," as Monford Harris says ("Purim," 161). In the medieval *Sefer Hasidim,* one finds the interesting statement, based on Genesis 5:1, that because the book of Esther is unconcerned with the generations (*toldot*) of Israel, it "does not (therefore) contain the Divine name (YHWH)" (Harris, "Purim," 165).

14. After all, Euripides wrote *Medea* and D. H. Lawrence *Lady Chatterley's Lover*!

15. Levenson, *Esther,* 90.

16. Despite the Greek A-T! Esther's delaying tactics make her "a foil for his [the king's] and Haman's customary rashness," as Yehuda Radday says ("Esther with Humour," in Radday and Brenner, *On Humour and the Comic,* 305).

17. Laniak, *Shame and Honor,* 89, note 67.

18. Alter writes, "Feasting in Esther is closely associated with sexual comedy, and the incentive deployment of sexual comedy in the story is not readily reconciled with the sober purposes of covenantal faith" (*The World of Biblical Literature* [New York: Basic Books, 1992], 31).

19. Alter, ibid., 32, 33.

20. On visibility in the book of Esther, see Mieke Bal, "Lots of Writing." The literary device of retardation is a very effective one. It adds a powerful note of suspense to the story, especially welcome in a fast-paced narrative. Carey Moore quotes David N. Freedman as saying, "The third time is the charm in literary accounts. It is like the acrobat or magician who deliberately fails twice in trying to perform his most difficult feat, before succeeding on the third try. This enhances the suspense and the expectation of the audience, as well as winning for the performance the applause he deserves but is not likely to get if the audience thinks that there is no danger or limited need of skill to succeed" (Carey A. Moore, *Esther,* 58 [no reference to source]).

21. A third and last crisis occurs in the book, but it has nothing (?) to do with sexuality. Those who plotted to impose on the Jews their version of the "final solution" become themselves the victims of their intended victims (9:5–16).

22. Ironically, scholars have proposed as an etymology for the name Agag a derivation from the Akkadian *agagum,* "to get angry, furious." In Esther 3:5, to recall, Haman is said to have become "furiously angry."

23. See Proverbs 29:22.

24. Jack Sasson counts among the "droll" and "comic" elements of the book

the question raised by the king, "Who is he and where is he who dares plan such a thing?" when the king might well be the one Esther is describing ("Esther," 337). Clines (*Ezra,* 311) rightly says that, "In the double question there is a double irony: the first that it is the king who has 'sold' the Jews (Haman has 'bought' them); the second that, whether the culprit is the king in his fickleness with his subjects or Haman in his genocidal design, both the conspirators are 'here.'" See the dramatic irony of Oedipus's question to Creon, "Where are they [Laius's murderers] upon the earth?" And, a little later, Oedipus imagines that "the slayer of Laius might wish to take vengeance on me also with a hand as fierce." The parallel with Ahasuerus's suspicions of Haman's evil designs is obvious.

25. Laniak, *Shame and Honor,* 111.

26. On this, see also Moore, *Esther,* 67.

27. Jack Sasson writes about Esther 6 that Haman suggests to the king that he, Haman, be honored by receiving a "treatment (we know from cuneiform evidence) [was] reserved for substitute kings" ("Esther," 341).

28. A spin-off of the Akitu, the Sacees festival, celebrated in Cappadocia and Asia Minor, was a kind of bacchanalia. For five days, a slave or a man on death row is made "king," with all consequent honors, including access to the royal concubines; then he is crucified (so Strabo xi.8, 4; see Esther 7:8–10). It is mentioned by Nietzsche in *The Birth of Tragedy* (sec. 2) with the judgment that "human beings regressed to the condition of tigers and monkeys."

29. In his book *Voprosy literatury i estetiki,* the section titled "Shapes of Time and Chronotope; The Functions of the Scoundrel, of the Buffoon, and of the Fool in the Novel." See *Mikhail Bakhtine, esthétique et théorie du roman,* 307–8.

30. Samuel Pagán, "Esther," 717b.

31. On the compounded irony of the whole scene, see Clines, *Ezra,* 312. I see that Adele Berlin understands the king's reaction the same way I do (*Esther,* 64–65, 70).

32. In the perspective of Solomon Alkabez's *Sefer Menot ha-Levi: Midrash Megillat Esther* [1522] (Jerusalem: Ofer ha-Ayalim, 1999), the king affected to be angry at Haman when he saw him bent over the couch of the queen.

33. One remembers the role played in the book of Judith by Judith's servant. See the eighteenth-century works of Marivaux and Lesage, among others (for example, see Marivaux, *Le Jeu de l'amour et du hasard,* 1730).

34. But no one, of course, can compete with Esther's use of rhetoric in presenting her "request" and "petition" to the king. Linda Day (*Three Faces,* especially 201) judiciously insists on Esther's balance in the MT. This, we add, is one of the main requirements of wisdom.

35. The Mishnah in j. Megillah 3.8 counts Harbona among the righteous gentiles.

36. In Esther 7:8, the LXX has Haman averting his face from the king.

37. Other biblical texts speak of covering the face. The most famous, of

course, is Exodus 34, in which Moses is compelled to veil his face (with a *misweh*) because of the blinding sheen of his skin after he has spoken with God "face-to-face" (Exod. 33:11). Another example appears in 1 Kings 19:13, in which Elijah covers his head to avoid looking at the theophany. By all the evidence, the author of Esther offers a parody or inverse meaning of those traditions.

38. Hosea 8:7.

39. As they do in Song of Songs 8:6, for example. During the defense of his dissertation on Rabelais's work, Bakhtin protested against the idea that the carnival of the Middle Ages was carefree. Laughter and death are intertwined, he said, death and pain, but death never has the last word. (See Emerson, *First Hundred Years,* 96.) Here again, a quote from Bakhtin's work is fitting: "Death is not the negation of life . . . but part of life as a whole—its indispensable component, the condition of its constant renewal and rejuvenation. . . . Death is included in life, and together with birth determines its eternal movement" (*RAHW,* 50).

40. *PDP,* 126. Bakhtin elsewhere and often speaks of "death pregnant with life." No renewal occurs, he says, but through death. (*PDP,* 127: "everything is reborn and renewed through death.")

41. This setting for the book distinguishes it from the picaresque, a related genre in which the hero is found in the streets or the marketplace.

42. The mysterious connection of woman with death and rebirth is emphasized by Bakhtin: "The popular tradition is in no way hostile to woman and does not approach her negatively. In this tradition woman is essentially related to the material bodily stratum; she is the incarnation of this stratum that degrades and regenerates simultaneously" (*RAHW,* 240).

43. Morson and Emerson, *Mikhail Bakhtin: Creation of a Prosaics,* 451, paraphrasing *RAHW,* 240.

44. See *RAHW,* 240.

45. See *RAHW,* 240–41.

46. Nicole Duran, "Who Wants to Marry a Persian King?" 74.

47. See Linda Day, *Three Faces,* 44.

48. See Klara Butting, "Esther: A New Interpretation of the Joseph Story in the Fight Against Anti-Semitism and Sexism," in Brenner, *Ruth and Esther,* 240. Judiciously, Butting adds, "This connection links the solution of the question of women's rights inseparably to the deliverance of the Jewish people from the threat of the other nations" (ibid., 244).

49. Interestingly enough, one finds the same kingly impotence in the Chanson de Roland (LXII, 779; late tenth century) when King Charlemagne, against his own will, must appoint Roland to command the rear guard.

50. See Daniel 6:9, 13.

51. See Mieke Bal, "Lots of Writing," 235: "the writ is issued (by whom?); it is drawn up in the king's name, which specifically means not by him but for him by

someone else; and it is sealed with the king's signet, which is no longer on his finger. The stamp intended to validate the identity of the writer becomes instead the index of anonymous writing."

52. See LaCocque, *Romance, She Wrote.*

53. See LaCocque, *Feminine Unconventional.*

54. Rounding up the empire's virgins required a military operation; they are brought to the palace by officers of the state (2:3).

55. The so-called Stockholm syndrome.

56. Hence, the scandal of Job's predicament.

57. In 3 Maccabees, King Ptolemy becomes the enemy of the Jews despite having been saved by a Jew (albeit an apostate). In this story as well, the potentate's plans are overturned and the Egyptian Jews' lament is changed into praise (1:32). An annual festival commemorates the Jews' vindication (6:36; see 6:31; 7:19: "as long as they live in a foreign land"). J. G. McConville writes, "The character of Haman would be unbelievable had he not been replicated countless times in history and most appallingly in our own century" ("Esther," in *Ezra, Nehemiah, and Esther,* 165).

58. The parallel between thralldom and murder is starkly drawn by Esther in her indictment of Haman before the king (7:4).

59. Levenson, *Esther,* 56.

60. A blatant example of this is provided by *The Merchant of Venice,* composed some three hundred years after the Jews' complete expulsion from England!

61. Pace Clines.

62. Corneille, *Le Cid.*

63. Crawford, "Esther and Judith," 69.

64. In fact, the traditionally keen interest in history of the Israel of old is now fading away, replaced by scrupulous fulfillment of the mitzvoth. For all practical purposes, the history "that counts" is deemed to have occurred in biblical times (see Yosef H. Yerushalmi, *Zakhor: Jewish History and Jewish Memory* [Seattle: University of Washington Press, 1982]).

65. As Baldwin writes, "Civil disobedience of a minor nature is seen to be justified in a greater cause, namely, the genuine good of the state (7:4)" (Joyce G. Baldwin, *Esther,* 28).

66. Laniak, *Shame and Honor,* 164.

67. About Esther 9:12, Clines (*Ezra,* 324) notes the absence of the king, in contradistinction to 5:1–2; 6:4–5; and 8:1, 15. We are less surprised than Clines at this eclipse of the king. For the Jewish sages, Ahasuerus is a *tipeš* (a moron), corresponding to the designation *kesil* (a fool) in Proverbs 29:11.

68. At one point, Ahasuerus is ironically presented as speaking like God. In Esther 7:8, the expression "the word came out of his mouth" is strikingly reminiscent of the word that comes out of the mouth of YHWH, according to Isaiah 55:11 or 45:23 (see also Mal. 2:7; Job 37:2).

69. All mention of Esther ceases after Esther 9:32; Esther 10 focuses on Ahasuerus and Mordecai. This is less surprising when tallied with the "disappearance" of Ruth once her self-assigned mission is accomplished (Ruth 4:13). With the crisis initiated by the Jews' "foe and enemy," Esther has risen to her full stature; she retires into the background with its end.

70. Quoted by C. Aviner, "Pourim: La lutte finale contre Amaleq,"in *Etincelles—Cinquante questions de pensée juive* (Beth-El: Sifriat Hava, 1998), 23–24.

71. In Exodus 5:19–21, for example, the Israelite "bosses" blame Moses and Aaron, rather than the Pharaoh, for the harsh conditions of their labor.

72. As we know, Haman's accusation against the Jews was a common one in the Hellenistic world. See chapter 2, note 17.

73. On this in particular, see Sandra B. Berg, *The Book of Esther,* 103–13, esp. 103 and 113.

74. So it would seem, based on Daniel 5:2, 3. The point is contradicted, however, by Herodotus 5.18 and Plutarch *Artaxerxes 5.* On Persians' notorious predilection for liquor, see Herodotus 10.133.

75. Aristotle, *Poetics* 1452 *a,* 24–26.

76. One could almost think that Bakhtin had the book of Esther in mind when he wrote, "Carnival is the festival of all-annihilating and all-renewing time" (*PDP,* 124).

77. *SG,* 168.

78. Mikhail Bakhtin, *Estetika,* 373 (also *SG,* 170).

Bibliography

Alkabez, Solomon (Rav Shlomo Halevi, 1505–76). *Sefer Menot ha-Levi: Midrash Megillat Esther.* Jerusalem: Ofer ha-Ayalim, 1999.

Allen, Leslie, and Timothy Laniak. *Ezra, Nehemiah, Esther.* New International Biblical Commentary. Peabody, Mass.: Hendrickson, 2003.

Alter, Robert. *The Art of Biblical Narrative.* New York: Basic Books, 1981.

———. *The World of Biblical Literature.* New York: Basic Books, 1992.

Alter, Robert, and Frank Kermode, eds. *The Literary Guide to the Bible.* Cambridge, Mass.: Harvard University Press, 1987.

Anderson, Bernhard W. *The Book of Esther: Introduction and Exegesis.* Interpreter's Bible 3. Nashville, Tenn.: Abingdon, 1954.

Auerbach, Erich. *Mimesis.* Princeton, N.J.: Princeton University Press, 1953.

Averintsev, Sergei. "Bakhtin, Laughter, and Christian Culture." In Felch and Contino, *Bakhtin and Religion,* 79–95.

Aviner, Chlomo. "Pourim: La lutte finale contre Amaleq." In *Etincelles—Cinquante questions de pensée juive.* Beth-El: Sifriat Hava, 1998.

Babcock, Barbara. "Arrange Me into Disorder: Fragments and Reflections on Ritual Clowning." In MacAloon, *Rite, Drama,* 102–28.

Bakhtin, Mikhail. *Art and Answerability: Early Philosophical Essays by M. M. Bakhtin.* Edited by Michael Holquist and Vadim Liapunov. Austin: University of Texas Press, 1990.

———. *The Dialogic Imagination: Four Essays by M. M. Bakhtin.* Edited by Michael Holquist. Translated by Caryl Emerson and Michael Holquist. Austin: University of Texas Press, 1981.

———. *Estetika slovesnogo tvorchestva.* Edited by S. G. Bocharov. Moscow: Iskusstvo, 1979. Translated as "Toward a Methodology for the Human Sciences," in Bakhtin, *Speech Genres,* 159–72.

———. *Esthétique de la création verbale.* Paris: Gallimard, 1984. Translated by A. Ancouturier. In English: "Author and Hero in Aesthetic Activity," in Bakhtin, *Art and Answerability,* 4–256.

———. *Mikhail Bakhtine, esthétique et théorie du roman.* French translation by Daria Olivier. Paris: Gallimard, 1978.

———. *Problems of Dostoevsky's Poetics.* Edited and translated by Caryl Emerson. Minneapolis: University of Minnesota Press, 1984.

———. *Rabelais and His World.* Translated by Hélène Iswolsky. Bloomington: Indiana University Press, 1984.

———. *Speech Genres and Other Late Essays.* Edited by C. Emerson and M. Holquist. Translated by V. W. McGee. Austin: University of Texas Press, 1986.

———. *Toward a Philosophy of the Act.* Translated and with notes by Vadim Liapunov. Austin: University of Texas Press, 1993. (In Russian, "K filosofii postupka," *Filosofiia i sotsiologiia nauki i tekniki.* Moscow: Nauka, 1984–85, 80–160.)

———. *Voprosy literatury i estetika: Issledovaniia raznykh let.* Moscow: Khudozhestvennaia literatura, 1975.

Bal, Mieke. "Lots of Writing." In Brenner, *Ruth and Esther,* 212–38.

Baldwin, Joyce G. *Esther: An Introduction and Commentary.* Tyndale Old Testament Commentaries. Leicester: Inter-Varsity Press, 1984.

Banon, David. *La Lecture infinie: Les voies de l'interprétation midrachique.* Paris: Seuil, 1987.

Bardtke, Hans. *Das Buch Esther.* Kommentar zum Alten Testament 17.5. Gütersloh: Mohn, 1963.

———. "Neuere Arbeiten zum Estherbuch: Eine kritische Würdigung." *Ex Oriente Lux* 19 (1965/66): 519–49.

Beal, Timothy K. *The Book of Hiding: Gender, Ethnicity, Annihilation, and Esther.* London: Routledge, 1997.

———. *Esther.* Berit Olam. Collegeville, Minn.: Liturgical Press, 1999.

Bechtel, Carol M. *Esther.* Interpretation: A Biblical Commentary for Teaching and Reading. Louisville, Ky.: John Knox Press, 2002.

Bennett, E. K. *A History of the German Novelle from Goethe to Thomas Mann.* Cambridge: Cambridge University Press, 1934.

Berg, Sandra B. *The Book of Esther: Motifs, Themes, and Structure.* Society of Biblical Literature Dissertation Series 44. Missoula, Mont.: Scholars Press, 1979.

Berlin, Adele. *The JPS Bible Commentary: Esther.* Philadelphia: Jewish Publication Society, 2001.

Bernstein, Michael André. "The Poetics of *Ressentiment.*" In Morson and Emerson, *Rethinking Bakhtin,* 197–224.

———. "When the Carnival Turns Bitter: Preliminary Reflections upon the Abject Hero." In Morson, *Bakhtin: Essays and Dialogues,* 99–122.

Berquist, Jon L. *Judaism in Persia's Shadow: A Social and Historical Approach.* Minneapolis, Minn.: Fortress Press, 1995.

Bickerman, Elias. "The Colophon of the Greek Book of Esther." *Journal of Biblical Literature* 68 (1944): 339–62.

———. *Four Strange Books of the Bible: Jonah, Daniel, Koheleth, Esther.* New York: Schocken Books, 1967.

———. *The Jews in the Greek Age.* Cambridge, Mass.: Harvard University Press, 1988.

Blanchot, Maurice. *Faux Pas.* Paris: Gallimard, 1993.

Blenkinsopp, Joseph. "Was the Pentateuch the Civic and Religious Constitution of the Jewish Ethnos in the Persian Period?" In Watts, *Persia and Torah,* 41–62.

Block, Haskell M., and Herman Salinger, eds. *The Creative Vision: Modern European Writers on Their Art.* New York: Grove Press, 1960.

Bloom, Harold. *Where Shall Wisdom Be Found?* New York: Riverhead Books, 2004.

Booth, Wayne C. "Freedom of Interpretation: Bakhtin and the Challenge of Feminist Criticism." In Morson, *Bakhtin,* 145–76.

Boriskin, Vladimir M. *Ateizm i tvorchestvo.* Saransk: Mordovskoe knizhnoe izdatel'stvo, 1986.

Branham, R. Bracht. "Inventing the Novel." In Mandelker, *Bakhtin in Contexts,* 79–88.

———, ed. *Bakhtin and the Classics.* Rethinking Theory. Evanston, Ill.: Northwestern University Press, 2002.

Breneman, Mervin. *Ezra, Nehemiah, Esther.* The New American Commentary. Nashville, Tenn.: Broadman Holman, 1993.

Brenner, Athalya, ed. *A Feminist Companion to Esther, Judith, and Susanna.* The Feminist Companion to the Bible 7. Sheffield, Eng.: Sheffield Academic Press, 1995.

———, ed. *Ruth and Esther.* Sheffield, Eng.: Sheffield University Press, 1999.

———. "Who's Afraid of Feminist Criticism? Who's Afraid of Biblical Humour? The Case of the Obtuse Foreign Ruler in the Hebrew Bible." *Journal for the Study of the Old Testament* 63 (1994): 38–55.

Britt, Brian. "Erasing Amalek: Remembering to Forget with Derrida and Biblical Tradition." Chap. 4 in *Derrida's Bible,* edited by Yvonne Sherwood. New York: Palgrave (Macmillan), 2004.

Bush, Frederic W. *Ruth, Esther.* Word Biblical Commentary 9. Dallas: Word Books, 1996.

Butting, Klara. "Esther: A New Interpretation of the Joseph Story in the Fight Against Anti-Semitism and Sexism." In Brenner, *Ruth and Esther,* 239–48.

Buttrick, George, ed. *Interpreter's One Volume Commentary.* Nashville, Tenn.: Abingdon Press, 1971.

Carroll, Michael P. "Myth, Methodology, and Transformation in the Old Testament: The Stories of Esther, Judith, and Susannah." *Studies in Religion* 12, no. 3 (1983): 301–12.

Cazelles, Henri. "Note sur la composition du rouleau d'Esther." In *Lex Tua Veritas: Festschrift for Hubert Junker,* edited by H. Gross and F. Mussner, 17–29. Trier: Paulinus, 1961.

Charles, Robert H. *The Apocrypha and Pseudepigrapha of the Old Testament.* 2 vols. Oxford: Oxford University Press, 1913.

Clark, Katerina, and Michael Holquist. *Mikhail Bakhtin.* Cambridge, Mass.: Harvard University Press, 1984.

Clines, David J. A. *The Esther Scroll: The Story of the Story.* JSOT Suppl. 30. Sheffield, Eng.: Sheffield University Press, 1984.

———. *Ezra, Nehemiah, Esther.* The New Century Bible Commentary. Grand Rapids, Mich.: Eerdmans, 1984.

———. "In Quest of the Historical Mordecai." *Vetus Testamentum* 41, no. 2 (1991): 129–36.

Coats, George W., ed. *Saga, Legend, Tale, Novella, Fable.* JSOT Suppl. 35. Sheffield, Eng.: Sheffield Academic Press, 1985.

Coggins, Richard J., and S. Paul Re'emi. *Israel Among the Nations: Nahum, Obadiah, Esther: Israel Among the Nations.* International Theological Commentary. Grand Rapids, Mich.: Eerdmans, 1985.

Cohen, Abraham D. "'Hu Ha-Goral': The Religious Significance of Esther." *Judaism* 23 (1974): 87–94.

Cohen, Arthur A. *The Tremendum: A Theological Interpretation of the Holocaust.* New York: Crossroad, 1981.

Cox, Harvey. *The Feast of Fools: A Theological Essay on Festivity and Fantasy.* Cambridge, Mass.: Harvard University Press, 1969.

Craghan, John F. "Esther: A Fully Liberated Woman." *Bible Today* (Jan.1986): 6–9.

Craig, Kenneth. *Reading Esther: A Case for the Literary Carnivalesque.* Literary Currents in Biblical Interpretation. Louisville, Ky.: Westminster / John Knox Press, 1995.

Crawford, Sidnie. "The Book of Esther: Introduction, Commentary, and Reflections." In *New Interpreter's Bible,* vol. 3, 855–941. Nashville, Tenn.: Abingdon, 1999.

———. "Esther." In Newsom and Ringe, *Women's Bible Commentary,* 131–37.

———. "Esther and Judith: Contrasts in Character." In Crawford and Greenspoon, *Esther in Modern Research,* 61–76.

Crawford, Sidnie, and Leonard J. Greenspoon, eds. *Esther in Modern Research.* JSOT Suppl. 380. New York: T. and T. International, 2003.

Crüsemann, Frank. "Le Pentateuque, Une Tora: Prolegomènes à l'interprétation de sa forme finale." In de Pury, *Le Pentateuque en question,* 339–60.

———. *The Torah: Theology and Social History of Old Testament Law.* Minneapolis, Minn.: Fortress Press, 1996.

Da Matta, Roberto. "Carnival in Multiple Planes." In MacAloon, *Rite, Drama,* 208–40.

Daube, David. "The Last Chapter of Esther." *Jewish Quarterly Review* 37 (1946–47): 139–47.

Davis, J. M. *Farce.* London: Methuen, 1978.

Day, Linda. *Esther.* Abingdon Old Testament Commentaries. Nashville, Tenn.: Abingdon Press, 2005.

———. *Three Faces of a Queen: Characterization in the Books of Esther.* Sheffield, Eng.: Sheffield Academic Press, 1995.

Dentith, Simon. *Bakhtinian Thought: An Introductory Reader.* London and New York: Routledge, 1995.

Dillard, Raymond B., and Tremper Longman III. *An Introduction to the Old Testament.* Grand Rapids, Mich.: Zondervan, 1994.

Dorothy, Charles V. *The Books of Esther: Structure, Genre, and Textual Integrity.* Sheffield, Eng.: Sheffield Academic Press, 1997.

Duran, Nicole. "Who Wants to Marry a Persian King?" In Kirk-Duggan, *Pregnant Passion,* 71–84.

Ehrlich, Ernst L. "Der Traum des Mardochai." *Zeitschrift für Religions und Geistesgeschichte*, 1955, no. 1: 69–74.

Eissfeldt, Otto. *The Old Testament: An Introduction*. New York: Harper and Row, 1965.

Emerson, Caryl. *The First Hundred Years of Mikhail Bakhtin*. Princeton, N.J.: Princeton University Press, 1997.

———. Introduction to Mandelker, *Bakhtin in Contexts*, 1–30.

Emerson, Caryl, and Michael Holquist, eds. *M. M. Bakhtin: Speech Genres and Other Essays*. Translated by Vern W. McGee. Austin: University of Texas Press, 1986.

"Esther, mémoire et résistance." Special issue, *Lumière et Vie* 260 (October–December 2003).

Felch, Susan M., and Paul J. Contino, eds. *Bakhtin and Religion*. Evanston, Ill.: Northwestern University Press, 2001.

Fewell, Danna Nolan, ed. *Reading Between Texts: Intertextuality and the Hebrew Bible*. Literary Currents in Biblical Interpretation. Louisville, Ky.: Westminster / John Knox Press, 1992.

Fisch, Harold. *Poetry with a Purpose: Biblical Poetics and Interpretation*. Bloomington: Indiana University Press, 1988.

Fishbane, Michael. *Text and Texture: Close Readings of Selected Biblical Texts*. New York: Schocken Books, 1979.

Fox, Michael. *Character and Ideology in the Book of Esther*. 2nd ed. Grand Rapids, Mich.: Eerdmans, 2001.

———. "The Religion in the Book of Esther." *Judaism* 39, no. 2 (issue 154, 1990): 135–47.

———. "The Structure of the Book of Esther." In *Isac Leo Seeligmann Volume*. Vol. 3, edited by Alexander Rofé and Yair Zakovitch. Jerusalem: Rubenstein, 1983.

———. "Three Esthers." In Crawford and Greenspoon, *Esther in Modern Research*, 50–60.

Frazer, James G. *Taboo and the Perils of the Soul: The Golden Bough, a Study in Magic and Religion, Part 1*. Oxford: Oxford University Press, 1994.

Freud, Sigmund. *Totem and Taboo*. Vol. 13, *The Standard Edition of the Complete Psychological Works of Sigmund Freud*. London: Hogarth Press, 1999.

Fuerst, Wesley J. *The Books of Ruth, Esther, Ecclesiastes, The Song of Songs, Lamentations: The Five Scrolls*. Cambridge: Cambridge University Press, 1975.

Gadamer, Hans-Georg. *Truth and Method*. New York: Continuum, 1975.

Gan, Moshe. "The Book of Esther in the Light of the Story of Joseph in Egypt" (in Hebrew). *Tarbiz* 31 (1961–62): 144–49.

García-Treto, Francisco O. "The Fall of the House: A Carnivalesque Reading of 2 Kings 9 and 10." In Fewell, *Reading Between Texts*, 153–72.

Gaster, Theodor H. *Myth, Legend, and Custom in the Old Testament*. 2 vols. New York: Harper and Row, 1969.

———. *Purim and Hanukkah in Custom and Tradition*. New York: Henry Shuman, 1950.

Gerleman, Gillis. *Esther.* Biblischer Kommentar, Altes Testament (BKAT), 21. Neukirchen-Vluyn: Neukirchener, 1973.

Ginzberg, Louis. *The Legends of the Jews.* Vol. 4. Philadelphia: Jewish Publication Society of America, 1913.

Girard, René. *Le Bouc émissaire.* Paris: Grasset, 1982.

———. *La Violence et le sacré.* Paris: Grasset, 1972.

Gogotishvili, Liudmila. "Varianty i invarianty M. M. Bakhtina." *Voprosy Filosofii* 1 (1992): 115–35.

Goitein, Shelomo D. *Iyunim ba-Mikra.* Tel-Aviv: Yibeneh, 1958.

———. "Omanuth hassippur ba-mikra." In *Torath shimushei ha-lashon ha-ivrith beyameinu,* vol. 1. Beer-Sheba: Ha Makhon Haskalah Gabohah Banegeb, 1967.

Good, Edwin M. *Irony in the Old Testament.* Sheffield, Eng.: Almond Press, 1981.

Gordis, Robert. *Megillat Esther, with Introduction, New Translation, and Commentary.* New York: Ktav, 1972.

———. "Religion, Wisdom, and History in the Book of Esther: A New Solution to an Ancient Crux." *Journal of Biblical Literature* 100, no. 3 (1981): 359–88.

———. "Studies in the Esther Narrative." *Journal of Biblical Literature* 95, no. 1 (1976): 43–58.

Grawe, Paul H. *Comedy in Space, Time, and the Imagination.* Chicago: University of Chicago Press, 1983.

Green, Barbara. *Mikhail Bakhtin and Biblical Scholarship: An Introduction.* Atlanta, Ga.: Society of Biblical Literature, 2000.

Greene, Thomas M. *The Light in Troy: Imitation and Discovery in Renaissance Poetry.* New Haven, Conn.: Yale University Press, 1982.

Greenstein, Edward L. "A Jewish Reading of Esther." In Neusner, *Judaic Perspectives on Ancient Israel,* 225–43.

Gunkel, Hermann. *Esther.* Tübingen: J. C. B. Mohr, 1916.

Haller, Max. *Die fünf Megilloth: Ruth, Hoheslied, Klagelieder, Esther der Prediger.* Handbuch zum Alten Testament. Tübingen: J. C. B. Mohr, 1969.

Hallo, William W. "The First Purim." *Biblical Archaeologist* 46 (1983): 19–27.

Hals, Ronald M. *The Theology of the Book of Ruth.* Philadelphia: Fortress Press, 1969.

Hambrick-Stowe, Charles E. "Ruth the New Abraham, Esther the New Moses." *Christian Century* 100 (1983): 1130–34.

Harris, Monford. "Purim: The Celebration of Dis-Order." *Judaism* 26 (1977): 161–70.

Harvey, Dorothea. "Esther, Book of." In *The Interpreter's Dictionary of the Bible,* vol. 2, 149–51. Nashville, Tenn.: Abingdon, 1962.

Herodotus. *The Persian Wars.* Translated by A. D. Godley. 4 vols. Loeb Classical Library. Cambridge, Mass.: Harvard University Press, 1924.

Heschel, Abraham Joshua. *The Wisdom of Heschel.* Translated by Ruth Marcus Goodhill. New York: Farrar, Straus and Giroux, 1970.

Holquist, Michael. *Dialogism: Bakhtin and His World.* 2nd ed. London and New York: Routledge, 2002.

———. Introduction to Emerson and Holquist, *Bakhtin: Speech Genres,* ix–xxiii.

Hugo, Victor. "The Contemplations" in *The Legend of the Centuries* (1856). *Les Contemplations. Oeuvres de Victor Hugo,* vols. 5–6. Paris: J. Lemonnyer, 1885–95.

Humphreys, W. Lee. "Esther, Book of." In *Interpreter's Dictionary of the Bible.* Suppl. vol., 279–81. Nashville, Tenn.: Abingdon, 1976.

———. "A Lifestyle for Diaspora: A Study of the Tales of Esther and Daniel." *Journal of Biblical Literature* 92, no. 2 (1973): 211–23.

———. "The Story of Esther and Mordecai: An Early Jewish Novella." In Coats, *Saga, Legend, Tale, Novella, Fable,* 97–113.

Hutcheon, Linda. "Modern Parody and Bakhtin." In Morson and Emerson, *Rethinking Bakhtin,* 87–103.

Hvidberg, F., and F. Loekkegaard. *Weeping and Laughter in the Old Testament.* Leyden: Brill, 1962.

Jacobs, Louis. "Purim." *Encyclopaedia Judaica,* vol. 13, 1390–95. New York: Macmillan, 1971.

Jensen, Peter. "Elamitische Eigennamen." *Wiener Zeitschrift für die Kunde des Morgenlandes* 6 (1892): 47–70, 209–26.

Jobes, Karen H. *Esther.* New International Version Application Commentary. Grand Rapids, Mich.: Zondervan, 1999.

Jones, Bruce William. "The So-Called Appendix to the Book of Esther." *Semitics* 6 (1978): 36–43.

———. "Two Misconceptions About the Book of Esther." *Catholic Biblical Quarterly* 39 (1977): 171–81.

Josephus, Flavius. *The Works of Josephus.* Rev. ed. Translated by William Whiston. Peabody, Mass.: Hendrickson, 1987.

Jung, Carl G. *Collected Works of C. G. Jung.* Vol. 11. Princeton, N.J.: Princeton University Press, 1969.

Kalimi, Isaac. "The Book of Esther and the Dead Sea Scrolls' Community." *Theologische Zeitschrift* 60, no. 2 (2004): 101–6.

Kautzsch, Emil, ed. *Die Apokryphen und Pseudepigraphen des Alten Testaments.* 2 vols. Tübingen: Mohr, 1900.

Kirk-Duggan, Cheryl, ed. *Pregnant Passion: Gender, Sex, and Violence in the Bible.* Semeia Studies. Atlanta, Ga.: Society of Biblical Literature, 2003.

Klein, Jacob. "Akitu." In *Anchor Bible Dictionary,* vol. 1, 138–40. New York: Doubleday, 1998.

Klein, Lillian R. "Honor and Shame in Esther." In Brenner, *Feminist Companion to Esther,* 149–75.

Klein, Richard. "Prolegomena to Derrida." *Diacritics* 2, no. 4 (1972): 31–32.

Knight, George A. F. *Esther, Song of Songs, Lamentations.* Torch Bible Commentaries. London: Student Christian Movement, 1955.

Kugel, James. *The God of Old.* New York: Free Press, 2003.

Kundera, Milan. *The Unbearable Lightness of Being.* New York: Harper and Row, 1984.

LaCocque, André. *Daniel in His Time.* Columbia: University of South Carolina Press, 1988.

———. "The Different Versions of Esther." *Biblical Interpretation* 7, no. 3 (1999): 301–22.

———. "Esther: Enjeux théologiques des déplacements." *Lumière et Vie* 260 (October–December 2003): 33–48.

———. *The Feminine Unconventional: Four Subversive Figures in Israel's Tradition.* Overtures to Biblical Theology (OBT). Minneapolis, Minn.: Fortress Press, 1990.

———, ed. *Guide des Nouvelles Lectures de la Bible.* Paris: Bayard, 2005.

———. "Haman in the Book of Esther." *Hebrew Annual Review* 11 (1987): 207–22.

———. "A Psychological Approach to the Book of Jonah." Chap. 6 in *Psychology and the Bible: A New Way to Read the Scriptures,* vol. 2, edited by J. H. Ellens and W. G. Rollins. Westport, Conn., and London: Praeger, 2004.

———. *Romance, She Wrote: A Hermeneutical Essay on Song of Songs.* Harrisburg, Pa.: Trinity Press International, 1998.

———. *Ruth.* Commentaire de l'Ancien Testament, xvii. Geneva: Labor et Fides, 2004. Published in English as *A Continental Commentary.* Translated by K. C. Hanson. Minneapolis, Minn.: Fortress Press, 2004.

———. *The Trial of Innocence: Adam, Eve, and the Yahwist.* Eugene, Ore.: Cascade Books, Wipf and Stock, 2006.

LaCocque, André, and Pierre-Emmanuel LaCocque. *Jonah: A Psycho-Religious Approach to the Prophet.* Columbia: University of South Carolina Press, 1990.

Laffey, Alice. *An Introduction to the Old Testament: A Feminist Perspective.* Philadelphia: Fortress Press, 1988.

Laniak, Timothy. "*Esther's* Volkcentrism and the Reframing of Post-Exilic Judaism." In Crawford and Greenspoon, *Esther in Modern Research,* 77–90.

———. *Shame and Honor in the Book of Esther.* Society of Biblical Literature Dissertation Series 165. Atlanta, Ga.: Scholars Press, 1998.

Lawrence, D. H. *Lady Chatterley's Lover.* Harmondsworth, Eng.: Penguin Books, 1960.

Lebram, Jürgen C. H. "Purimfest und Estherbuch." *Vetus Testamentum* 22 (1972): 208–22.

Levenson, Jon D. *Esther: A Commentary.* Old Testament Library. Louisville, Ky.: Westminster / John Knox Press, 1997.

Levit-Tawil, Dalia. "The Enthroned King Ahasuerus at Dura in Light of the Iconography of Kingship in Iran." *Bulletin of the American Schools of Oriental Reseach* 250 (Spring 1983): 57–78.

Lewy, J. "Old Assyrian puru'um and purum." *Revue Hittite et Asianique* 35 (1939): 117–24.

Licht, Jacob. *Storytelling in the Bible.* Jerusalem: Magnes, 1986.

Loader, James A. "Esther as a Novel with Different Levels of Meaning." *Zeitschrift für die Alttestamentliche Wissenschaft* 90 (1978): 417–21.

Lock, Charles. "Carnival and Incarnation: Bakhtin and Orthodox Theology." *Journal of Literature and Theology* 5, no. 1 (1991): 68–82.

Luther, Martin. *Table Talk.* Philadelphia: Fortress Press, 1967.

MacAloon, John J., ed. *Rite, Drama, Festival, Spectacle: Rehearsals Toward a Theory of Cultural Performance.* Philadelphia: Ishi, 1984.

Malina, Bruce J. "Dealing with Biblical (Mediterranean) Characters: A Guide for U.S. Consumers." *Biblical Theology Bulletin* 19 (1989):127–41.

Mandelker, Amy, ed. *Bakhtin in Contexts: Across the Disciplines.* Evanston, Ill.: Northwestern University Press, 1995.

Mann, Thomas. "The Art of the Novel." In *The Creative Vision: Modern European Writers on Their Art,* edited by Haskell M. Block and Herman Salinger. New York: Grove, 1960.

Matthews, Victor H., and Don C. Benjamin. *Old Testament Parallels: Laws and Stories from the Ancient Near East.* Rev. ed. New York: Paulist Press, 1997.

McCarthy, Carmel, and William Riley. *The Old Testament Short Story: Exploration into Narrative Spirituality.* Message of Biblical Spirituality 7. Wilmington, Del.: Michael Glazier, 1986.

McConville, J. Gordon. *Ezra, Nehemiah, and Esther.* Daily Study Bible Series. Edinburgh: St Andrew's Press; Philadelphia: Westminster Press, 1985.

McCracken, David. "Character in the Boundary: Bakhtin's Interdividuality in Biblical Narratives." *Semeia* 63 (1993): 29–42.

McKane, William. "A Note on Esther IX and 1 Samuel XV." *Journal of Theological Studies* 12 (1961): 260–91.

Medvedev, Pavel. *The Formal Method in Literary Scholarship: A Critical Introduction to Sociological Poetics.* Translated by Albert J. Wehrle. Baltimore: Johns Hopkins University Press, 1978.

Meinhold, Arndt. "Die Gattung der Josephgeschichte und des Estherbuches: Diasporanovelle I." *Zeitschrift für die Alttestestamentliche Wissenschaft* 87 (1975): 306–24.

———. "Die Gattung der Josephgeschichte und des Estherbuches: Diasporanovelle II." *Zeitschrift für die Alttestamentliche Wissenschaft* 88 (1976): 72–93.

Mendilow, Adam. *Time and the Novel.* London and New York: P. Nevill, 1952.

Meyers, Carol. "Esther." In *The Oxford Bible Commentary,* edited by John Barton and John Muddiman, 324–30. Oxford: Oxford University Press, 2001.

Midrash Rabba. "Esther." Translated by Maurice Simon. London: Soncino, 1939.

Midrash Shoher Tov. Jerusalem: Midrash, 1968.

Montaigne, Michel de. *Essays* [1575]. Translated by John M. Cohen. New York: Penguin, reprint 1993.

Montefiore, Claude G., and Herbert Loewe. *A Rabbinic Anthology.* New York: Schocken, 1974.

Moore, Carey A. "Additions to the Book of Esther." In *The Anchor Bible Dictionary,* vol. 2. New York: Doubleday, 1992.

———. "The Book of Esther." In *The Anchor Bible Dictionary,* vol. 2. New York: Doubleday, 1992.

———. *Daniel, Esther, and Jeremiah: The Additions.* Anchor Bible 44. Garden City, N.Y.: Doubleday, 1977.

———. *Esther: A New Translation with Introduction and Notes.* Anchor Bible 7B. Garden City, N.Y.: Doubleday, 1971.

———. "Esther Revisited Again: A Further Examination of Certain Esther Studies of the Past Ten Years." *Hebrew Annual Review* 7 (1983): 169–86.

———, ed. *Studies in the Book of Esther: Selected with a Prolegomenon.* The Library of Biblical Studies. New York: Ktav, 1982.

Morson, Gary Saul, ed. *Bakhtin: Essays and Dialogues on His Work.* Chicago: University of Chicago Press, 1986.

Morson, Gary Saul, and Caryl Emerson. *Mikhail Bakhtin: Creation of a Prosaics.* Stanford, Calif.: Stanford University Press, 1990.

———, eds. *Rethinking Bakhtin: Extensions and Challenges.* Evanston, Ill.: Northwestern University Press, 1989.

Muecke, D. C. *Irony.* The Critical Idiom Series. London: Methuen, 1970.

Murphy, Roland E. *Wisdom Literature: Job, Proverbs, Ruth, Canticles, Ecclesiastes, Esther.* Forms of the Old Testament Literature, vol. 8. Grand Rapids, Mich.: Eerdmans, 1981.

Myerhoff, Barbara G. "A Death in Due Time: Construction of Self and Culture in Ritual Drama." In MacAloon, *Rite, Drama,* 149–78.

Neher, André. *The Exile of the Word: From the Silence of the Bible to the Silence of Auschwitz.* Translated by David Maisel. Philadelphia: The Jewish Publication Society of America, 1981.

Neusner, Jacob, ed. *Judaic Perspectives on Ancient Israel.* Philadelphia: Fortress Press, 1987.

Newsom, Carol A. "Bakhtin, the Bible, and Dialogic Truth." *Journal of Religion* 76, no. 2 (1996): 290–306.

———. "Review of *Character and Ideology in the Book of Esther,* by Michael V. Fox." *Journal of the American Academy of Religion* 63, no. 3 (1995): 618–21.

Newsom, Carol A., and Sharon H. Ringe, eds. *The Women's Bible Commentary.* Louisville, Ky.: Westminster / John Knox Press, 1998.

Niditch, Susan. "Legends of Wise Heroes and Heroines." In *The Hebrew Bible and Its Modern Interpreters,* edited by Douglas E. Knight and Gene M. Tucker, 445–63. Philadelphia: Fortress Press; and Chico, Calif.: Scholars Press, 1985.

———. *Underdogs and Tricksters: A Prelude to Biblical Folklore.* San Francisco: Harper and Row, 1987.

Niditch, Susan, and Robert Doran. "The Success Story of the Wise Courtier: A Formal Approach." *Journal of Biblical Literature* 96 (1977): 179–93.

Nietzsche, Friedrich, *The Birth of Tragedy and the Genealogy of Morals.* Translated by Francis Golffing. Garden City, N.Y.: Doubleday, 1990.

Nollan, Valerie Z. *Bakhtin: Ethics and Mechanics.* Evanston, Ill.: Northwestern University Press, 2004.

Pagán, Samuel. "Esther." In *The International Bible Commentary,* edited by William Farmer, Sean McEvenue, Armando Levoratti, and David L. Dungan. Collegeville, Minn.: Liturgical Press, 1998.

Paton, Lewis B. *A Critical and Exegetical Commentary of the Book of Esther.* International Critical Commentary. Edinburgh: T. & T. Clark, 1908.

Paul, Shalom M. "Adoption Formulae: A Study of Cuneiform and Biblical Legal Clauses." *Maarav* 2 (1980): 173–85.

Pechey, Graham. "Philosophy and Theology in 'Aesthetic Activity.'" In Felch and Contino, *Bakhtin and Religion,* 47–62.

Peristiany, J. G., ed. *Honour and Shame: The Values of Mediterranean Society.* Chicago: University of Chicago Press, 1965.

Pitt-Rivers, Julian. "Honour and Social Status." In Peristiany, *Honour and Shame,* 19–77.

Porten, Bezalel. "Haman." *Encyclopedia Judaica,* vol. 7, 1222–24. New York: Macmillan, 1971.

———. "Mordecai." *Encyclopedia Judaica,* vol. 12, 307–9. New York: Macmillan, 1971.

Preminger, Alex, and Edward L. Greenstein, eds. *The Hebrew Bible in Literary Criticism.* New York: Ungar, 1986.

Pröbstle, Martin. "Is There a God Behind This Text? A Closer Look at Esther 4:14 and 16." In *Creation, Life, and Hope: Essays in Honor of Jacques Doukhan,* edited by Jiri Moskala, 147–68. Berrien Springs, Mich.: Andrews University, 2000.

Propp, Vladimir. "Ritual Laughter in Folklore: A Propos of the Tale of the Princess Who Would Not Laugh, Nesmejana." In *Theory and History of Folklore,* edited by Anatoly Liberman, 124–46. Manchester: University of Minnesota Press, 1984.

Pury, Albert de, ed. *Le Pentateuque en question.* Geneva: Labor et Fides, 1989.

Rabelais, François. *Pantagruel* [1532] and *Gargantua* [1534]. *Oeuvres de Rabelais, avec introduction et notes critiques.* Edited by Abel Lefranc. Vols. 1 and 2. Paris: Champion, 1912. Edited and translated by Samuel Putnam, in *The Portable Rabelais* (New York: Penguin Books, 1978).

Racine, Jean. *Esther* [1689]. Classiques Larousse. Paris: Larousse, 1933.

Radday, Yehuda. "Esther with Humour." In Radday and Brenner, *On Humour and the Comic,* 295–313.

———. "Humour in Names." In Radday and Brenner, *On Humour and the Comic,* 59–98.

Radday, Yehuda T., and Athalya Brenner, eds. *On Humour and the Comic in the Hebrew Bible.* Sheffield, Eng.: Almond Press, 1990.

Reed, Walter. "The Bible According to Mikhail Bakhtin." In *Dialogues of the Word: The Bible as Literature According to Bakhtin.* New York and Oxford: Oxford University Press, 1993.

Re'emi, S. Paul. "The Faithfulness of God." Commentary on Esther, in Coggins and Re'emi, *Israel Among the Nations,* 103–40.

Reiner, Jacob. "The Original Hebrew Yosippon in the Chronicle of Jerahmeel." *Jewish Quarterly Review* 60 (1969–70): 128–46.

Rhode, Irwin. *Der griechische Roman und seine Vorläufer.* 4th ed. Hildescheim: Georg Olms, 1960.

Richardson, H. Neil. "The Book of Esther." In *Interpreter's One Volume Commentary,* edited by George Buttrick, 232–37. Nashville, Tenn.: Abingdon, 1971.

Ringgren, K. V. Helmer. "Das Buch Esther." In *Das Hohe Lied, Klagelieder, Das Buch Esther,* edited by K. V. H. Ringgren and Arthur Weiser, 113–44. Das Alte Testament Deutsch (ATD), 16. Göttingen: Vandenhoeck and Ruprecht, 1958.

———. "Esther and Purim." *Svensk exegetisk årsbok* 20 (1955): 5–24.

Roberts, Mark D. *Ezra, Nehemiah, Esther.* The Communicator's Commentary. Dallas: Word, 1993.

Rosenthal, Ludwig A. "Die Josephgeschichte, mit den Büchern Ester und Daniel verglichen." *Zeitschrift für die Alttestamentliche Wissenschaft* 15 (1895): 278–84.

Rubenstein, Jeffrey, "Purim, Liminality, and Communitas." *AJS Review* 17, no. 2 (1992): 247–77.

Ryklin, Mikhail. "Bodies of Terror: Theses Toward a Logic of Violence." *New Literary History* 24 (1993): 51–74.

Sanders, James. "The Canonical Process." In LaCocque, *Guide des Nouvelles Lectures,* 67–94.

Sandmel, Samuel. *The Hebrew Scriptures: An Introduction to Their Literature and Religious Ideas.* New York: Oxford University Press, 1978.

Sasson, Jack M. "Esther." In Alter and Kermode, *The Literary Guide to the Bible,* 335–42.

Shea, William H. "Esther and History." *Andrews University Seminary Studies* 14 (1976): 227–46.

Sieber, Harry. *The Picaresque.* London: Methuen, 1977.

Ska, Jean Louis. "Persian Imperial Authorization, Some Question Marks." In Watts, *Persia and Torah,* 161–82.

Sophocles. *Oedipus the King.* Translated by R. C. Jebb. In *Seven Famous Greek Plays,* ed. Whitney J. Oates and Eugene O'Neill Jr. New York: The Modern Library: 1938.

Sternberg, Meir. *The Poetics of Biblical Narrative.* Bloomington: Indiana University Press, 1985.

Stiehl, Ruth. "Das Buch Esther." *Wiener Zeitschrift für die Kunde des Morgenlandes* 53 (1956): 4–22.

Striedl, H. "Untersuchungen zur Syntax und Stilistik des hebräischen Buches Esther." *Zeitschrift für die Alttestamentliche Wissenschaft* 55 (1937): 82–108.

Talmon, Shemaryahu. "'Wisdom' in the Book of Esther." *Vetus Testamentum* 13 (1963): 419–55.

Thompson, Stith. *The Folktale.* Los Angeles: University of California Press, 1985.

Torrey, Charles C. "The Older Book of Esther." *Harvard Theological Review* 37 (1944): 1–40.

Tov, Emmanuel. "The 'Lucianic' Text of the Canonical and the Apocryphal Sections of Esther: A Rewritten Biblical Book." *Textus* 10 (1982): 1–25.

Turner, Victor. "Liminality and the Performative Genres." In MacAloon, *Rite, Drama,* 19–41.

———. *The Ritual Process: Structure and Anti-Structure.* Chicago: Aldin, 1969.

Ungnad, Arthur. "Eponymen." *Reallexikon der Assyriologie* 2 (1938): 412–57.

———. "Keilinschriftliche Beiträge zum Buch Ezra und Esther." Pts. 1 and 2. *Zeitschrift für die Alttestamentliche Wissenschaft* 58, no. 1 (1940): 240–44; no. 59 (1942–43): 219.

Van Wijk-Bos, Johanna W. H. *Ezra, Nehemiah, and Esther.* Louisville, Ky.: Westminster / John Knox Press, 1998.

———. *Ruth and Esther: Women in Alien Lands.* Nashville, Tenn.: Abingdon, 2001.

———. *Ruth, Esther, Jonah.* Atlanta, Ga.: John Knox Press, 1986.

Von Wilamowitz-Moellendorf, Ulrich. *Die griechische und lateinische Literatur und Sprache.* Leipzig: Teubener, 1912.

Walfish, Barry D. *Esther in Medieval Garb.* Albany: State University of New York, 1993.

Watts, James W., ed. *Persia and Torah: The Theory of Imperial Authorization of the Pentateuch.* Atlanta, Ga.: Society of Biblical Literature, 2001.

Whedbee, J. William. *The Bible and the Comic Vision.* Minneapolis, Minn.: Fortress Press, 2002.

Wiebe, John M. "Esther 4:14: 'Will Relief and Deliverance Arise for the Jews from Another Place?'" *Catholic Biblical Quarterly* 53, no. 3 (1991): 409–15.

Wills, Lawrence M. *The Jew in the Court of the Foreign King.* Minneapolis, Minn.: Fortress Press, 1990.

Yerushalmi, Yosef H. *Zakhor: Jewish History and Jewish Memory.* Seattle: University of Washington Press, 1982.

Zeitlin, Solomon. "The Books of Esther and Judith: A Parallel." In *The Book of Judith,* edited by Morton S. Enslin, 1–37. Jewish Apocryphal Literature 7. Leiden: Brill, 1972.

Zimmern, Heinrich. "Zur Frage nach dem Ursprung des Purimfestes." *Zeitschrift für die Alttestamentliche Wissenschaft* 11 (1891): 157–69.

Zlotowitz, Meir. *The Megillah.* New York: Mesorah, 1979.

Index

About the Author

André LaCocque is professor emeritus of Hebrew Scriptures at the Chicago Theological Seminary and director emeritus of its doctoral Center for Jewish-Christian Studies. He is the author of many books, including *Thinking Biblically: Exegetical and Hermeneutical Studies* with Paul Ricoeur.